Digital Media Ethics

Second Edition

CHARLES ESS

polity

First edition published in 2009 by Polity Press
This edition first published in 2014 by Polity Press

Polity Press
65 Bridge Street
Cambridge CB2 1UR, UK

Polity Press
350 Main Street
Malden, MA 02148, USA

ISBN-13: 978-0-7456-5605-2
ISBN-13: 978-0-7456-5606-9 (pb)

A catalogue record for this book is available from the British Library.

Typeset in 9.5 on 12.5 pt FF Scala by
Servis Filmsetting Ltd, Stockport, Cheshire
Printed and bound in Great Britain by Clays Ltd, St Ives plc

For further information on Polity, visit our website: www.politybooks.com

Digital Media Ethics

Second Edition

Digital Media and Society Series

For Mom (1927–2008) and Dad (1925–2010), my first and most
important ethics teachers

For Conni, best beloved, wonderful mother, grace-ful minister

For Joshua and Kathleen, our children, now young adults, who
bring overwhelming joy and hope

Contents

Foreword

Luciano Floridi

A common risk, run by many forewords, is to bother the reader by repeating, sometimes less accurately, what the table of contents of the book already specifies or (and unfortunately this is often an inclusive or) by eulogizing the text and the author, plastering comments that look like semantic clones lifted from a myriad of other texts. It is in order to try to avoid both pitfalls that I shall skip here the usual hypes – which the book and its author do deserve, make no mistake – in order to speak to the reader a bit more frankly and hence, I hope, less uninformatively.

The book has all the usual virtues of a good textbook: it is carefully researched, clearly written, and argued intelligently. Yet these are basic features that we have come to expect from high-standard scholarship and do not make it special. That Charles Ess has written a good textbook is uninteresting. That he might have written an excellent one is what I would like to argue. What the book offers, over and above its competitors, are some remarkable and, to my knowledge, unique features. Let me be schematic. The list is not exhaustive, nor do the listed features appear in order of importance, but there is a good narrative that keeps them together.

First, the topic. The book addresses the gray but crucial area of ethical concerns raised by digital media. Of course, it is flanked on the shelf by many other textbooks in information and computer ethics but, as Charles Ess well explains, this is not one of them, and it sticks out for its originality. For the book tackles that messy area of our ordinary lives where ethical issues are entangled with digital mass media, communication artifacts, information technologies of all sorts, computational processes, computer-mediated social interactions, and so forth. Indeed, it is one of its virtues that it tries to clarify that "so forth" which I have just somewhat surreptitiously added in order to spare myself the embarrassment of a lack of a clear definition. As Schrödinger once said in a different context, this is a very sharp picture of a rather fuzzy subject.

Second, the approach. The book has all the required philosophical rigor, but, once again, this is not its most impressive feature. It is also graced by a light touch, which means that Ess has avoided being either *prescriptive* or *proscriptive* (you will not be told what to do and what not to do), opting in favor of an enlightened (liberal, in his own words), *critical description* of the problems discussed. This is a noteworthy advantage, since the author empowers the reader, as should be (but often is not) the case with similar texts. Having said all this, the feature that I find absolutely unique and outstanding (in the literal sense that it makes this book stand out on the ideal shelf of other comparable books) is its capacity to combine a pluralistic approach – without the bitter aftertaste of some crypto-relativism – with a well-informed and timely look into non-Western views on the ethical issues it tackles. This is crucial. Following a remarkable tradition of German philosophers (Nietzsche, Schopenhauer, Hegel), Ess makes a sustained and successful effort to bring together Eastern and Western ethical traditions in an enriching and fascinating synthesis. And he achieves all this thanks to his extended, international experiences with a variety of cultures. If you wish to see how masterfully he avoids syncretism, relativism, and dogmatism and succeeds in shaping an overview of the field which is both captivating and ethically robust, you need to read the book.

Third, the style. This is a reader-friendly book that teaches without patronizing, with a didactic style that can only be the result of decades of care and experience in guiding students and readers through difficult topics. Its degree of accessibility is as misleading as the ability of an acrobat to make her performance look effortless.

Someone once told me that digital media are like pornography: it is very difficult to define them, but you recognize them immediately when you see them. Because we all know what digital media are, even if it is hard to determine the boundaries of their nature, applications, evolutions, and effects on our lives, I am confident that the reader will understand why I would recommend this book not only inside but also outside the classroom. Given its topic, its approach, and its style, this is a book for the educated public as well. It should be read by anyone interested in the development and future of the information society and our moral lives within it.

Preface to the Second Edition

Why this book?

The first edition of *Digital Media Ethics* was the culmination of several developments. The first was my increasingly urgent sense that the various topics and issues developed by friends and colleagues over the past several decades in the domains of information and computing ethics (ICE) and intercultural information ethics (IIE) were no longer the concerns solely of the relatively small communities of professional philosophers and computer scientists. Rather, the explosion of digital media, most especially as interconnected via the Internet and the Web, had pushed (and still pushes) digital and computational devices from a few research labs into the lives and (quite literally) the pockets of the majority of the planet's population. They have brought in their trail at least some of the ethical issues and concerns originally taken up in research labs and philosophy conferences. This means, in my view, that these ethical matters are matters that concern "the rest of us" – i.e., all of us who pick up and use such devices and networks and thus encounter these issues in our daily lives. Most of "the rest of us," however, do not enjoy the privileges and pleasures of a good applied ethics class where these matters can be taken up with the careful attention they require. A primary goal for the first edition was then to develop a textbook that would make the requisite philosophical tools and insights accessible and thereby useful to students and faculty across a range of disciplines. The larger goal – in keeping with my teaching applied ethics over some three decades, principally in the liberal arts tradition – was not to tell anyone what to think. Rather, my aim was to provide the sorts of information, arguments, philosophical frameworks, and, above all, opportunities to practice using especially the ethical decision-making frameworks that, taken together, would enhance readers' abilities to choose and decide for themselves.

Such a goal reflects first my own deepest beliefs in the sorts of ethical autonomy, freedom, equality, and emancipation stressed in (especially, but by no means exclusively) Western philosophical traditions from Socrates through feminism. It further reflects my teaching experience, which, if evaluations and student comments are to be believed, indicates that these goals can indeed be realized in praxis, at least on a good day and for a good number of students.

For this classroom teacher, it was hence a most astonishing but deeply gratifying experience to learn from my editors at Polity that the first edition of the book had become sufficiently popular as to warrant a second. To be sure, I'm quite wary of confusing success in the marketplace with any other forms of success. But, when coupled with the compliments as well as critical suggestions that I've received for the book, I can take all of this together in the Danish Jutland way: perhaps it's not so bad . . . (*det var ikke så slemt . . .*).

Moreover, to state the obvious, things move quickly in the worlds of technology. This was made clear to me in painful detail as I reviewed the first edition and was struck, to begin with, by how many examples and case-studies would need updating – or simply replacing – for the book to remain relevant to our contemporary experiences and possibilities. I was even more struck, however, by how much has changed over the past five years or so in both the literatures of Internet studies (as providing much of the empirically oriented understanding of our lives online) and information and computing ethics. In particular, virtue ethics has developed into an increasingly significant ethical decision-making framework.

Hence, many of the revisions made for this second edition have been substantial: but I very much hope, of course, that they work effectively towards the same goals defining the first edition.

Changes in the second edition

It may be helpful to note these revisions in at least summary form. In chapter 1, I've replaced the original opening case-study with one focusing on cyberbullying and what some call "trial by Internet." This is inspired by current events as well as the recent *EU Kids Online* report (Livingstone et al. 2011) that identifies cyberbullying as the top concern of young people these days. Moreover, I have more fully developed a critical theme from the first edition – namely, attention to our basic assumptions and views regarding our personal identities and capacities as moral agents. I now draw this thread throughout the volume, first of all because these assumptions are foundational for how we think about ethics as well as politics. Further, these assumptions – involving a continuum between emphases on more individual or more relational dimensions of selfhood – vary from culture to culture: understanding cultural differences in these terms both gives us vital insight into diverse traditions and views and is essential to digital media ethics as a globally oriented ethics. Finally, these views appear to be shifting in both "Western" and "Eastern" countries – and thereby so will our ethics (and politics) shift. (The scare quotes are to indicate that whatever these terms may have meant in the days of Western colonization, they can now be used, if at all, only in heavily qualified ways, beginning precisely with determining the changing conceptions of selfhood and identity that once defined differences between "East" and "West.")

This new theme is immediately at work in chapter 2 as taking up the core issue of privacy. To be sure, as digital media – most especially in the form of mobile and locative media – diffuse ever more into what were once "private" spaces, the ethical issues have grown more complex in any event: these developments have led to remarkable changes in our basic philosophical conceptions of what "privacy" means and why it might (still) be valuable. At the same time, as our conceptions of selfhood and identity shift in diverse cultures and countries, these correlate with dramatic shifts in attitudes, policies, and legislation regarding privacy.

By contrast, chapter 3, on copyright, has required fewer changes. I have updated the chapter mostly in light of more recent battles over familiar claims and arguments, including the rise of the Pirate Party. Unfortunately, these expansions have forced deletion of the earlier discussion of the digital divide and ICT4D (ICTs for development). This was not an easy choice, especially in the face of the fact that such disparities tend strongly to grow only worse.

Chapter 4 has been completely rewritten. As with the digital divide and ICT4D, the themes of the first edition chapter – the cultural dimensions of technology design and the requirements for becoming better *cosmopolitans*, citizens of a world increasingly interwoven by digital media – are critical ones. But the explosion of social networking sites (SNSs), the rise of "citizen journalism," and the role of digital media in, e.g., the Arab Spring of 2011, all followed on by a correlative explosion in the relevant ethical (and political) literatures, seemed to me more urgently to require our attention. And so I've focused on the ethics of friendship online and then the ethics of democracy and citizen journalism.

As with copyright issues, some aspects of pornography and violence, the foci of chapter 5, have remained fairly constant. But significant revisions were required nonetheless – to begin with, as some of the earlier debates over pornography included in the first edition have given way to more recent discussions between third-wave feminists and postfeminists. I've also expanded the philosophical analyses offered here – primarily from phenomenological and feminist directions – in part reflecting my students' (generally) very positive responses to these. As with the other chapters, I've also updated the suggested resources to reflect more recent scholarship, empirical findings, and debate.

Finally, chapter 6 has been modestly updated. Based on comments and suggestions offered in response to the first edition, this chapter appears to have been consistently successful and useful as it stood. At the same time, however, in concert with the rapid changes in these technologies and their affordances and uses in our lives, ethical discussion of digital media has expanded dramatically since the first edition appeared. Again, virtue ethics has become strikingly more significant since the writing of the first edition. Finally, I round out the themes of selfhood and identity with recent work on notions of relational autonomy and its correlates of distributed responsibility and morality.

Acknowledgments

What I observed in my acknowledgments to the first edition is only all the more true for the second: "the rise of computer networks is leading many of us in the West to recognize something called 'distributed responsibility' – the understanding that, as these networks make us more and more interwoven with and interdependent upon one another, the ethical responsibility for a given act is distributed across a network of actors, not simply attached to a single individual." Awareness of these interconnections is further amplified by our awareness of how far we are relational selves. Such awareness is rarely more acute than when attempting to acknowledge the very large number of persons who have contributed to this volume in both its first and now its second edition.

First of all, I'm deeply grateful to Andrea Drugan, Lauren Mulholland, and Jonathan Skerrett at Polity Press, who steadfastly carried me through the complexities and chores of both editions of this volume. Second, I remain profoundly grateful to the communities of scholars, researchers, colleagues, friends, and students who contributed so extensively to the first edition. The list here begins with John Lawrence, my first guru in the then (1980s) nascent field of humanities computing; Preston Covey (1942–2006), whose pioneering work and generous friendship in computing and applied ethics inspired and encouraged so many of us in these fields; and Henry Rosemont, Jr., whose patient mentoring in Confucian thought has been exemplary indeed.

The first edition built upon work undertaken in part during a 2007 stay at the Institut for Informations- og Medievidenskab – the "good old" (*gammeldags*) IMV (Institute of Information and Media Studies), University of Aarhus, Denmark. The second edition is even more the product of the IMV and my colleagues there. Among others, Pia Majbritt Jensen Azzolini, Anja Bechmann, Niels Brügger, Niels Ole Finnemann, Jakob Linaa Jensen, Stine Lomborg, Randi Markussen, Poul Erik Nielsen, Finn Olesen, Anne Marit Waade, and institute head Steffen Ejnar Brandorff have contributed in numerous ways. As well, many conversations and workshops with (then) PhD students Henrik Smid Nielsen, Rikke Toft Nørgaard, Line Hassall Thomsen, and Rune Veerasawmy, among others, helped enormously to move me beyond 2007.

Two other communities have also shaped this book in important ways. The colleagues gathered by Nicole Dewandere and Luciano Floridi to pursue the Onlife Initiative (https://ec.europa.eu/digital-agenda/en/onlife-initiative) have constituted one of the most remarkable scholarly projects of my experience. Especially the work of Mireille Hildebrandt (Radboud University, Nijmegen; Erasmus School of Law, Rotterdam; Vrije Universiteit, Brussels) and Judith Simon (Karlsruhe Institute of Technology [Germany] and Department of Philosophy, University of Vienna) has substantively enhanced and improved the sections on EU data protection law and guidelines (chapter 2) and distributed responsibility and morality (chapter 6) respectively.

Second, the final research and writing of this edition occupied my first months as a *førstamanuensis* (associate professor) in the Department of Media and Communication, University of Oslo. I am profoundly grateful for the warm and most supportive welcome given to me here by academic and administrative colleagues alike, including Niamh Ní Bhroin, Dagfinn Hagen, Arne Håskjold Krumsvik, Knut Lundby, Maren Kristine Moen, Eli Skogerbø, Kristin Lomo Sandberg, Elizabeth Staksrud, Tanja Storsjul, and Espen Ytreberg: their patience, insight, and encouragement have been simply essential.

My Drury colleagues – Peter Browning, Lisa Esposito, Chris Panza, Richard Schur, and Ted Vaggalis – have continued to provide invaluable insight. Susanna Paasonen (University of Helsinki) has remained a patient guide through the complicated and often murky waters of pornography (chapter 5). Mia

Consalvo (Concordia University) and Miguel Sicart (IT University, Copenhagen) were equally generous and helpful with the section on games (chapter 5). Rich Ling (IT University, Copenhagen) has served as a rich source for all things mobile. I am also grateful to several colleagues who shared their forthcoming manuscripts and comments, most especially Herman Tavani (Rivier College), Julie Cohen (Georgetown University), and Zisi Papacharissi (University of Illinois at Chicago).

Finally, of course, my family played the most important roles. My brother Robert (Director, IT Operations, Fujitsu Network Communications) provided most helpful technical insight as well as a vital professional corporate perspective. My sister Dianne Kaufmann shouldered the lion's share of burdens on our family's home front, freeing me up to research, travel, and write. My wife, the Reverend Conni Ess, put up with the workaholic practices and schedules needed to bring a book like this to fruition; her exceptionally sharp eye for imperfect grammar, typos, and the all-too-frequent unclear sentence also directly benefited the manuscript. Our son Joshua, now a professional technical support person, helped especially with the more arcane technical details that often prove essential to digital media ethics. Our daughter Kathleen, pursuing her career as a classics and religion scholar, provided invaluable assistance with both Greek philosophy and English style.

The deepest gratitude goes of course to my parents, Bob and Betty Ess. My Mom was especially pleased to see me working on the first edition of this volume. Like any mother, she was always pleased and proud of her children's accomplishments – especially those that sought to be of use to others. At the same time, in many ways she was the single person most responsible for my pursuing philosophy: she loved discussing ideas and current events from a variety of perspectives – a practice hence deeply interwoven in our lives. My father provided unfailing care and encouragement throughout his life, including the most exemplary kind – namely, supporting my ethical and political choices even when they differed sharply from his own. My parents' exemplars of practice were thus the foundations of the core values motivating this book

– beginning with keen interest in different approaches and views, and the spirit of enacting deep care for Others.

Insofar as this volume reflects and helps foster such virtues – Mom, Dad, this is for you.

Chapter Synopses

Chapter 1: Central Issues in the Ethics of Digital Media

This chapter introduces us to some of the characteristics of digital media that give rise to both familiar and novel ethical challenges. We further examine in an initial way how popular media report in the form of "moral panics" – i.e., stories that highlight apparent risks and dangers of digital media; such reporting may entail ways of thinking that can obstruct or short-circuit the sorts of ethical reflection needed to resolve ethical problems more effectively. The chapter concludes with an overview of the organization of the book and its chief pedagogical approaches and apparatus.

Chapter 2: Privacy in the Electronic Global Metropolis?

This chapter addresses the challenges to modern Western notions of individual privacy presented by contemporary digital media, most especially networked communications media such as the Internet and the Web. It then explores diverse cultural attitudes towards and understandings of individual and collective privacy in non-Western cultures in order to raise a central problem for contemporary digital media ethics – namely, is it possible to develop ethical frameworks for the use of digital media that conjoin norms shared globally along with the irreducible differences that define distinctive individual and cultural identities? The meta-theoretical approach of ethical pluralism is highlighted here, as contemporary intercultural dialogues show how such ethical pluralism resolves this central problem.

Chapter 3: Copying and Distributing via Digital Media: Copyright, Copyleft, Global Perspectives

Digital media make copying and distributing information – in the form of music, videos, or texts – far easier than previous media. We explore some of the common ethical aspects of copying and distributing music and other forms through three main frameworks for interpreting and regulating these as intellectual property: current copyright law (especially in the US and the EU), various "copyleft" schemes, and Confucian tradition as shaping many non-Western approaches and attitudes.

Chapter 4: Friendship, Democracy, and Citizen Journalism

Friendship online – most notably, on social networking sites (SNSs) such as Facebook – opens up a range of ethical issues, including potential for cyberbullying. The design of SNSs involves further ethical matters in terms of underlying assumptions regarding what constitutes "friendship" and, more fundamentally, how human identity is constituted and expressed. Virtue ethics is particularly useful for analyzing and resolving some of the ethical challenges here. How democratization and citizen journalism may be fostered through digital media is then explored, with a primary focus on the ethical requirements for citizen journalism if it is to serve democratic ends.

Chapter 5: Still More Ethical Issues: Digital Sex and Games

This chapter takes up two of the most likely topics of digital media ethics: pornography online and violence in video games. We begin with the difficulties of defining pornography, especially given diverse cultural perspectives and norms regarding more foundational conceptions of embodiment, sexuality, and gender. Central ethical issues are then examined through the frameworks of utilitarianism, deontology, feminist ethics and ethics of care, and virtue ethics. We turn finally to debates surrounding violence and rape in video games. Here, utilitarianism, deontology, and virtue ethics are applied.

Chapter 6: Digital Media Ethics: Overview, Frameworks, Resources

This chapter introduces and illustrates by way of several examples the frameworks applied in the topics chapters (2–5). These are the widely used ethical frameworks of utilitarianism, deontology, feminist ethics/ethics of care, virtue ethics, and Confucian and African frameworks, which prescribe distinctive approaches to analyzing and resolving ethical difficulties. Moreover, three major meta-theoretical frameworks – those of ethical relativism, ethical monism/absolutism, and ethical pluralism – are likewise introduced and examined with some care.

CHAPTER ONE

Central Issues in the Ethics of Digital Media

Chapter overview

We open with a case-study intended to introduce us to representative ethical issues brought about by digital media, beginning with cyberbullying. This case-study is accompanied by one of the primary pedagogical/teaching elements of the book – questions designed to foster initial reflection and discussion (for individuals, small groups, or a class at large), followed by additional questions that can be used for further reflection and writing.

After an introduction to the main body of the chapter, the section "(Ethical) life in the digital age?" provides a first overview of digital media and their ethical dimensions. I also highlight how more popular treatments of these, however, can become counterproductive to clear and careful ethical reflection. We turn next to some of the specific characteristics of digital media – convergence, digital information as "greased," and digital media as communication technologies – that highlight specific ethical issues treated in this volume. We then take up initial considerations on how to "do" ethics in the age of digital media. Finally, I describe the pedagogical features of the book and provide some suggestions for how it is designed to be used – including specific suggestions for the order in which the chapters may be read.

Case-study: Amanda Todd and Anonymous – an introduction to issues in digital media ethics

When Amanda Todd was twelve years old and "fooling around" with friends, including someone looking on via a webcam, the someone asked Amanda to show him her breasts. She lifted her top: the result was a video and pictures that began circulating on the Internet – distributed in part as her stalker would develop a new Facebook profile when Amanda moved to a new school. Once friended with Amanda's new friends, the stalker would distribute the video and photos again, as well as send them to teachers and parents. One of the consequences of the online stalking was offline bullying – not unusual, unfortu-nately, for young adolescents, but now laced with taunts of "porn star" (Bleaney 2012). At one point, Amanda made her first suicide attempt: part of the online response included a series of "jokes" facilitated by tumblr.

Her stalker did not go away, and Amanda's responses became more and more desperate. In September, 2012, she posted a video on YouTube that described her experience (https://www.youtube.com/watch?v=KRxfTyNa24A). On October 10, Amanda, now fifteen years old, committed suicide. Her death – including her video – attracted significant attention. At the time of this writing, the video has logged over 4 million views. Alongside the official investigations, the group Anonymous claimed to have identified her stalker and published his name and address – not surprisingly, he received death threats. Meanwhile, "Amanda Todd jokes" – and, presumably, the original pictures and video – continue to circulate online (Warren and Keneally 2012).

First questions for discussion

Amanda Todd's (cyber)bullying and the multiple layers of responses surrounding it constitute a complex case. We will explore, for example, the issues it raises concerning privacy in chapter 2, and then more fully as a case of cyberbullying in chapter 4, as part of the discussion of friendship. Here, we begin with it as an episode of cyberbullying. We will also take an initial look at two additional topics evoked here – namely, the risks of "moral panics" in media reporting on such events and new forms of "vigilante justice" facilitated by Internet-connected digital media.

1. Given your experiences – and those of your friends and family – how do you react to Amanda Todd's suicide after some three years of cyberbullying? For example, does it seem to you that this is a serious problem for those of us living in "a digital age" – i.e., as immersed in a world of digital media more or less seamlessly interconnected and interwoven with our offline lives? Remember here that part of Amanda's difficulty was that, while she could – and did – physically move and change schools – her stalker was always able to find her again easily through her online profile and activities.

A) Insofar as you agree that such cyberstalking is problematic – make a first effort at identifying more precisely just what's wrong here. Of course, there are a wide range of ethical points you can make – beginning with the exploitation (including sexual exploitation) of vulnerable persons (certainly including young girls, but not exclusively so – plenty of young boys get bullied as well) by more powerful ones. Moreover, it seems clear that, if Amanda deserved privacy and anonymity – as we will see, argued by deontologists as basic rights of persons – she was not able to have such rights in her online environments. As a last suggestion, what about the ongoing taunts and "jokes" that circulated – and still circulate – in connection with Amanda's video and suicide: are these sorts of responses ethically problematic, in your view, and/or, as a utilitarian might argue, simply the price to be paid for free speech online?

B) Whatever your responses to "A)," now go back and do your best to provide whatever reasons, grounds, feelings, and/or other sorts of claims and evidence that can you offer at this stage to support these first points.

2. As we will explore below, a common phenomenon in reporting on new technologies in "the media" is that of a "moral panic." That is, stories are often developed around sensational – and so very often the sexual – but risky possibilities of a new technology. Sometimes a panic ensues – e.g., cries for new efforts somehow

to regulate or otherwise restrain clearly undesirable behaviors and consequences. Such panics are not always misplaced: they can sometimes inspire responses and changes that may effectively improve our social and ethical lives. But one of our concerns is that such "moral panic" reporting style has us frame (if we don't think about it too much) new technologies and their possibilities in a kind of "either/or" dilemma: we are caught between having to reject new technologies – e.g., as they lead, in this case, to the stalking and suicide of a young girl – or defending these technologies wholesale (as, for example, the US National Rifle Association finds itself compelled to do in the wake of the Newtown, Connecticut, school shooting – manifestly with great difficulty; Raasch and Johnson 2012).

Reflect on some of the examples of media coverage given here, as well as others that you can easily find on your own, perhaps with the help of the Wikipedia article on Amanda Todd (http://en.wikipedia. org/wiki/Suicide_of_Amanda_Todd#cite_note-ottawacitizen1-22).

Does it seem to you that this coverage provides a much needed and useful service in calling our attention to the sorts of social and ethical problems that new media make possible? And/or: do you see any risks here of such coverage falling into a "moral panic" style of reporting? Either way, the key point is to provide evidence – including examples (carefully cited, please) that support your claims and observations.

3. Especially in the face of what seems to be (a) the clear injustice of stalkers and pedophiles using Internet-connected digital media and the sorts of anonymity afforded in online communication, including popular social network sites (SNSs) to harass young people to the point of suicide, vis-à-vis (b) the apparent inability of "traditional" law-enforcement agencies to identify and track down such perpetrators, it is tempting to applaud the efforts of Anonymous to do what the authorities apparently can't. But in this instance, rather than speeding up justice, the "trial by Internet" – beginning with the "outing" of the alleged stalker online, followed by quick condemnation – resulted in a second injustice. Despite their prodigious hacking abilities, Anonymous apparently erred,

and the wrong man was targeted with death threats and other harassment (Warren and Keneally 2012).

How do you respond to this set of problems? That is, does it sometimes seem justified for groups such as Anonymous to intervene in such cases – i.e., when the legal authorities appear to lack the technical sophistication needed to track down stalkers such as the one who pursued Amanda Todd? And/or: might the risks of such "trial by Internet" – beginning with the erroneous accusation of the wrong person – outweigh its possible benefits (such as – occasionally – getting the right person when the authorities can't)?

Again, the key point is to provide support for your claims and observations, beginning with evidence (e.g., how often does a group such as Anonymous succeed where others fail?) and arguments that will hold up to critical scrutiny.

ADDITIONAL REFLECTION/WRITING SUGGESTIONS:
MEDIA LOG

Develop a log – a description of what digital devices you use, for how long, and for what purpose – for a given period (e.g., 24 hours/three days/one week). Try to be specific here. Identify as clearly and in as much detail as you can what you do – e.g., scan for friends' updates, post a status update, tweet or retweet an interesting comment or story, upload an important photograph or video you have produced, text-message, call, play games (either by yourself or with others), look up locations or information, post your location for friends or on a tourism site, check a bank balance or pay a bill, shop and order a product or service, "micro-coordinate" a meet-up with friends, use an "augmented reality" app on your phone to explore a museum or tourist site, etc., etc.

WRITING – CLASS DISCUSSION QUESTIONS

A) As you review this log, any surprises – e.g., are you using (a) device(s) significantly more or less than you might have originally thought?

B) Can you determine how you're using these devices – specifically, what kinds of communication are you using them for?

C) Are there any obvious ethical aspects and/or problems that you notice and/or encounter in your use of these technologies? Identify these as carefully as you can.

Class discussion: Collect the ethical aspects/problems of your uses of digital media onto a commonly shared list. These will be useful to refer to as examples as you work through this text – both as some of these are likely to be discussed in the following chapters and as some may not be explicitly covered here. The latter will be especially interesting for further individual and class analysis, discussion, and writing – particularly as you and your colleagues develop greater skill and ability in grappling with such ethical issues and challenges.

D) How does your use of digital media compare with that of:
  (i) your older and/or younger siblings (if you have any)?
  (ii) your parents and/or parents' friends?
  (iii) your grandparents and/or grandparents' friends?

This question asks you to consider the demographics of digital media use – on the presumption that there will be striking differences – e.g., between the usage rates of adolescents and twenty-somethings vis-à-vis[1] people in their forties and fifties, and then people in their sixties and seventies (and older).

---

1 Vis-à-vis: "face-to-face" (French). I use this phrase a lot – e.g. ". . . very different understandings of the role of the state vis-à-vis the life of the individual." It may be tempting to say something like "versus" the life of the individual – but I intend to avoid precisely the presumption of opposition or conflict that "versus" implies. Rather, I intend "vis-à-vis" as referring to the whole range of possible relationships (e.g., as equals, as superior/inferior, as complementary, as oppositional, etc.) between any two things that we may want to think about together. I thereby want to insist that we cannot assume we already know what these relationships may be. Rather, part of our work involves attempting to discern just what these relationships may be in fact.

E) If there are such differences, what are your thoughts about
the possible ethical implications of these differences? Does it
seem that our ethics indeed change from generation to generation? And, if so, what does that imply regarding claims
that ethics should be universal – i.e., applicable in all times
and places to all people? (Hint: we will take this up later on in
terms of the meta-ethical positions of ethical absolutism, relativism, and pluralism; see chapter 6 for more discussion.)

Introduction

In the industrialized world, our lives are inextricably interwoven
with what are sometimes called "New Media" or digital media.
(We will explore the meaning of these terms more carefully in a
bit.) So we sometimes call the current generations "digital natives"
to point out that they have been born into and grown up in a
world saturated with these technologies. More broadly, a recent
European Commission "Digital Futures" project uses in its title the
term "Onlife," as developed by information philosopher Luciano
Floridi to highlight how the once distinct domains of "life online"
and "life offline" are now (more or less) seamlessly interwoven in
an "Onlife" (Broadbent et al. 2013). Certainly, if we pay attention
to contemporary media coverage of digital media, such reports
frequently highlight important, often frightening, ethical issues.
Beyond our opening examples of cyberbullying and "trial by
Internet," it is easy to find stories highlighting, e.g., how violence
in games appears to lead to horrific, real-world violence, ranging
from school shootings to the July 22, 2011, killings in Norway,
including sixty-nine young people on the island of Utøya (Daily
Mail Reporter 2012). Similarly, sexually explicit materials (SEMs)
online are claimed to lead to sexual aggression against women and
young girls (Martin 2012).

These are certainly critical ethical issues – ones that we will
explore more fully in chapter 5, in particular. At this point, these
examples are important not only as identifying pressing ethical
concerns, but also as they illustrate a tendency of popular media
to call our attention to such issues in ways that run the risk of

fostering what are called "moral panics." That is, in order to attract our attention, such stories sometimes focus unduly on the sensational (if not the sexual). But, thereby, they tend to appeal to a deep-seated fear that our new technologies are somehow getting out of control (a fear that has been expressed in the modern West since Mary Shelley's *Frankenstein* ([1818] 1933)) – in part as these new technologies apparently threaten to corrupt our ethical and social sensibilities.

To be sure, we will work to explore these (and similar important issues, such as privacy (chapter 2) and intellectual property rights (chapter 3)) in this volume. But, before doing so, it is helpful to begin, rather, by examining how such a "moral panic" style of reporting both furthers and frustrates careful ethical reflection on digital media. On the one hand, such reporting usually succeeds in getting our attention – and is thereby useful as it catalyzes more careful reflection on important ethical issues evoked by digital media. On the other hand, by highlighting especially the potentially negative effects of digital media, such reporting fosters a polarized way of thinking – a framework that could be character-ized as "technology good" (because it brings us important benefits) vs. "technology bad" (because it threatens the moral foundations of society, most especially the morality of young people). The problem is that such a framework for thinking about important ethical issues is simply misleading. As we will see – and as most of us probably already know full well – whatever truths may be dis-cerned about the ethics of digital media often lie somewhere in the middle between these two extremes. But, if we are presented only with the simple choice between "technology good" and "technology bad," it is tempting to think that these are indeed our only choices, and so we get needlessly stuck in trying to choose between two compelling alternatives. Getting stuck this way short-circuits what we need to do if we are to move beyond such either/or thinking – a movement that requires more careful and extensive reflection.

One way to see how to move beyond such polarities is first to examine more carefully some of the important characteristics of digital media, along with the specific sorts of ethical issues that these characteristics often raise for us.

(Ethical) life in the digital age?

"Digital media" are the subject of an ever growing range of analyses in a number of disciplines (e.g., Lievrouw and Livingstone 2006; Couldry 2012). This book, however, takes the standpoint of an interest in digital media *ethics*; thereby, at least at the beginning, we are interested in seeing the distinctive features of digital media – what sets them apart from earlier media – that make them ethically challenging and interesting.

To be sure, digital media represent strong continuities with earlier forms of communication and information media such as printed books, journals, and newspapers, what we now call "hardcopy" letters, and, for example, traditional forms of mass media that include not only newspapers but also "one-to-many" broadcast media such as radio and TV. We will note and explore these continuities more fully in our efforts to evaluate one of the larger ethical questions we will confront – namely, do digital media present us with radically new kinds of ethical problems that thereby require absolutely new ethical approaches? (See Preliminary exercise, below, p. 13.) For now, we can note that these questions are driven in good measure by rather emphasizing the important differences between earlier media and digital media. (Such an emphasis, by the way, also drives the "either/or" approach underlying much popular media reporting.) In particular, these differences often are part of why new ethical issues come up in conjunction with digital media. Exploring these differences at the outset is hence a good starting point.

Here, then, we will consider three distinguishing characteristics of digital media (though others are important): how digital media (in contrast with analogue media) foster convergence; digital information as "greased"; and digital media as (global) communication media.

1. Digital media, analogue media: convergence and ubiquity

To begin with, digital media work by transforming extant information (e.g., voices over a phone, texts written on a wordprocessor, pictures of an impressive landscape, videos recorded and broadcast, etc.) into the basic informational elements of electronic computers and networks, using binary code (1s and 0s – bits on and off), and the definition of how such code is to be manipulated within a given application. Digital media contrast in this way with analogue media – such as an old-fashioned vinyl record – which capture, store, and make information accessible by producing specific artifacts that are like the original. In the case of music, recording equipment, beginning with microphones and concluding with a storage medium such as audiotape, translates the vibrations of an original sound into magnetically stored information, corresponding to specific sound pitches and volumes, which is then "written" onto a tape that passes by a recording head at a specific speed. These *analogues* of an original sound are in turn transformed into further analogues, as they are mechanically carved onto the grooves of a vinyl record in the form of bumps and valleys that correspond to (i.e., are analogues of) the high and low frequencies and volumes of the original sound. These physical variations are further translated by a phonograph needle into electronic impulses that likewise mimic the original variations of a sound. Finally, these impulses are transformed back into sound by an amplifier and speaker(s) – again, as an analogue or copy of the original that, if all goes well, is as close to the original as possible.

One way to think about analogue media is that they work by capturing, recording, and replaying information as a smooth, continuously variable content. That is, there are comparatively continuous variations as a series of musical notes, first low and soft and then high and loud, are captured and replayed as moving evenly from the one to the other. In this sense, the contents of analogue media are more or less infinitely variable. By contrast, digital media capture, store, and make accessible their contents based entirely on a binary code of 1s and 0s.

More importantly, analogue media always involve some loss of information across the various processes of collecting, recording, and storing it. This means – and this is particularly critical to the ethical discussions of copying – that each analogue copy of an original is always less true to the original; and the more copies made – e.g., a tape copy of a record as a copy of a tape of an original performance – the less faithful (and satisfying) the resulting copy will be. By contrast, once information is transcribed into digital form, each copy of the digital original will be (more or less) a perfect replica of the original. Copy an MP3 version of your favorite song a thousand times and, if your equipment is working properly, there will be no difference between the first copy and the thousandth copy.

Even more importantly, analogue media are strongly distinct systems: how information is captured and replayed on a vinyl record is not immediately compatible – and, thereby, not easily exchangeable – with how information is captured and replayed in a newspaper or printed book. By contrast, once information is translated into digital form, such information – whether destined for an MP3 player as an audio recording or a wordprocessor as text – can be stored on and transmitted through a shared medium. Hence the same computer or smartphone can capture, create, process, and distribute digital photos and music, along with a thousand other forms of information held distinct in analogue media, from simple emails to wordprocessing files to maps to . . . "you name it."

To be sure, the distinctions between analogue and digital media are only one side of the coin. It is important to keep in mind that, however much our media technologies have changed in recent decades, the human eyes, ears, and voices have not – that is, we as *embodied* beings still generate and receive information in resolutely *analogue* form. The digital codes, for example, that pass between two computers or smartphones, whether in the form of a Skype call, Facebook update, or phone call, begin and end for their human users as analogue information. The emergence of "the digital," in short, does not mean the quick and complete end of "the analogue" (cf. Massumi 2002). This is critical to keep in mind especially from an ethical perspective: as digital media build on and enhance – rather than replace – our analogue modes of communication and experiences, they thereby call into play experiences and communication that have been part and parcel of human ethical reflection and frameworks for millennia. This is good news ethically, insofar as it means that the emergence of digital media does *not* require us to throw out all previous ethical reflections and views and somehow try to start *de novo*, from the beginning.

Nonetheless, as once distinct forms of information are translated into a commonly shared digital form, this establishes one of the most important distinguishing characteristics of digital media, namely, convergence (e.g., Briggs and Burke 2005: ch. 7; Jenkins 2006; Storsul and Stuedahl 2007). Such convergence can be (literally) seen in a rich webpage that contains text, video, and audio sources, as well as possibilities for sending email, remotely posting a comment, etc. These once distinct forms of information and communication are now conjoined in digital form, so that they can be transmitted entirely in the form of 1s and 0s via the Internet. Similarly, a contemporary smartphone exemplifies such convergence: as a highly sophisticated computer, it is capable of handling digital information used for a built-in camera (still and/or moving video), MP3 player, web browser capable of capturing text, GPS navigation, and many other sorts of information – and, oh yes, it will also make phone calls.

This means, then, that digital media bring together both traditional and sometimes new sorts of information sources. In particular, what were once distinct kinds of information in the analogue world (e.g., photographs, texts, music) are now no longer strongly distinct; rather, they share the same basic form of information. What does this mean, finally, for ethics? Here's the key point: what were once distinct sets of ethical issues now likewise converge – sometimes creating new combinations of ethical challenges that we haven't had to face before.

For example, societies have developed relatively stable codes and laws for the issue of consent as to whether or not someone can be photographed in public. (In the US, generally, one can photograph people in public without asking for their consent, while, in Norway, consent is required.) Transmitting that photo to a larger public – e.g., through a newspaper or a book – would then require a different information system, and one whose ethical and legal dimensions are addressed (however well or poorly) in copyright law. But, as many people have experienced to their regret, a contemporary smartphone can not only record their status and actions, but further (more or less immediately) transmit the photographic record to a distribution medium such as a Facebook profile or an even more public website. The ethics of both consent in photography and copyright in publication are now conjoined in new ways that we simply have not had to think through before.

PRELIMINARY EXERCISE:
DO WE REALLY NEED A (NEW) DIGITAL MEDIA ETHICS?

In response to these sorts of new ethical challenges brought about by digital media (and new technologies more generally), two sorts of arguments have emerged.

1. The new possibilities of photographing people in both public and more intimate situations, coupled with more or less immediately posting such photographs and/or videos to a forum such as a social networking site or more public webpage, mean that people are now more vulnerable to violations of privacy.

   That is, where privacy can be minimally defined as the capacity to control information about oneself, the new ability of others to record and quickly distribute potentially embarrassing information about oneself thereby decreases one's control over such information (e.g., in the form of permission to take a photograph, much less permission to distribute the photograph in a semi-public or public forum).

   A general guideline in many ethical systems, as we will see, is that increased vulnerability requires increased responsibility. So, for example, parents have greater responsibilities for their children as infants that they do not have for their children as young adults, because children as infants are vulnerable in many ways that young adults are not.

On this line of thinking, the fact that others around me are more vulnerable in the presence of my smartphone argues that I as the owner/operator of the device need to be more responsible for how I use it. This might mean, for example, paying increased attention both to whether or not what I'm recording and distributing might harm the person in some way and to the need for others to have and maintain control of information about themselves, etc.

More generally, this line of argument suggests that we now face a pressing need for careful and systematic ethical reflection, so as to develop the sorts of guidelines, codes, and laws that can help us work through especially the new sorts of ethical issues that digital media evoke.

2. Alternatively (but not necessarily to the exclusion of the first line of argument above), the history of technology is in part a history of people learning how to use new technologies in ethically appropriate ways – though often only after sometimes terrifically damaging (perhaps even fatal) experiences with them. On this view, we "muddle through" as a species, learning more from our experience than from careful reflection on how to utilize new technologies in ways that minimize harm, protect rights, etc.

From this perspective, there is no real need to undertake ethical reflection on the new situations confronting us as new technologies enter our individual and social lives. Rather, we can generally rely on people's common sense and previous ethical experiences and judgment to help forge the new ethical guidelines that will become generally known and respected. For example, if I post an embarrassing photograph or video of a friend on the Web, thinking it's all in good fun, but thereby manage only to make my friend really angry and upset with me, I'll eventually figure out that I shouldn't do such things. While, with the advantage of hindsight, I may well look back on such an act as a mistake, at least I'll avoid such errors in the future. There's no need for extensive ethical reflection ahead of time; rather, we will simply learn from our mistakes.

1. Of the two positions outlined above, which better describes your approach to the ethical dilemmas that arise as you take up new technologies in your life? Provide an example of this if you can.
2. Do you have a reason or sense for why your approach might be better than the alternative? Explain your view here as fully as you can.
3. Can you think of an instance or example – whether in relation to digital media technologies or to other new technologies – where your approach might not work as well as the alternative?
4. Do you have other thoughts and suggestions for how we – both individually and as a society and species – might best approach the ethical dimensions of digital media (and/or other new technologies)?

2. Digital media and "greased information"

A second characteristic of digital media is that the information they capture, record, and transmit is "greased." That is, as James Moor (2000) has observed, "When information is computerized, it is greased to slide easily and quickly to many ports of call." As anyone who has hit the "post" button on an status update too quickly knows all too well, information in digital form can spread more or less instantaneously and globally, whether we always want it to or not.

As the example of uploading potentially embarrassing photos or videos from a smartphone suggests, the capacity of digital informa-tion to move quickly from one place to another raises especially serious ethical issues surrounding privacy. That is, where it was once comparatively difficult to capture and then transmit infor-mation about a person that she or he might consider private, the advent of digital media, beginning with computer systems that can store and make easily accessible a wide range of information about persons, has resulted in a vast spectrum of new threats to what was once clearly personal and private information. Moreover, digital information as "greased" likewise makes it easy to copy and distribute, say, one's favorite songs, movies, or texts. To be sure, it has always been possible to copy and distribute copies of a given text, song, or film. But the ease with which we can do so by way of digital media appears to be one factor that makes such copying and distribution an even more pressing ethical problem these days.

3. Digital media as communication media: global scope, interactivity, and selfhood/identity

The emergence of digital media – along with the Internet and the Web as ways of quickly transporting digitized information – thus gives rise to strikingly new ways of communicating with one another at every level. Emails, SNSs (Facebook, MySpace, etc.), photo and video distribution sites (Flickr, YouTube, etc.), and personal blogs provide ways for people – especially in the developed world but also increasingly in developing countries – substantially to enhance existing relationships and to develop new ones with persons often far removed from their own geographical/cultural/ linguistic communities. Especially as the Internet and the Web now connect more than one-*third* of the world's population, they thereby make possible cross-cultural encounters online at a scope, speed, and scale unimaginable even just a few decades ago.

Along these lines, two additional features of digital media become crucial. To begin with, digital media enjoy what Phil Mullins (1996) has characterized as a kind of fluidity: specifically, a biblical text in digital form – either on one's smartphone or as stored on a website – becomes, in his phrase, "the fluid Word." In contrast to a biblical text as fixed in a strong way when inscribed on parchment (the Torah) and/or printed on paper, a biblical text encoded on a flash memory or server hard drive in the form of 1s and 0s can be changed quickly and easily. This fluidity is highlighted by a second characteristic of digital communication media – namely, interactivity. Both a printed Bible and the daily newspaper are produced and distributed along the lines of a "top-down" and "one-to-many" broadcast model. While readers may have their own responses and ideas, they can (largely) do nothing to change the printed texts they encounter. By contrast, I can change the biblical text on my smartphone if I care to (e.g., if I think a different translation of a specific word or phrase might be more precise or illuminating) – and, by the same token, a community of readers can easily amend and modify an online text; they might also be able to post comments and respond to a given text in other ways that are in turn "broadcast" back out to others. To put it differently, digital communication media provide us with new possibilities of "talking back": posting comments, or even a blog, in response to a newspaper story, now reproduced online; voting for a favorite in a TV-broadcast contest by way of SMS messaging; organizing "smart mobs" via the Internet and smartphones (as well as older media such as fax machines) to protest – and, in some cases, successfully depose – corrupt politicians, etc.

At the same time, the diffusion of Internet- and Web-based connectivity by way of smartphones and other digital devices (e.g., the sensor devices a jogger wears to track and record a run in exquisite detail, including precise location, time, speed, etc.) makes increasingly real for us the *ubiquity* of digital media. That is, we are increasingly surrounded by an envelope of interacting digital devices – meaning first of all that we are "always on," always connected (unless we take steps to go offline – steps that are increasingly difficult to accomplish). The ubiquity of our interactive devices means that we are increasingly both the subjects and the objects of what Anders Albrechtslund (2008) has aptly identified as "voluntary surveillance." To be sure, such voluntary or lateral surveillance can certainly be enjoyable, even life-saving – e.g., as we keep up with distant friends and family through a posting on a social networking site such as Facebook. At the same time, however, the mobile or smartphones we carry with us into more or less every corner of our lives – including the (once?) most intimate spaces of the bathroom and the bedroom – open up our lives in those spaces to new possibilities of tracking and recording. For example, a number of recent research projects utilize apps similar to "Device Analyzer" to collect an impressive range of data about the phone's use, including such details as whether the phone "is ringing normally, is silent or on vibrate," "the times when phone calls are made and text messages are sent and received as well as the number of characters per text message," "the amount of data transferred over 3G and wifi," "hashed values [i.e., replaced with an identifying number for the sake of anonymity] for the phone numbers involved," and much, much more (see http://device-analyzer.cl.cam.ac.uk/collected.htm). To be sure, the researchers involved go to great lengths to ensure that your personal identity remains protected. In addition to assigning hash values to the numbers you call, the project assigns hash values both to the wifi networks and Bluetooth devices you connect with and to the GSM cell your phone connects to (thereby indicating your location). The app also gives you considerable control over the data record-ing and what data you allow to be collected. Nonetheless, insofar as our smartphones open up access to those spaces of our lives previously out of reach (more or less) – both for researchers and for others with less benign intentions – they thereby evoke a new range of issues and questions regarding privacy in a digital age (Bechmann et al. under review). In particular, as we will explore more fully below, such surveillance is not always voluntary, and our online and offline lives risk becoming more and more like those in a medieval village in which "everybody knows everything about everybody." As the phenomena of "trial by Internet" and cyberbullying make clear, our increasing *inability* to hide or get away from those who seek to do us harm in such a medieval village – including, worst case, a self-righteous mob inspired by unproven allegations, e.g., of sexual assault – opens up a number of critical ethical (and political) concerns (Jensen 2007).

Moreover, especially as fluid and interactive digital media simul-taneously enjoy a global scope, they evoke a host of important ethical issues: because our communications can quickly and easily reach very large numbers of people around the globe, our use of digital communication technologies thus makes us *cosmopolitans* (citizens of the world) in striking new ways. In this new context, we are forced to take into account the various and often very diverse cultural perspectives on the ethical issues that emerge in our use of digital media. So I will stress throughout this book how the assumptions and ethical norms of different cultures shape specific ways of reflecting on such matters as privacy (chapter 2), copyright (chapter 3), and pornography and violence (chapter 5).

Finally, our engagements with digital media appear to have consequences for nothing less foundational than our most basic conceptions of selfhood and identity – of who we are as human beings. To be sure, questions such as "Who am I – really?" and "Who ought I to be?" are among the most abstract and difficult ones we can ask as human beings. Indeed, outside of an occasional philosophy class or, perhaps, a mid-life crisis, we may rarely raise such questions with the sort of sustained attention and informed reflection that they deserve and require. At the same time, however, there are strong theoretical and urgently practical reasons for taking up such questions here. To begin with, the Medium Theory developed by Harold Innis, Elizabeth Eisenstein, Marshall McLuhan, Walter Ong (1988), and Joshua Meyrowitz (1985) and, more recently, Naomi Baron (2008) and Zsuzsanna Kondor (2009), demonstrates strong correlations between our diverse modalities of communication and our sense of selfhood. These correlations begin with the stage of orality and what is characterized as a relational sense of selfhood. The emergence of literacy appears to correlate with more individual understandings of selfhood – so much so that Foucault has characterized writing as a "technology of the self" (1987, 1988). Emphases on individual aspects of identity emerge in conjunction with the Protestant Reformation and then as underlying both much of modern ethical theory and political theories justifying democratic regimes. With the rise of the "secondary orality" of electric media – beginning with radio, movies, and TV and then extending into the age of networked digital media – there appears to be a shift in Western societies (back) towards more relational emphases of selfhood and identity (Ess 2010). In addition, it is a commonplace in philosophy that our sense of human nature and selfhood drive our primary ethical assumptions and frameworks. In particular, we will begin exploring more fully below how questions of identity immediately interact with our most basic assumptions regarding ethical agency and responsibility. We will further see in our ethical toolkit (chapter 6) that our emphases on either more individual or more relational aspects of selfhood and identity are definitive for (more individually oriented) utilitarian and deontological ethics, in (some) contrast to (more relationally oriented) virtue and feminist ethics and the ethics shaped by Buddhist, Confucian, and African traditions, for example. While questions of identity are, again, among the most difficult we can raise and seek to resolve, our responses to those questions are crucial if we are to make coherent choices regarding the ethical frameworks we think best suited to help us analyze and resolve the ethical challenges evoked by digital media.

Lastly, our assumptions regarding identity and selfhood have immediate and practical import when we begin to think about, to begin with, the nature of privacy – specifically, if what we feel and think we need to protect is a more individual and/or more shared or collective sense of privacy (chapter 2). Similar questions hold for our understandings of who should have – and should not have – access to our intellectual property – i.e., whether we hold to more traditional (meaning, more individual and exclusive) conceptions of property, so that we transfer rights to its use to others only in exchange for monetary or other sorts of considerations, or to more inclusive notions of property, e.g., as an inclusive good to be shared freely, as we routinely do when giving copies of our favorite music and films to friends, for example (chapter 3). By the same token, our underlying notions of selfhood and identity will prove critical to our analyses of the issues surrounding friendship, democracy, and citizen journalism (chapter 4) and those evoked by pornography and violence in digital environments (chapter 5).

In short, there are perhaps no harder questions for us to confront than those surrounding our own identity – but such questions also seem unavoidable if we are to make progress in responding to the multiple ethical issues we encounter in a digital age.

Digital media ethics: how to proceed?

At first glance, developing such an ethics would seem to be an impossible task. Again, digital media remain *analogue* media in essential ways – the music arriving at our ears remains analogue, etc. And so the "lifeworlds" of human experience that digital media now increasingly define remain connected with the lifeworlds of earlier generations and cultures: this means that there remain important *continuities* with earlier ethical experience and reflection as well. At the same time, digital media often present us with strikingly new sorts of interactions with one another. So it is not always clear whether – and, if so, then how – ethical guidelines and approaches already in place (and comparatively well established) for traditional media would apply.

In addition, digital media as global media thus force us to confront culturally variable views – regarding not simply basic ethical norms and practices but, more fundamentally, how ethics is to be done. In particular, we will see that non-Western views – represented in this volume by Confucian, Buddhist, and African perspectives – challenge traditional Western notions of the primary importance of the individual, and thereby Western understandings of ethical responsibility as primarily individual responsibility. That is, while we in the West recognize that multiple factors can come into play in influencing an individual's decision – e.g., to tell the truth in the face of strong pressures to lie, to violate another's rights in some way, etc. – we generally hold individuals responsible for their actions, as the individual agent who both makes decisions and acts independently of others. But, these days, our interactions with one another increasingly take place via digital media and networks. This means, more specifically, that multiple actors and agents – not only multiple humans (including software designers as well as users) but also multiple computers, networks, bots, etc. – must work together to make specific acts (both beneficent and harmful) possible. So it appears that, in parallel with the distribution of information via networks, our ethical responsibility may be more accurately understood in terms of a distributed responsibility. That is, in contrast to a single person taking all the responsibility for his or her actions, ethical responsibility for the various actions we are able to undertake via digital media and networks may be shared, so to speak, across the network. We will see that this understanding of distributed responsibility is, in fact, not a new idea; rather, it is one shared with both pre-modern Western philosophies and religions and multiple philosophies and religions around the globe.

On the one hand, this is a Very Good Thing, as it may point towards important ethical norms and practices that can be shared among the multiple cultures and peoples now brought into communication with one another through the Internet and the Web. But, on the other hand, it represents a major challenge especially to Western thinkers used to understanding ethical responsibility in primarily individualistic terms.

Is digital media ethics *possible?* Grounds for hope

These challenges are certainly daunting; indeed, when we first begin to grapple with digital media ethics, especially with a view towards incorporating a range of global perspectives and changing notions of selfhood and responsibility, the tasks before us may seem to be overwhelming and, we may be tempted to think, futile.

But both our collective experience with earlier technological developments and more recent experience in the domain of information and computing ethics (ICE) suggest that, despite the considerable challenges of developing new ethical frameworks for new technologies, we are nonetheless able to do so. Indeed, this experience provides us with a number of examples of ethical resolutions that "work" both globally (as they involve discerning shared norms and understandings) and locally (as they further involve developing ways of interpreting and applying shared norms in specific cultural contexts – and thereby preserving the distinctive ethical differences that define diverse cultural identities).

Two examples are useful here. To begin with, as the Internet and Web first emerged in the 1990s, more and more researchers from a range of disciplines and cultures/countries sought to study the rapidly expanding ways in which humans interacted with one another online. Internet research thus developed and expanded – leading, for example, to the founding of the international Association of Internet Researchers (AoIR) in 1999. Along the way, however, more and more researchers were forced to wrestle with often new ethical issues concerning, for example, whether or not they were obliged to protect the identity and privacy of their subjects, whether or not their subjects enjoyed the right to informed consent, and so forth. These ethical demands were familiar to researchers in medicine and the social sciences, but precisely only as they were developed and applied to embodied subjects in real-world experiments and research. Some argued that, insofar as researchers examined only what happened online, especially in "virtual" environments and communities, no "real" human subjects were involved – and hence the ethics of traditional human subjects' protections did not apply. Others argued – supported by growing evidence that, in fact, our online behaviors and expressions are closely tied to our offline lives and selves – that some version of human subjects' protections should apply to online research as well.

In 2000, the AoIR began a two-year project to develop ethical guidelines for Internet researchers. Briefly, in this project we (I was chair of the committee, 2000–5) faced the range of difficulties that confront similar efforts to develop ethics for digital media, beginning with the need to determine how far established ethical frameworks may – and may not – successfully resolve the issues evoked by digital media and their new possibilities for communication, human interaction, and so forth. In addition, research on Internet-based phenomena is undertaken by individuals from around the globe; this means that when these researchers encounter ethical difficulties, they thus bring to bear on their ethical reflections a wide range of culturally variable ethical traditions and frameworks, along with often diverse laws (e.g., concerning privacy and data privacy protection).

In the face of such disciplinary and cultural diversity, how on earth could anyone imagine developing a single set of ethical guidelines that could be endorsed by researchers from around the globe?

Within two years, however, an interdisciplinary and international committee (representing eleven countries, both East and West) developed a set of ethical guidelines for Internet research that were in fact endorsed by the AoIR membership (AoIR Ethics

Working Group 2002). The AoIR guidelines have subsequently found extensive use by students and researchers across a range of countries and cultures, strongly suggesting that they are indeed useful in resolving a number of ethical issues evoked in Internet research, even though these may arise in widely diverse cultural and national domains.

By the same token, the emergence around 2005 of "Web 2.0" – i.e., those range of applications most of us use these days, beginning with SNSs and other forms of social media such as sites featuring user-developed content (think YouTube), micro-blogging (think Twitter), and so on – opened up a new array of ethical challenges for researchers. Building on the findings and procedures of the first AoIR document, a second set of guidelines has been developed over the past few years designed to address the newer sorts of ethics problems encountered by researchers investigating these more contemporary communicative environments. Of course, the original challenges of disciplinary and cultural diversity are only that much more complex as the Internet and the Web – and, with them, researchers intrigued by what we do there – have grown to encompass ever larger and ever more diverse populations and cultures around the globe. Nonetheless, the new set of guidelines was approved by the AoIR membership towards the close of 2012 (see Markham and Buchanan 2012).

More broadly, an emerging global dialogue among philosophers and ethicists regarding privacy and data privacy protection rights has highlighted, as we might expect, considerable differences between diverse cultures regarding our understandings and expectations surrounding individual and collective privacy. But, as we will see in more detail in chapter 2, this global dialogue appears to be converging on a set of shared norms and agreements regarding the nature of privacy. Importantly, these shared norms and agreements are understood, interpreted, and applied in different ways in different cultures and nations. That is, "privacy" in Thailand, China, and Japan is understood in ways that reflect the basic cultural assumptions and national norms of these countries – and thereby preserve the distinctive identities and traditions of these cultures. Again, these understandings of privacy differ considerably from their counterparts in Western countries, such as the United States and the European Union, where, as we would expect, prevailing understandings of privacy reflect the underlying cultural assumptions and norms of these nations. Nonetheless, insofar as both Eastern and Western understandings derive from shared norms and conceptions of privacy, the result is an ethical pluralism that thereby conjoins shared ethical norms alongside important (indeed, defining) cultural differences.

How to do ethics in the new mediascape: dialogical approaches, difference, and pluralism

These examples of the AoIR guidelines and an emerging pluralism regarding privacy suggest that we can undertake the enterprise of digital media ethics with some hope of success. As well, I think that we can further draw from these examples important suggestions for how to proceed. Both examples, in fact, share two elements in common. To begin with, they each incorporate what we can think of as dialogical approaches – approaches that emphasize the importance of listening for and respecting differences between our diverse ethical views.

Ordinarily – especially if our thinking is shaped by a polarized "either/or" common in popular media reporting – we tend to understand the difference between two views in only one possible way: if the two views are different, one must be right and the other wrong. As we will explore more carefully in chapter 6, such an approach is called ethical absolutism or ethical monism. Such absolutism or monism may work well in certain contexts and with regard to some ethical matters. But, especially in a global context, a frequent, limiting consequence of such ethical monism is to force us into thinking that one and only one particular ethical framework and set of norms and values (usually, those of the culture(s) in which we grew up) are right, and those that are different can only be wrong.

Oftentimes, in the face of such monism and its intolerance of different views, we are tempted to take a second position – one called ethical relativism. Ethical relativism argues that beliefs, norms, practices, frameworks, etc., are legitimate solely in relation to a specific culture; in this way, ethical relativism allows us to avoid the intolerance of ethical monism and to accept all views as legitimate. Such an approach is especially attractive as it prevents us from having to judge among diverse views and cultures: we can endorse all of them as legitimate in at least a relative way (i.e., relative to a specific culture, time, and/or place).

But the examples we have seen of ethical pluralism in both Internet research ethics and emerging understandings of privacy and data privacy protection make clear that such pluralism stands as a third possibility – one that is something of a middle ground between absolutism and relativism. That is, to begin with, such pluralism avoids the either/or of ethical monism – an either/or that forces us to choose between two different views, endorsing one as right and the other as wrong. Rather, pluralism shows how different views may emerge as diverse interpretations or applications of shared norms, beliefs, practices, etc. To be sure, not all of our differences can be resolved so neatly: but, when pluralism succeeds, the differences between two (or more) views thus do not force us to accept only one view as right and all the others as wrong. Rather, we can thereby see that many (but not necessarily all) different views may be right, insofar as they function as diverse interpretations and applications of shared norms and values.

In addition (though this may be a little confusing at this stage), ethical pluralism thereby overcomes a second "either/or" – namely, the apparent polarity between ethical monism and ethical relativism themselves. That is, when we first encounter these two positions – and, once more, especially if our thinking has been shaped by prevailing dualities in the thinking of those around us, including popular media reports – our initial response may again be either/or: either monism is right or relativism is right, but not both. In important ways, ethical pluralism says that both are right, and both are wrong. From a pluralist perspective, monism is correct in its presumption that universally valid norms exist, but mistaken in its insistence that the differences we observe between diverse cultures in terms of their practices and behaviors must mean that only one is right and the rest are wrong. Similarly, from a pluralist perspective, ethical relativism is correct in its attempt to endorse a wide range of different cultural norms and practices as legitimate, but mistaken, first of all, in its denial of universally valid norms.

Again, we will explore these theories of absolutism, relativism, and pluralism in much more detail in chapter 6. Here it suffices simply to introduce these possibilities of thinking in an initial way as we seek to move beyond the either/or thinking that tends to prevail in popular media and thereby tends to shape our own thinking.

Given this first introduction, perhaps we can now see more clearly why the "either/or" underlying much of popular media report works against our best thinking. Ethical pluralism requires us to think in a "both/and" sort of way, as it conjoins both shared norms and their diverse interpretations and applications in different cultures, times, and places. But if the only way we are able to think about ethical matters is in terms of the "either/or" of ethical monism, then we literally cannot conceive of how to move beyond the right/wrong dualisms with which it often confronts us. That is, we will find it difficult conceptually to move towards pluralism and other forms of middle grounds, because our either/or thinking insists that we can only have either unity (shared norms) or difference (in interpretation/application), but not both.

Stated differently: in dialogical processes we emphasize learning to listen for and accept differences – rather than rejecting them from the outset because different views must thereby be wrong (ethical monism). But neither do we come to endorse all possible views as correct (ethical relativism), because not every view can be understood as a legitimate interpretation or application of a shared norm. Rather, dialogical processes help us sort through, on the one hand, which views may stand as diverse interpretations of shared norms in a pluralism and, on the other, those views (e.g., endorsing genocide, racism, violence against women as inferior, etc.) that cannot be justified as interpretations of shared norms.

Further considerations: ethical judgments

Another difficulty with the "moral panics" approach to ethical issues in the new mediascape is that it suggests that "ethics" works like this:

1. There are clear, universally valid norms of right and wrong that we can take as our ethical starting points – as premises in an ethical argument.[2]
2. All that "ethics" really involves is applying these initial premises to the particulars of the current case in front of us – in a straightforward deduction that concludes the right thing to do, as based on our first premises.
3. Once we have our ethical answers in this way, we can be confident that our answers are right; those who disagree with us must be wrong.

This approach to ethics, I would suggest, is not necessarily mistaken; on the contrary, it seems to me that, much of the time, most of us in fact do not perceive an ethical problem or difficulty in the situation we're facing – because our ethical frameworks already provide us with reasonably clear and straightforward answers along just these lines. Most of us, for example, do not routinely lie, steal, or kill – despite sometimes what may be considerable temptations to do so – because we accept the general norms and principles that forbid such acts.

At the same time, however, this initial understanding of ethics obscures a number of important dimensions of ethical reflection.

---

2 Here I use the terms "premise," "argument," "conclusion," etc., in their logical sense. An understanding of the basic element of logic is essential for undertaking ethics – and many ethics texts include an introduction to logic (e.g., Boss 2005; Tavani 2013: ch. 3, etc.). For the sake of brevity I have chosen instead to introduce and discuss a minimal number of logical elements: analogy and questionable analogy in chapter 3; the distinction between exclusive and inclusive "or"s in chapter 5; and the basic fallacy of affirming the consequent in chapter 6. Otherwise, in addition to any preferred resources of instructors, I would further recommend some of the excellent introductions to logic that already exist (e.g., Weston 2000; Bowell and Kemp 2005; Possin 2005).

Among other things, this initial approach runs counter to what seems actually to happen when we encounter genuine ethical problems and puzzles. Take, for example, the notorious problem of downloading music illegally from the Internet. More or less everybody knows that this is illegal, but we are also pulled and influenced in our thinking by other considerations, e.g.:

I'm not likely to get caught, so there's virtually no possibility that this will actually hurt me in some way.

The internationally famous musicians – and the multinational companies that sell their music as product for profit – are certainly wealthy enough. They won't feel the loss of the 2 cents profit they would otherwise enjoy if I paid for the music.

Copyright laws are unfair in principle: they are written for the advantage of the big and already wealthy countries. Thus I think illegal downloading by a struggling student in a developing country is a justified form of protest against multinational capitalism and its exploitation of the poor.

Whatever the law says, the law is the law: I think it should be respected so far as possible – not only in order to avoid punishment, but in order thereby to contribute to good social order.

Even if the chances of getting caught are vanishingly small, if I do get caught, the negative consequences would be enormous (fines, possibly problems at work, maybe even jail time). It's not worth breaking the law to save a few bucks on music.

While internationally famous artists may not miss my contribution to their royalties, local and/or new artists certainly will. I'll not rip them off by illegally copying their music – I'll just order the song online or buy the CD instead.

The point here is not only that we are often pulled in competing directions by values and principles that appear to contradict one another; the more fundamental problem is:

given the specific details of our particular situations, how do we know *which* principle, value, norm, rule, etc., is in fact relevant to our decision?

This is to say, in direct contrast to the "top-down" deductive model of ethical reasoning – i.e., one that moves from given general principles to the specifics of our particular case – this second ethical experience begins with the specifics of our particular case, in order then to try to determine ("bottom-up") which general principles, values, norms, etc., in fact apply.

This second maneuver is thereby far more difficult, as it first requires us to judge – based on the particulars of our case – which general principles, norms, values, etc., apply to our case. Clearly, without such general principles, we cannot make a reasoned decision. But the great difficulty is this:

> there is no general rule/procedure/algorithm for discerning which values, principles, norms, approaches *apply*; rather, these must be discerned and *judged* to be relevant in the first place, *before* we can proceed to any inferences/conclusions about what to do.

Aristotle referred to the kind of judgment that comes into play here as *phronesis* – a term often translated as "practical judgment." For Aristotle (and for many ethicists in multiple traditions around the world), the development of this sort of practical judgment – i.e., one that can help us discern in the first place just which norms and values do apply to the particulars of a specific case – is an ongoing project that continues throughout one's entire life. This is in part because it requires experience – both of successes and failures – as these help us learn (oftentimes, the hard way) what "works" (is relevant) ethically and what doesn't. The first time we try to learn a new skill or ability – say, ice-skating – we are certain to stumble and fall, perhaps catastrophically, and almost certainly more than once. Analogously, our first efforts to grapple with difficult ethical issues that require *phronesis* do not always go well: we are caught in the ethical "bootstrapping" problem of needing precisely the ability to judge that is robust enough to help only after it has been developed and honed through many years of (sometimes hard) experience.

But, as we also say: we have to start somewhere . . .

Overview of the book, including suggestions for use

By now, I hope readers have a reasonably clear idea of the features of digital media that lead to specific sorts of ethical issues that we will explore more fully in subsequent chapters. I also hope that you are beginning to have a sense that, especially with regard to digital media that interconnect us globally, it is important to do so in ways that go beyond the either/or polarities that tend to dominate popular media reporting.

At this stage, it is also important to understand why the chapters are arranged as they are. The book is organized in a somewhat unusual way, but one that has generally proven to be more effective and useful. I follow here what I think of as a "circle" approach to exploring and teaching ethics, one that intentionally moves back and forth between (a) specific, real-world examples from how we actually use digital media, and thereby encounter specific ethical problems and (on a good day) legitimate resolutions, and (b) a number of relevant theories precisely about how we are to resolve such ethical challenges and difficulties. Certainly, this differs from a more common approach: ethics texts often begin with a rather complete listing and discussion of the important theories, on the very sensible view that students can come to grips with specific ethical difficulties only if they are first familiar with a complete range of ethical theories. Here, I've done the reverse, and placed the resources on ethical theory at the end of the text (chapter 6). The idea is to encourage students and instructors to take up just two or three of these theories at the beginning and then apply them to the specific cases taken up in each of the chapters. After students are thereby comfortable with how two or three theories work in their application to real-world cases, they can return with their instructor to take up additional theories – and then apply these theories to additional cases. While I offer a specific reading plan in this direction (below), by placing the theory/meta-theory chapter at the end of the text, I hope to provide students and their instructors with more flexibility in determining for themselves as they go along just how much theory they wish to absorb vis-à-vis specific issues and problems.

This organization reflects my own (several decades of) teaching experience. After some years of attempting the more usual approach of "first, all the theories, then the applications," my students made it clear that they were more likely to learn both an extensive range of theories and how to apply them if we instead began with just two or three theoretical frameworks and then applied these to specific cases. To be sure, our grappling with specific cases early in the course will thus be hampered in the sense that my students will not have a more complete range of theory at their disposal. But, at the same time, it often happens that they will discover that the theories they initially bring to bear on a given case are not adequate – i.e., the initial theories do not allow them to resolve the problems in ways that better fit their own ethical intuitions and sensibilities. In short: from here, they see on their own the need for further theory/theories, and so, as we return from specific cases to more theories (making the circle from praxis to theory), they are characteristically more interested in and open to learning about new theories than they would be if we simply worked through all of them from the outset.

By the same token, nothing prevents us from going back to reconsider earlier cases in light of more recently acquired theories – and thereby seeing these cases in a new light (making the circle from theory to praxis). Indeed, when things work well, our doing so helps us come to resolutions of the ethical problems involved in more satisfying ways than previously. Such resolutions thereby enhance our appreciation not only for how a specific theory may offer distinctive advantages vis-à-vis a specific case, but also for how a now greater range of theories work in their application to real-world issues and problems.

Suggested reading plans

Circle method

Instructors and their students who want to follow this approach can do so by moving into chapter 2 (privacy), before turning to chapter 6 for a first run at some of the most important theories. For both chapters 2 and 3 (copyright and intellectual property), you will find the introductions to utilitarianism and deontology to be the minimum needed from chapter 6; but you may, depending on your interests and contexts, find other(s) to be of importance and interest in this first exploration as well. It's also the case that ethical pluralism is central to chapter 2, and so it will be helpful to take up the section on ethical pluralism in chapter 6 in conjunction with chapter 2.

From there, you can return to chapter 3 – and/or turn further in chapter 6 for more theory, meta-theory, and especially the material on non-Western ethical traditions (Buddhism, Confucian thought, and African thought). This much from chapter 6 should be completed prior to chapter 4 (friendship, democracy, and citizen journalism). As well, the material on virtue ethics from chapter 6 is presupposed for chapters 4 and 5 (pornography and violence). But some readers may prefer to go to chapter 5 before chapter 4 (or 3, for that matter), as more concrete and specific in certain ways, before taking up chapter 4 (or 3).

"Traditional" method

Instructors and students who prefer to plunge first into matters of ethical theory and meta-theory should simply start with chapter 6 first, before turning to any of the specific chapters (2–5).

Case-studies; discussion/reflection/writing/ research questions

Each chapter includes real-world examples intended to elicit initial reflection; and so these are accompanied by often an extensive series of questions and suggestions for "reflection/ discussion/writing/research." These questions and suggestions can be used by students and classes as initial catalysts for reflection, discussion, and perhaps informal writing. Instructors may also find useful suggestions here for questions and material that they can develop into formal writing and research assignments more precisely tuned to their own curriculum and goals. But these are only "starters" and examples. Instructors and students will certainly come up with their own preferred questions, case-studies, etc.

In general, I suggest that students have a chance to reflect and write through their initial responses to opening case-studies and examples prior to further reading into the chapter. The intention is to help students (and their instructors) articulate their initial intuitions and sensibilities as a starting point for discussion and further reflection. Of course, students (and their instructors) may eventually change their views, but our initial intuitions and views are where we must start, and it helps to articulate these as fully and clearly as possible before moving on.

OK – enjoy!

CHAPTER TWO

Privacy in the Electronic Global Metropolis?

Everyone has the right to respect for his private and family life, his home and his correspondence.

> (Council of Europe, European Convention for the Protection of Human Rights and Fundamental Freedoms, Section I, Article 8 [1950])

In a democracy, privacy is a basic political right that cannot be sold out in the marketplace.

> (Reidenberg 2000)

Under *ubuntu* [an African worldview emphasizing connectedness and community welfare over individual welfare], personal identity is dependent upon and defined by the community. Within the group or community, personal information is common to the group, and attempts to withhold or sequester personal information are viewed as abnormal or deviant. While the boundary between groups may be less permeable to information transfer, *ubuntu* lacks any emphasis on individual privacy.

> (Burk 2007: 103)

Every teenager wants privacy. Every single last one of them, whether they tell you or not, wants privacy. – "Waffles"

> (boyd and Marwick 2011)

Chapter overview

This sampling of diverse perspectives on privacy leads us into initial reflections and then exercises on privacy and anonymity online. Following some cautions regarding the notion and possible (mis)uses of "culture," we explore how different people in different cultures understand and value "privacy" and private life in different ways – including important differences between Eastern and Western conceptions, as well as between the United States and the European Union. In this context, finally, we first examine the important meta-ethical positions of ethical absolutism, ethical relativism, and ethical pluralism. We see how these positions shape our responses to the diversity of cultural views and beliefs regarding privacy – diversity that must be preserved, in my view, alongside any effort to establish a global ethics of norms and practices that are shared around the world.

Information and privacy in the global digital age

1. "Privacy" and anonymity online – is there any?

As the 2012 scandal concerning General Petraeus (now former director of the US Central Intelligence Agency) makes clear, even very smart and well-informed people may mistakenly assume that their email communications are more or less private. We all know, of course, that someone with specialized software and hardware tools (such as a hacker and/or a government agency "sniffing" for information) may look into your email. Apart from these sorts of positive actions, though, we might assume that we can trust that our email is sent and received as private information.

In addition, many users may believe that they can send and receive information via email with their identity protected. Indeed, we know how easy it is to set up a free email account with a popular service such as Gmail: we can choose any user name we like, for example – including simple pseudonyms that appear to hide our real identity. Such pseudonymity or anonymity might be very helpful – especially for political purposes. Democratic activists in countries with authoritarian regimes have used email (along with social media and other technologies) to exchange ideas and information considered by the authorities to be dangerous, to help organize protests and other important actions, etc. With their real identities hidden behind a pseudonym, they can do so with greater freedom and safety. (This sort of scenario, in fact, is part of the original intuitions as to why privacy is a crucial right to be protected in democratic societies.)

But many users do not seem to be aware, for example, that their email contains a great deal of information about them – including information that can be used to determine their identity – and that such information is essentially public.

For example, most email clients (i.e., the software packages such as Outlook, Outlook Express, Entourage, [Apple] Mail, and Thunderbird) are set to show users only the basic contents of an email: sender, recipient, cc's, subject line, and email body. But look again: these clients also allow you to review the complete contents of your email – usually by selecting, e.g., "Source" under the view menu in Thunderbird or "Internet Headers" in Entourage, once a given message is selected.

Initial reflection/discussion/writing

Select a recent email from a friend, and then view the complete source of the email as outlined above. (Nota bene: if you use a webmail application such as Gmail, you may not be able to see the complete source in any easy or straightforward way. As we are about to see, there is good reason for this.)

A) What strikes you about the information contained here in the lines before the usual information about sender and receiver addresses?

B) Notice that each email includes here a history of how it was sent, usually in a format like this (from a recent email using a free guest account):

```
Received: by 10.49.108.69 with SMTP id
hi5csp744895qeb;
Wed, 14 Nov 2012 01:13:20 -0800 (PST)
Received: by 10.180.92.103 with SMTP id
cl7mr24734170wib.16.1352884399902;
Wed, 14 Nov 2012 01:13:19 -0800 (PST)
Return-Path:<charles.ess@--.com>
Received: from mailout--.--.com (---.--.com.
[213.165.64.43])
by -.----.com with SMTP id j5si22736062
eeo.62.2012.11.14.01.13.18;
Wed, 14 Nov 2012 01:13:19 -0800 (PST)
```

In particular, notice the IP (Internet Protocol) address: 213.165.64.43. What, if anything, does this IP address tell you? (Nota bene: if you are not able to find this information easily using your mail client and/or in a specific email – i.e., depending on how your friend's email service works – again, we are about to see there may be a very good reason for this.)

ADDITIONAL INFORMATION, DISCUSSION

You may already know that such an IP address is essential to each and every transmission of information – whether an email, the text of a chat message, video, music, etc. – that takes place via the Internet. You may further know that your computer is assigned an IP address by your Internet service provider (ISP) – usually a "dynamic" address, one that changes in a small way each time you log in to the ISP. Sometimes, the address is "static" – one permanently assigned to your particular machine.

But if you've ever wondered why, when you're browsing a website, you receive ads (either within a page and/or as a pop-up) that seem to "know" your physical location, the simple fact is: they do. That is, as your machine exchanges information with a website through your browser, your IP address is sent along as well. Even if you have a dynamic address, this change still belongs within a set of addresses assigned to a given ISP in a given area. And so if you look up the IP address that accompanies your mail (using any of the web-based services found by searching for "IP address lookup"), you may be surprised to discover how close the resulting physical location is to your own physical address.

It is for this reason, then, that Gmail – at least on occasion but by no means always, as we will see – justifies not revealing users' IP addresses in mail headers: "IP addresses can be considered sensitive information. As such, Gmail may hide sender IP address information from outgoing mail headers in some circumstances" ("Seeing a sender's IP address", http://support.google.com/mail/ bin/answer.py?hl=en&topic=1278&answer=26903, accessed November 14, 2012). The service I used to create the above example is even better at not revealing my physical location. Because it is located in a European Union country and thus bound to strict data protection laws, looking up the IP address will reveal only the loca- tion of the mail server (in said country), not the machine I used to send it. (In General Petraeus's case, however, his more easily dis- cernable IP address contributed to the discovery of his extramarital affair; Perlroth 2012.)

And what about your web-browsing?

Second reflection/discussion/writing

If you use the web browser Firefox, download and install the add-on "Collusion." (Under the "Tools" menu, select the "Add- ons" tab, which should take you to an introductory page that explains what add-ons are. Look for the link that allows you to "Browse all add-ons": this will take you to a second page that includes a search box. Type in "Collusion" and follow the direc- tions from there.) As Collusion runs, it tracks the websites that are tracking you as you navigate through the Web – and presents its findings in a graph that shows the increasingly complex set of links to the sites you have visited and the services they use to record your browsing activities.

After a few days of letting Collusion run, have a look at the graph. And/or: if you are interested in seeing more of the details of how such tracking works, you can install an add-on such as "NoScript." NoScript gives you control over the mini-programs or scripts (built in the program language Java) that are required for many of the conveniences a given website offers, such as search functions – as well as those used to track your web-browsing. The add-on specifically warns web servers that you do not want to be tracked, thus giving you the possibility to "opt in" to such tracking, rather than accede to it unawares and without explicit consent (the current default – one we will explore more fully below).

C) What strikes you about the resulting patterns and connections that Collusion (and/or NoScript) presents to you? Are there any surprises here?

D) As we will explore more fully below, "privacy" online is not simply a matter of protecting personal or sensitive information – information that increasingly seems to define our identity or sense of selfhood, and thus information that could be used to harm us in some way, beginning with simple identity theft and extending to worse instances such as cyberbullying and surveillance by oppressive governments. In addition, especially in an age dominated by our use of social media such as social networking sites, micro-blogging services such as Twitter, shared video sites such as YouTube, etc. – our Internet use and web-browsing also reveals a great deal about those to whom we are closest. In at least some cultures and contexts, such as Denmark and Norway, what we want to protect is not solely the personal or sensitive information of an individual but also the personal information of those within our "intimate sphere" (*intimsfære*) – our close circle of friends and family. In these contexts, what is important to protect is not simply individual privacy but our "private life" (*privatlivet*) as made up by these close relationships.

So, before going much further in thinking about privacy, we need to be clearer about just *what* we want protected and/or what we have a *right* to have protected. Hence two questions here:

(i) In terms of the information available about you as you send email and use the Web, just *what* do you think/ feel needs to be kept within your control? Personal and sensitive information about you – and, if so, what counts as such information? And/or personal and sensitive information about those with whom you communicate and interact in various online environments, beginning with your close circle of friends and family?

(ii) Given the amount of information you supply – in the form of your IP address that accompanies your email, and especially the picture of your web-browsing habits and patterns created as various websites and services record your IP address along with your specific visits – how much "privacy" do you appear to have online? More specifically: given your response to the first question above, do online environments allow you to control and protect the kinds of information you think/feel *should* be protected, e.g., as a *right*?

E) Whatever your responses in (D), explain why. That is, what arguments/evidence/reasons and/or other grounds, including feelings or intuitions, can you appeal to that would justify your response(s)?

Of course, it is no surprise (at least to most of us) that companies, governments, and some savvy individuals have access to extensive databases that record and document individual web-browsing: when coupled with other databases that record, say, your purchases at your favorite store (whether online or offline) and increasingly powerful "data-mining" techniques that cross-correlate this information, such institutions (and at least some hackers) thus learn an astonishing amount of detail about you as an individual consumer. And so it is that Amazon or Facebook, for example, along with thousands of other corporations, are able to "micro-target" advertising precisely to you and tailored to meet your apparent interests and needs. While much of this may be useful to interested shoppers, or at least benign, it is certainly not without its risks and discomforts. To cite a prominent example in the US: early in 2012, Target sent coupons for baby cribs and clothes to a high-school girl. Target's sophisticated software analysis of the young girl's shopping activities indicated a high probability that she was pregnant – but the coupons came as a less than pleasant surprise to her father who, until their arrival, had not been informed of the situation (Duhigg 2012). Still more darkly, such abilities to track persons through their online lives – lives that become ever more extensive as digital media become ever more ubiquitous – further allows for vicious forms of cyberbullying, various forms of identity theft, and the activities of groups such as Anonymous (see the opening discussion in chapter 1).

All of this makes clear that IP addresses – especially when coupled with other information collected about us – are indeed "sensitive and personal" (to use the language of EU data privacy protection laws). But this further helps highlight the fact that there are important differences between how diverse countries and cultures decide to treat IP addresses. US-based Google has long held that IP addresses are not "personal information": by contrast, European Union data commissioners ruled in 2008 that IP addresses are indeed personal information and thus require data privacy protection (White 2008). More broadly, the EU is moving towards protecting data privacy in positive ways – much to the consternation of US-based companies such as Google. In 2012 the EU introduced legislation requiring websites to request the explicit consent of users to the use of cookies – specifically those required for third-party advertising and related functions, including "financial logging, ad affiliation, click fraud detection, research and market analysis, product improvement and debugging" (Article 29 Data Protection Working Party 2012a: 11). Those of us accessing the Web within the domains defined by this legislation will notice, indeed, occasional requests for such consent. This is the sort of consent that folk outside the EU can now give – or not, depending on the website and their interests and needs – if they choose to install a security add-on such as NoScript. But, according to Google, such a requirement would "break the Internet" (Gapper 2012). Mine still seems to be working – but, in the meantime, the EU has drafted even more stringent data privacy regulations that are scheduled for implementation in 2015 (Article 29 Data Protection Working Party 2012b). Industry opposition to these laws can be expected to be quite fierce: for the first time, the regulation will hold for all member states of the EU, with no exceptions for more lenient interpretations, for example. At the same time, "The Regulation has much more rigorous sanctions: in case of substantive violations data controllers can be fined up to 2% of their global turnover" (Mireille Hildebrandt, personal communication, December 16, 2012). (See also Gilbert 2012: my very great thanks to Mireille for suggesting these resources.)

More broadly, we have begun to see that there are indeed strong cultural influences on how we understand and value "privacy" – beginning with strong differences between the United States and the European Union, as reflected in and suggested by this example. However these contrasting views may be resolved (if at all), here we can continue by noting that it is possible to establish and sustain at least some level of anonymity online: in addition to using security add-ons such as NoScript, you can explore using "anonymizer" software and webmail and web-browsing services that hide this sort of information, beginning with Tor (https://www.torproject.org/index.html.en). As well, by using encryption software (e.g., the freely available "Pretty Good Privacy" software), users can send emails that can be easily deciphered and read only by recipients who have been given the required encryption key, thereby assuring themselves a reasonably strong degree of privacy. But unless users take these unusual – and, in my experience, not widely familiar – steps, their transmissions across the Internet will thus be more or less open to anyone who cares to look.

Similar comments hold, by the way, for people using their computers to share information through peer-to-peer (p2p) networks – such as those used, for example, in downloading and uploading music and other files through a network such as BitTorrent, but also in instant messaging exchanges, including the use of video cameras for video chat and conferencing. Not to mention doing all of this more and more on your smartphone. (Tor, for example, is available for Android devices.) Be careful out there!

Look up the privacy policies of the email service you use – whether it's a university-related service and/or one of the many "free" services such as Gmail, Yahoo, etc. Beyond what these policies say regarding what information about you is collected and shared, be sure to notice the justifications for various forms of information-sharing.

REFLECTION/DISCUSSION/WRITING

F) Any surprises here? In particular,
   (i) is there either a kind of information about you and/or
   (ii) a use of that information allowed for under the privacy policy that is news to you – i.e., that you were not aware of?
   Identify these clearly.
G) Insofar as the policy you examine offers an ethical justification for its practices, highlight at least one of these.
      Either individually and/or as a small group/class, analyze the argument(s) at work here, especially with a view towards
   (i) discerning what kind of ethical argument is offered (e.g., utilitarian, deontological, etc.); and
   (ii) determining whether or not you (and your cohorts) find the argument persuasive.
   If so, explain why. If not, explain why not.

2. *"Privacy": a matter of culture*

As the example of Google vs. the EU regarding IP addresses suggests – and as we might expect – our understandings of privacy vary widely, not simply from individual to individual but also from culture to culture. The following exercise is intended to give you and your cohorts an initial set of indicators of where your sensibilities regarding privacy might lie upon a continuum of possibilities. It may also help you begin to think about what you mean by "privacy" as a concept or notion.

Consider the "smart ID" project of Thailand – a project that aims to create and issue national identity cards that contain the following information:

Name _____
Address _____
Date of Birth _____
Religion _____ .
Blood Group _____
Marital Status _____
Social Security _____
Health Insurance _____
Driver's License _____
Taxation Data [income bracket, taxes paid/owed] _____
Health-care Entitlements _____
Officially Registered Poor Person? _____

(Kitiyadisai 2005: 22)

REFLECTION/DISCUSSION/WRITING

A) Where do you draw the line? Beginning with your own responses, which of these elements of identity would you be comfortable having encoded on a chip in a national ID card? Which of these elements do you think/feel/believe should not be included in a national ID card?

B) Why? In both cases, what arguments/evidence/reasons and/or other grounds, including feelings or intuitions, can you appeal to that would justify your response(s)?

C) You may want to compare your and your cohorts' sensibilities with the following that I've observed in using this example with students and faculty from a variety of cultural backgrounds.

Roughly, reactions/responses range from a minimum to a maximum amount of information designated as public or private. These variations, moreover, appear to correlate with a number of values and sensibilities that are known to vary from culture to culture. One of the most important is suggested in the set of quotations at the beginning of this chapter, in the contrast between the Council of

Europe's articulation of what amounts to individual privacy as a human right vis-à-vis a lack of emphasis on individual privacy in the worldview of *ubuntu*, for example. Indeed, we will see that this lack of emphasis on individual privacy – in part because of a greater emphasis on community harmony and integration – is characteristic of a wide range of non-Western cultures and traditions.

And within the domain of Western countries and cultures, there are further variations in our expectations regarding privacy that correlate with often very different understandings of the role of the state vis-à-vis the life of the individual.

So, for example, most US students – if they accept the idea of a national identity card at all – are moderately comfortable with a card that would contain name, address, date of birth, and social security number. Perhaps religion. Perhaps blood group (in case of a medical emergency). Perhaps driver's license. Perhaps marital status. But it becomes unclear how much the federal government – or anyone else, for that matter, besides the person who handles my medical bills – needs to know about my health insurance. As for taxation data, including income data – no thank you! (And, of course, while there are plenty of poor people in the US, they are not "officially registered" – nor, I imagine, would anyone be eager to have that registration included in their identity card.) In Norway, by contrast, everyone's tax records are published annually online – in part, I am told, so that everyone can see that everyone else is contributing their fair share to the common good.

Danish students and faculty draw the line quickly at religion. This is in keeping with a strong Danish sensibility – encoded in Danish data protection laws (and, for that matter, in those of the European Union) – that insists on a (more or less) absolute freedom of belief and viewpoint in matters of political ideology and religion. But if we are to enjoy such freedom (as we will explore more fully below), our beliefs and viewpoints must be protected as personal information.

What about Thai people? Roughly speaking, while there is a strong opposition among some activists and academics to the national "smart ID card," they have been accepted by the majority of the population as necessary – in part, for example, as such cards, the government has argued, will help in the fight against domestic terrorism.

Finally, if you come from a culture shaped by emphases on community harmony – as the *ubuntu* example suggests, you may see no (good) reason at all for wanting any form of individual privacy.

Overall, then, there emerge these points along a continuum of possible responses:

Minimal info . . . Moderate info . . . Maximum info
(Denmark)   (US)   (Thailand)   (*ubuntu*)

Given this continuum and set of points for the sake of specific national/cultural references, where have you and your cohorts drawn the line?

So far as you can tell at this point, how might your sensibilities regarding privacy be connected with the larger national, political, and cultural environments in which you find yourselves?

Interlude: can we meaningfully talk about 'culture'?

Q: How do you tell the difference between an introverted Norwegian and an extroverted Norwegian?

A: The extroverted Norwegian looks at your shoes when he's talking to you.

This joke was told to me by Johnny Søraker in 2005, in response to a joke I passed on from Minnesota: "Did you hear about the Norwegian man who loved his wife so much he almost told her?" Both jokes trade on the cultural stereotype of Norwegians as very reserved; both are funny, in my view – especially if they are told by Norwegians (or their descendants) as a way of poking fun at their own tendencies and habits.

These jokes help make a larger point: there are sets of behavior patterns (beginning with language), norms and values, preferences, communication styles, and judgments regarding what counts as beauty, good taste, etc., that are characteristic of one group of people in contrast with others. Since the nineteenth century, anthropologists and other social scientists have accustomed us to thinking of these sets in terms of "culture." We have just seen an effort to associate specific attitudes and beliefs regarding privacy with larger (primarily national) cultures. We will continue to pay attention to "culture" in these ways throughout this volume, but it is important to make clear from the outset how far such references are useful and in what ways these uses of "culture" are limited and, indeed, potentially misleading, if not simply destructive.

To begin with, as I hope these Norwegian jokes suggest, such generalizations about (national) cultures contain at least some grains of truth. In this case, that is, it seems safe to say – as a generalization – that indeed many (if not most) of the people born and raised in Norway are, in comparison with, say, the average Midwestern American, more shy and reserved. Such generalizations are useful – not only for the sake of good humor, but also as starting points for thinking through our differences and similarities. Indeed, for many (most?) people, our culture (however difficult it is to define) usually serves as a core component of our identity, one that demarcates in various ways how we are both alike (in relation to those who share at least many of the elements of the same culture) and different (from those shaped by different cultures).

So, for example, as a Midwesterner, I know that (most of) my East Coast friends will speak and walk more quickly than is the norm in Springfield, Missouri. It is also the case, of course, that these sorts of differences are the occasion for our judging (or, as frequently happens, misjudging) one another on the basis of what is normal (in at least a statistical sense) for our own culture. As in many (most?) other small towns in the US Midwest, the norm is to be "friendly" with, e.g., cashiers and sales clerks, so as to spend a little time in conversation during the course of an otherwise commercial exchange. This friendliness is often (mis)interpreted as time-wasting superficiality by some of my East Coast friends.

In turn, their tendency to avoid such small talk might tempt a Midwesterner to (mis)judge them as abrupt, unfriendly, aloof, perhaps arrogant.

And, of course, as we move across national cultures, the differences become even more striking. So, as the jokes above suggest, Norwegians tend to be much more reserved, for example, than Southern Europeans. And so on.

I hope these examples illustrate three critical points that should be kept in mind any time the word "culture" appears in this text. First, up to a point at least, these sorts of generalizations are useful – perhaps even essential – if we are to understand and communicate respectfully with one another. That is, if I understand these sorts of cultural differences, I can better anticipate how to communicate appropriately with those who do not share my own cultural values and communicative preferences. So, for example, I am less likely to misinterpret my East Coast friend's curt response (curt, that is, as compared with the norm for a Midwesterner) as rude or unfriendly, and more likely to understand it as intended, i.e., as efficient, to the point, and thereby respectful of our time as a limited and thus valuable commodity.

More broadly, these differences are interesting and enriching, as they make us aware of what deeply shapes our individual identities and group norms, and thereby of the incredible richness and diversity of the human family. In particular, these generalizations should thus be helpful to us in coming to understand both ourselves and the multiple Others around us, as we are both similar and irreducibly different in critical ways. Doing so, finally, is necessary if we are to overcome the twin dangers of ethnocentrism (assuming our own ways of doing things are universal) and then judging Others as inferior because their ways are different from our own. Human history is too full of the sorts of warfare, colonization, enslavement, and imperialism that follow upon such ethnocentrism. As Ames and Rosemont put it: "the only thing more dangerous than making cultural generalizations is the reductionism that results from not doing so" (1998: 20). That is, as risky, difficult, and inevitably incomplete as an attempt to characterize culture may be, it seems a necessary exercise if we are to avoid assuming that all others must be like us, and that they are less than fully human if they are not.

But, second, when we use such generalizations, we obviously run the risk of turning them into simple and unfair stereotypes that may foster unjust prejudices rather than intercultural understanding. Hence it must be remembered: every generalization, most especially the generalizations that we think may help characterize a given "culture," by definition entails multiple exceptions to the general rule. In statistical terms, there are always "outliers" – those persons who stand outside the statistical norm as defined by the standard bell curve. So, while many Midwesterners may seem friendly, open, and extroverted as compared with many Norwegians, of course there will be at least a few introverted Midwesterners and at least a few extroverted Norwegians who simply confound the generalization. In other words, we must never mistake a generalization for anything other than a generalization – not, for example, some sort of universal category that somehow captures an eternal and immutable essence of Midwestern-ness, Norwegian-ness, etc. This is the difference, in short, between a possibly useful generalization and a potentially misleading and destructive stereotype.

Third, however far we can fairly make such generalizations about a given culture, we must further keep in mind that, for every individual who may share such national characteristics, she or he is further shaped by a very complex range of additional differences and variations both within and beyond national categories. Folk in Eastern Oklahoma are clearly distinct from folk in Western Oklahoma, just as people in Aarhus (Denmark) have distinct (and not always positive) impressions of how Copenhageners, while clearly Danes, at the same time differ from them (and vice versa, of course). Immigrant communities are distinct in multiple ways, while simultaneously including people seeking either to assimilate to or hybridize with the larger national culture. Indeed, in any given city, a specific neighborhood features a specific set of cultures or subcultures as affiliated with age, ethnicity, and class. And then, of course, gender – generally – makes a difference as well. Oh yes: all of these change over time, of course – some elements more quickly than others – complicating the picture still further.

All of this means, again, that any generalizations we make about a culture can be taken only as starting points – and as dynamic concepts (i.e., concepts open to change), not static concepts. That is, while potentially useful for our initial reflections and encounters with one another, further exploration almost always leads us to more complex and nuanced understandings. As a result, we will almost always modify and perhaps reject altogether elements of these starting points. In fact, we are about to see an example of this sort of modification shortly, in Soraj Hongladarom's account of Buddhist understandings of the person and privacy – an account that will nicely complicate the basic differences between Thai and US culture that we have started with here (see pp. 45–7). At the same time, however, some notion of culture remains useful when handled with care, beginning with current work in intercultural communication (e.g., Cheong et al. 2012; see also Cohen 2012: 17 for a postmodernist account).

In our context, then, I believe (judge) that the grains of truth underlying cultural generalizations, and their utility in helping us to overcome ethnocentrism, to come to more respectful understandings of Others as Other (i.e., as genuinely and irreducibly different from ourselves), and to communicate with one another more effectively, help offset the risks and limitations of such generalizations. But this means that, if these generalizations are indeed to be useful, they must be employed with great care, beginning with always keeping in mind the several caveats highlighted here.

By keeping these comments and caveats in mind, I hope that readers will never be tempted to mistake what I intend as an initial, dynamic, always incomplete, and exception-laden generalization for a stereotype.

"Privacy" in the global metropolis: initial considerations

In the developed world, we increasingly are the digital information that facilitates our lives and engagements with one another. Luciano Floridi has made this point most strongly: a person is her or his information. "My" in "my information" is not the same as "my" in "my car" but rather the same as "my" as in "my body" or "my feelings"; it expresses a sense of constitutive belonging, not of external ownership, a sense in which my body, my feelings, and my information are part of me but are not my (legal) possessions. (2005: 195)

On first glance, this claim may seem too strong. To be sure, as more and more of our entertainment and communication take place via digital media, and as more and more of our lives are captured in digital form, our "digital footprint" expands dramatically. As a simple but telling measure: when the first hard drives became available for PCs in the early 1980s, 10MB or, even more staggering, 20MB seemed to offer more than enough data storage for a lifetime's worth of text files. Three decades later, as the personal computer, tablet, or even smartphone is the "digital hub" of a life involving TV, radio, personal photographs and videos, commercially produced music and movies, emails, and web-browsing – and, oh yes, text files – required personal data storage is measured in hundreds of gigabytes. At the time of this writing, hard drives with a terabyte (1,000 gigabytes) on notebook computers are not uncommon, and the latest smartphones can be ordered with 64GB of storage and be supplemented with a 64GB microSD card. At the same time, as more and more of us store important information in "the cloud" – i.e., web-based services as Dropbox, iCloud, Microsoft's SkyDrive, etc., which provide data storage that we can access through our devices wherever there is an Internet connection – so our digital footprint continues to expand accordingly.

But is all of this information primarily our property in the sense of an external, legal possession, and/or is Floridi correct to suggest that at least some elements of "our" information are who we are, in the same way as we think of ourselves in terms of our own bodies and feelings, for example?

Floridi's claim becomes more persuasive when we consider how much of our lives in the developed world – beginning with, but by no means limited to, important governmental identity information (e.g., Social Security numbers in the US, CPR numbers in Denmark, Fødselnummer in Norway, etc.), bank and credit card accounts (e.g., the RIB number in France, IBAN and SWIFT numbers, etc.), and so forth – are digitized, processed, and trans-mitted electronically. Couple this with the metaphor introduced by James Moor (as we saw in chapter 1), such information is "greased": it is (almost) as easily copied and transmitted to those whom we may not want to see it as to those whom we do want to see it. As the aptly named phenomenon of identity theft suggests, losing these sorts of information about ourselves – what we think of as private information – to others may well feel and result in harms more like a direct assault on our own bodies and feelings rather than solely the theft of external property.

To use another example: simply ask your neighbor if you can have access to his or her mobile or smartphone – i.e., to the text messages, contact list, phone numbers, perhaps emails, documents, etc., that are stored there. Especially if you ask this of a relative stranger, it seems likely that he or she will refuse: you're asking for information that is private – information that increasingly defines our sense of identity in a digital age.

You don't have to be paranoid – but it helps . . .

Whatever our individual ethical assessments and responses to these situations may be, many familiar threats to privacy are well known. Most of us know, for example, to be careful with passwords to important accounts, with PIN numbers for debit and credit cards, and so forth. Most of us are aware that both commercial and governmental databases containing our personal information are the targets of sometimes successful attacks by hackers: once a database is broken into, others are then able to use this informa-tion about us – enacting what is rightly called identity theft not only to take money from our bank accounts and charge purchases to our credit cards, but also thereby, in some cases, to jeopardize our own claims to our own identity.

In addition to these sorts of major but comparatively occasional threats, we are constantly vulnerable when we may think that we are safest – i.e., sitting in front of our personal computer, sending information via email, engaging in web-browsing (perhaps for shopping), perhaps doing banking transactions. Especially – but by no means exclusively – users of Windows machines face a constant barrage of Trojan horses, worms, and viruses that can, for example, capture and then transmit critical banking information to a third party.

If you're not paranoid yet . . . terrorism and state surveillance

Many of us are further aware that, beyond criminals and hackers, as citizens we face additional threats to our privacy – e.g., from corporations that collect data on individual purchasing choices (usually by consent in exchange for modest discounts or other economic incentives). Governments may be (somewhat ironically) the worst culprits. On the one hand, the modern liberal state exists to protect basic rights – including rights to privacy; but, to protect our rights – especially so-called positive or entitlement rights, e.g., to education, health care, disability assistance, family benefits such as child support and salary offsets for maternity and paternity leave, etc. – governments clearly require a great deal of personal information about us. How governments ought to and actually do protect that information from illicit and potentially devastating use against their own citizens varies widely from country to country. Somewhat more darkly, especially following the September 11, 2001, attacks in the United States, governments throughout the world justify ever greater surveillance of their own (and other) citizens in the name of fighting terrorism. And so unknown (because secret) quantities of personal information – as transmitted through emails, phone calls, faxes, etc. – are collected and scrutinized for potential threats. By the same token, surveillance of citizens through security cameras – distributed ever more densely throughout the world – continues to expand.

About that phone, laptop, tablet, and/or camera you're carrying . . .

Finally (for now, at least), digital media beyond computers and computer networks put our privacy and private lives at risk in other ways. In 2010, for example, a Philadelphia school district issued laptops to its students that incorporated a security feature – namely, the ability to photograph the user remotely via the laptop's webcam. Very useful for identifying a thief in case the laptop were to be stolen: but several students launched complaints that the school district was instead using the laptops to spy on them. (The courts eventually agreed with the students, resulting in over US$1.6 million in fines, settlements, and legal fees for the school district in question; Martin, 2011.) For its part, Apple Computers has patented what the Electronic Frontier Foundation (EFF) has characterized as "spyware" and "traitorware." The software allows Apple "to record the voice of the device's user, take a photo of the device's user's current location or *even detect and record the heartbeat of the device's user*" (Samuels 2010). This biometric information can be used to determine whether the current operator of an Apple device is its legitimate owner – and/or whether the owner is using the device in ways Apple does not approve (e.g., by "jailbreaking" or unlocking it so as to be able to install software Apple otherwise forbids – hence the term "traitorware"). Under these circumstances, the company can then use the software to wipe out "sensitive data" on the device and/or shut it down. Still more aggressively, reporters for the UK Sunday tabloid the *News of the World* were discovered, in the name of gathering news, to have hacked into mobile phones as early as 2002 – among them those of a young murder victim and several celebrities and politicians. The resulting scandal forced the closure of the paper in 2011; the investigation continues at the time of this writing (BBC News, 2012b).

"Privacy" and private life: changing attitudes in the age of "Big Brother" and mobile phones

At the same time, however, these manifest threats to personal privacy and private life appear to be accompanied by changing attitudes towards privacy in both "Western" and "Eastern" societies – perhaps as an artifact of our growing use of digital media (Ess 2010). For example, in 2007, Antonin Verrier received first prize at the French "Festival Pocket Films" for an eight-minute video shot with his mobile phone, entitled *Porte de Choisy*. The video focuses entirely on his girlfriend, first as she is talking on her phone while sitting in the bathroom, and then as she moves into their bedroom. We see the girlfriend entirely unclothed as well as some apparent sex play, followed by her sitting in front of a computer, still trying to determine the location of an upcoming appointment (Verrier 2007). In her analysis of the film, Gabriela David (2009: 79) points out that it thereby violates two of the otherwise most private spaces (as developed in Western modernity) – namely, the bedroom and the bathroom. To be sure, some will respond to such a film as a marker of a "pornographic turn" in contemporary society (Röttgers 2009: 89). By contrast, David (2009: 80) traces this growing willingness to put what was once private into the public eye to the rise of, e.g., "Big Brother" reality shows and the so-called WebCam girls of the 1990s and early 2000s – beginning with J. K. Ringley and her JenniCam.org. She uses the term "publicy" to describe what in the film thus exemplifies in contemporary cultures – namely, a complete blurring of earlier public/private boundaries (ibid.: 86).

In sharp tension, then, with worries about hierarchical forms of surveillance by states and corporations, a growing number of scholars and researchers document how we increasingly engage in what Anders Albrechtslund (2008) calls "voluntary" and "participatory surveillance." Such lateral surveillance is apparent on sites such as Facebook and YouTube – where, as Patricia Lange (2007) has characterized it, savvy users manage their personal information as either "publicly private" or "privately public." The former includes videos on YouTube that are "hidden" by tagging so that only ("close-tie") friends and relatives would know how to find them. The latter refers to information made available to one's less intimate (or "weak-tie") "friends": this information is still relatively private, e.g., one's real name, sexual orientation, and relationship status – but not strongly, such as one's home address.

In part, these shifts in our sensibilities surrounding earlier notions of privacy and intimacy may have to do with our efforts to retake control over our personal lives, precisely because we are aware of how much we are the targets of state and corporate surveillance (Reading 2009). More broadly, it seems clear that, with the rise of mobile and locative media – namely, those digital devices such as mobile phones, tablets, cameras, and related gadgets such as the runner's GPS watch that records his or her runs in great detail – we increasingly find ourselves "always on." That is, in what now seem to be the ancient days of landline phones and Internet access primarily through desktop computers, we could move "off the grid" simply by leaving the desk or stepping away from the phone. Now, of course, most of us carry mobile phones with us more or less everywhere, including, as *Porte de Choisy* exemplifies, bedrooms and bathrooms as once places of privacy *par excellence*. (How many of us have overheard someone carrying on a conversation while using the toilet in a public restroom?) As Theptawee Chokvasin (2007) has pointed out, this inverts our earlier context, in which a ringing but unanswered phone could signal the real unavailability of the person we wanted to speak with: with mobile phones, everybody knows that, if we do not answer a call to our mobile phone, it may well be because we choose not to, even though we're physically available to do so. What this means, Chokvasin points out, is that, in the era of the mobile phone, we are always "there": our "default setting" is to be connected to the communication network – and disconnected usually just by choice.

More starkly: as it inverts the earlier context – as being "on the grid" is now the norm, such that being off the grid or offline can signal a positive desire not to communicate – the mobile phone has turned traditional notions of "public" and "private" upside down. Earlier, privacy in the form of being "off the grid" of a public communications network was commonplace. And, especially for the sorts of philosophical and political reasons we will explore more fully below, the capacity to be incommunicado in this way was seen to be essential to being human. First of all, such privacy makes possible the sort of space and time needed for the development of an autonomous self, one capable of reflecting on and carefully choosing among the multiple acts and values available to human beings, both in solitude and in community with others. As Virginia Woolf (1929) famously advised, women seeking their own self-development, creativity, and freedom need "a room of one's own." In this way, privacy is an essential condition for our creating our selves. Such autonomy, moreover, is not only a necessary condition for our being suited to living and acting in a democratic society; most fundamentally, as modern political theory emphasizes, only such autonomous selves can justify the existence of democratic societies.

By contrast, the mobile phone – and, increasingly, its GPS-equipped cousins such as tablets and runners' watches – have made publicity our default setting. We are always "on the grid" in the developed world – often by choice, to be sure, but not always. This inverts or turns upside down earlier understandings of who we are and of our relationships with others. As we are about to see, this inversion and transformation means first of all that we have to rethink our conceptions of privacy in dramatic ways. It may also well mean that we will likewise need to revisit and perhaps revise our earlier ethical and political philosophies.

"Privacy" and private life: cultural and philosophical considerations

It is important to note that these shifts towards "publicy" and the "publicly private/privately public" do not, at least so far, mean that young people in "Western" societies and cultures have abandoned earlier notions of strongly individual privacy. For example, in the US context, research by the Pew Internet and American Life Project suggests a complex picture regarding teenagers and privacy expectations. On the one hand, the majority of teenage users take steps to protect their privacy – e.g., by limiting access to their profiles, using fake names or first names only, etc. (Lenhart and Madden 2007: i–iv). More recently, as "Waffles" reminds us at the opening of this chapter, individual privacy remains a core concern of contemporary teenagers – whatever their worried parents may think.

While the generations may disagree on the nature and limits of privacy, it is clear that we all nonetheless expect, and, in some cases at least, require, some form of privacy and data privacy protection. The key question is: what do we mean by "privacy"?

In the US context and tradition, our conception of privacy begins with primarily physical notions: as the examples of bedroom and bathroom privacy exemplify, what we initially wanted to protect was the privacy of spaces, first of all our homes. That is, "privacy" does not appear as a basic right in the US Constitution or Bill of Amendments: rather, it emerges only gradually as a concept to be defended in legal terms in the seminal paper by Samuel Warren and Louis Brandeis in 1890. As Bernhard Debatin points out, the concept is rooted in Fourth Amendment protections against "unreasonable search and seizure" of private property, among others (2011: 49).

Such a spatially oriented conception may have worked well in the days before electric media (such as telegraph and radio) and the Internet. But with the advent of electric and then electronic media, such as phone calls or radio transmissions that could be intercepted and recorded unbeknown to their primary senders and receivers, it gradually becomes clear that "privacy" is not simply a matter of protecting specific spaces. Rather, as we have seen, Luciano Floridi makes clear that what we want protected in an information age is precisely our information – information that, in digital form, is that much easier to access, copy, and distribute.

But why would we worry? As Judith DeCew points out: "The expectation of privacy is grounded in the fear concerning how the information might be used or appropriated to pressure or embarrass one, to damage one's credibility or economic status, and so on" (1997: 75). In short, we are afraid that someone and/or some organization will be able to use information about us to harm us – and/or those close to us – in some way.

We will explore the legal and philosophical dimensions of privacy more fully below. But let's continue here with the cultural aspects, remaining with "Western" societies. To begin with, in Norwegian and Danish, for example, there is no direct counterpart to the English term "privacy." Rather, what is at the heart of "privacy" discussions in these languages and cultures is *privatlivet* – "private life" – where such private life encompasses not simply the interests and pursuits of a solitary individual: in addition, *privatlivet* is understood to involve one's *intimsfære*, an "intimate sphere" of close friendships and relationships. These concepts thus do not map neatly onto earlier US notions of privacy as primarily an individual private space. In contrast to such a static or substantive conception, these notions of *privatlivet* and the *intimsfære* bring to the foreground our close relationships – relationships that are ongoing, evolving, and in some important ways negotiated over time. (A once distant stranger becomes accepted as an important member of one's *intimsfære*; a parent or sibling or child or close relative may suddenly and tragically pass away; a long-time friend may move to a distant country, making it difficult to sustain a sense of closeness and intimacy.) In these cultural contexts, then, it is not simply important to protect "privacy" for the individual – specifically, to find ways to ensure that personal or sensitive information about the individual is not taken up by those who would use it to harm that individual. At the same time, what we want to protect from harm includes these close relationships and the private life they constitute. So it is, then, that among the guidelines issued by the National Committees for Research Ethics in Norway is "The obligation to respect individuals' privacy and close relationships" – i.e., not simply an individual privacy (NESH 2006: 17).[1]

As the example of *ubuntu* suggests, when we turn to what we once thought of as non-Western cultures and traditions, what counts as even a rough approximation of "privacy" becomes still more complicated. As we will see more fully in the next section, in those cultures shaped by Buddhist and Confucian conceptions, the stress is on the self as a relational self – i.e., a sense of identity that is more or less fully constituted precisely by the extensive relationships that define us as members of families and larger communities. To use the example of a once classic form of Chinese introduction: such an introduction would recount my primary relationships, beginning with my parents, siblings, aunts and uncles, and (perhaps) children. This sense of selfhood thereby stresses the importance of sustaining harmonious relationships

---

[1] I am grateful to Niamh Ní Bhroin, University of Oslo, for pointing me towards this resource.

with the family and larger community and includes an exquisitely developed attention to the moods and wishes of others – what a Japanese student once described as the need to "read the atmosphere" or even to "read the minds" of those around one, with the goal of attuning one's behavior so as to avoid conflict or disharmony. In this context, some notion of *individual* "privacy" – a desire to hold something of oneself apart from the group – can be seen only in negative terms. As in the Western Middle Ages – i.e., before the rise of modern conceptions of individuals as rational autonomies who thereby require privacy – the notion seems to be rather: "the only reason you would want privacy is if you have something bad (or illegal) to hide."

At the same time, however, the shifts we are starting to see in "Western" societies towards "publicy" and the "publicly private/ privately public" suggest a correlative shift in our underlying assumptions regarding selfhood and identity – namely, from an earlier emphasis on strongly individual notions of selfhood towards a greater emphasis on more relational notions of selfhood. In this sense, (recent) "Westerners" are becoming more like (older) "Easterners." At the same time, we will see more fully below that (recent) "Easterners" are likewise shifting – from a greater emphasis on relational selfhood to a greater emphasis on more individual selfhood: this shift is apparent first of all in the changing demands in "Eastern" cultures towards (older) "Western" notions of individual privacy as a positive good.

For the moment, however, we see another continuum emerging here:

(Strongly) individual conception of self → (strongly) relational conception of self

    Individual privacy → Group privacy → "Publicy" (no privacy)

US (protection of spaces) . . . Norway (protection of *intimsfære*) . . . Confucian, Buddhist societies

REFLECTION/DISCUSSION/WRITING

A) In light of the above discussion, what are your intuitions regarding
  • your sense of selfhood or identity, and

- your sense of privacy (and/or private life) – that is, what kind(s) of privacy (if any) and/or private life (if any) do you feel/think requires protection?

B) Are your intuitions consistent with your historical/linguistic/communicative backgrounds – i.e., as shaped primarily by the "culture(s)" of a specific nation-state such as the US, Scandinavia, "Eastern" societies, etc.?

C) Whatever account of selfhood and privacy you offer, can you further provide arguments, evidence and/or some other forms of support that would somehow justify these conceptions?

(As we will see, these conceptions further correlate with our assumptions regarding the most appropriate or desirable forms of social structures and governance – broadly, a continuum that emphasizes equality and democracy vis-à-vis hierarchy and more authoritarian regimes. Our preferences in these domains may provide us with an important set of arguments for the kinds of selves and privacies/private lives we think are justified.)

Privacy and private life: first justifications, more cultural differences – transformations and (over?)convergence

As we have seen, strongly individual notions of "privacy" have emerged in the modern West as one of the basic rights of individuals. But justifications for this right vary. As Deborah Johnson (2001) has pointed out, in the United States, privacy is seen as an intrinsic good (something we take to be valuable in and of itself) and as an extrinsic good – something valuable as a means for another (intrinsic or extrinsic) good.[2] In particular: we need

---

2 We easily recognize that some things are valuable primarily as they serve as means to other goods or ends: so, commonly, many students value their education as an extrinsic good – i.e., something that is valuable as a means to achieving some other good, such as a job, a good salary, etc. But these in turn may be simply extrinsic goods – i.e., goods that are likewise valuable not so much in themselves (e.g., few of us – unfortunately – think of our work as an intrinsic good, as something worthwhile in itself, whether or not we are paid for it). So it seems that, somewhere, the chain of justifications for extrinsic goods must come to a rest at

privacy to become autonomous selves. That is, we need privacy to cultivate and practice our abilities to reflect and discern our own ethical and political beliefs, for example, and how we might enact these in our daily lives. Privacy is thus a means for the autonomous self to develop its own sense of distinctive identity and autonomy, along with other important goods such as intimate relationships. Only through privacy, then, can the autonomous self develop that has the capacity to engage in debate and the other practices of a democratic society (Johnson 2001: ch. 3). In Germany, rights to privacy are likewise considered as a basic right of an autonomous person qua citizen in a democratic society. Privacy is also seen as an instrumental good – primarily as it serves to protect autonomy, the freedom to express one's opinion, the "right of personality" (*Persönlichkeitsrecht*), and the freedom to express one's will. Finally, privacy protection – specifically, data privacy protection – is seen as a means necessary for the development of e-commerce (Bizer 2003).

By contrast, "privacy" in many Asian cultures and countries has traditionally been understood first of all as a collective rather than an individual privacy – e.g., the privacy of the family vis-à-vis the larger society (Ramasoota 2001: 97f., 100f.; cf. Kitiyadisai 2005). Insofar as something resembling individual privacy was considered, such privacy was looked upon in primarily negative ways. For example, Japan's Pure Land (*Jodo-shinsyu*) Buddhist tradition emphasizes the notion of *Musi*, "no-self," as crucial to the Buddhist project of achieving enlightenment – precisely in the form of the dissolution of the "self," understood in Buddhism to be not simply an illusion, but a most pernicious one. That is, as the elemental "Fourfold

---

an intrinsic good – something that is simply worthwhile in and of itself. Or else, as Aristotle famously argued, we are faced with an infinite regress of an extrinsic good being justified by a further extrinsic good, etc. Then the difficulty becomes one of finding such an intrinsic good – indeed, one that all of us would agree is valuable in and of itself. But, as Aristotle further argued, *eudaimonia* – often translated as "happiness," but better translated as "contentment" – is a good we all recognize as intrinsically valuable. That is, we may well ask someone why they want to attend university – i.e., what further good justifies such attendance if she or he believes that attending university is only an extrinsic good. But we don't seem to need to ask why someone would want to be happy or content: that is, happiness or contentment appears to be good in itself, and thus does not require further justification as a means to some further end.

Truths" of Buddhism make clear, our discontent or unhappiness as human beings can be traced to desire that can never be fulfilled (because either we will never obtain those objects or, if we do, we will lose them again, especially as time and death take them from us). But such desire, in turn, is generated by the self or ego. Hence, to eliminate the unhappiness of unfulfilled/unfulfillable desire, all we need do is eliminate ego or self. The Buddhist goal of nirvana, or the "blown-out self," thus justifies the practice of what from a modern Western perspective amounts to intentionally violating one's "privacy": in order to purify and thus eliminate one's "private mind" – thereby achieving *Musi*, "no-self" – one should voluntarily share one's most intimate and shameful secrets (Nakada and Tamura 2005). Similarly negative attitudes towards individual privacy have marked China for most of its history – in part because of the Confucian emphasis on the good of the larger community (see the discussion of Confucian ethics in chapter 6). Hence, until only relatively recently, the Chinese term correlating with individual "privacy" (*Yinsi*) held only negative connotations, i.e., of a "shameful secret" or "hidden, bad things" (Lü 2005). Finally, a similar emphasis on community is apparent in many indigenous traditions. So *ubuntu*, as we saw Dan Burk characterize it at the beginning of this chapter, understands personal identity as "dependent upon and defined by the community" – in part, as we will see in more detail in chapter 6, as this African tradition shares with Confucian thought an understanding of the individual as a relational being, i.e., as defined by the multiple relationships with others in the larger community. In this light, it makes sense that

> Within the group or community, personal information is common to the group, and attempts to withhold or sequester personal information are viewed as abnormal or deviant. While the boundary between groups may be less permeable to information transfer, *ubuntu* lacks any emphasis on individual privacy. (Burk 2007: 103)

At the same time, however, these understandings of privacy are undergoing dramatic changes. This is in part because globalization, as itself driven by the rapid diffusion of digital media, often thereby increases our awareness of and interactions with one another cross-culturally. This in turn leads to a hybridization of diverse cultural values and practices. In particular, as young people in Asia enjoy a growing material wealth and thereby a growing physical personal space (i.e., their own room in a family dwelling – something more or less nonexistent a few decades ago), and as they are ever more aware, thanks to global media, of Western notions and practices regarding individual privacy, they increasingly insist on personal and individual privacy in ways that are baffling (at best) and frustrating (at worst) to their parents and their parents' generation (e.g., Lin and Henkes 2004; Kitiyadisai 2005; Lü 2005; cf. Yan 2010; Hansen and Svarverud 2010)

These shifts can be seen most dramatically in terms of the laws surrounding privacy: indeed, following these changing understandings of selfhood, and thus what counts as "privacy" in both "Western" and "Eastern" countries, privacy laws have changed so much over the past decade or so that they move, in effect, ever closer to one another. To see how this is so, we take a brief look first at the European Union and then at the United States.

Very briefly, the European Union has encoded in law since 1995 very strong personal data privacy protections (European Union 1995). The EU Data Privacy Directives define what counts as personal and sensitive information (e.g., not simply name and address, but also regarding health status, religious and philosophical beliefs, trade union membership, and sexual identity) and require that individuals be notified when such information is collected about them. Individuals further have the right to review and, if necessary, correct information held about them. As Dan Burk (2007: 98) emphasizes, individuals have the right to consent – they must agree to the collection and processing of their personal information. And as we have seen, recent legislation makes these rights to consent – to "opt in" to, e.g., data collection as you browse a website – even stronger. Finally, the directives insist that the transfer of personal information to third parties outside the EU can occur only if the recipient countries provide the same level of privacy protection as that encoded in the EU directives. This last requirement, as Burk further explains, means that the EU approach to privacy is spreading more quickly around the world than its US counterpart (ibid.: 100f.). As we will see, this requirement is making especially dramatic impacts in Asia.

Finally, in ethical terms that may now be familiar to you from chapter 6, Burk characterizes the EU approach as strongly deontological: it rests upon a conviction that privacy is an inalienable right – one that states must protect, even if at considerable economic and other sorts of costs. This is in part because of the recognition, as articulated by Joel Reidenberg at the beginning of the chapter, that, "In a democracy, privacy is a basic political right that cannot be sold out in the marketplace" (2000). That is, as we will explore more fully below, privacy is essential to democratic processes: to compromise privacy for any reason is thereby to compromise democracy itself.

In the United States, by contrast, data privacy protection is something of a patchwork. In general, national or federal regulations address privacy issues with regard to health matters (e.g., the Health Insurance Portability and Accountability Act, 1996 [www.hhs.gov/ocr/hipaa]) and some financial information (e.g., banking and credit information), leaving the rest to individual states and/or businesses to work out (the latter through so-called aspirational models of good practice – see Burk 2007: 97; Debatin 2011: 49). The default setting here is the exact opposite of the EU model: rather than asking individuals to "opt in" to having their information collected, processed, and distributed in specific ways, the US approach requires individuals to "opt out" if they have reservations about how information about them is being collected and possibly used (Burk 2007: 97). So it is, then, that, if you are sitting in the US and would like the "opt-in" approach more characteristic of the EU codes, you'll need to install the sorts of security software discussed above.

As Burk goes on to observe, this "business-friendly" attitude appears to be the result of a utilitarian approach to the issues of data privacy protection. Simply put, the US preference is for minimal governmental involvement and maximum freedom for businesses, in hopes of minimizing the economic – and other – costs of implementing and enforcing more rigorous data privacy protections, such as those of the European Union, and thereby maximizing business efficiencies and profitability. Presumably, doing so will lead to the utilitarian goal of realizing the greatest good for the greatest number – at least in terms of economic gains and benefits. (See Burk 2007: 98f.)

Finally, we take up Asia – meaning here, the People's Republic of China (PRC) and surrounding countries, including the two special administrative regions of Hong Kong and Singapore, as well as Taiwan and South Korea. As we would expect in light of the greater emphases in these societies on a relational self, the greater priority of community harmony, and hence traditional attitudes towards individual "privacy" as only something hidden or bad (see above, p. 64), legal definitions of and protections for individual privacy rights have emerged only relatively recently. In Hong Kong, for example, individual privacy protections were first intro- duced as a *means* necessary to the development of e-commerce (Tang 2002) – that is, not, as in earlier Western justifications, for the sake of individual autonomy, etc. But the Supreme Court of the PRC established individual privacy rights as "attached" to "repu- tation right" – i.e., the right to have one's reputation protected from slander or defamation. Privacy violations that lead to serious damage to reputation are thus considered a *tort*, a personal injury for which the agent can be sued for damages in a civil court. By 2001, the Supreme Court established privacy as its own independ- ent right, justified in part by the view that a violation of individual privacy amounted to a "spiritual harm." By 2010, new tort liability law was enacted that established privacy as a right among other civil rights. Something close to an EU-style law regarding "protec- tion of personal information," as well as a proposed "online rights of minors," are, at the time of this writing, still pending (Sui 2011). Whatever caveats must be made regarding the critical difference between a law on the books and its enforcement in society, these shifts nonetheless represent remarkable transformations over a relatively short time. Indeed, legal scholar Graham Greenleaf sees these developments as marking out a striking convergence with EU law:

> In North Asia almost all countries bordering the People's Republic of China (PRC) [have] enacted or revised data privacy laws recently, including the two

> Special Administrative Regions of the PRC. If China ever goes in the same
> direction, North Asia will become the most 'data privacy intensive' region
> outside Europe. (Greenleaf 2011: 2)

Perhaps most striking in the example of the PRC is that legal
scholars such as Professor Sui (2011) are arguing for due process
rights – rights established in the United States in the Fifth and
Fourteenth Amendments – that seek to restrict the power of
the government to override individual rights. Specifically, she
argues that state interests should not supersede the individual
right to privacy without following a legal procedure that would
first examine justification for such infringement and then make a
judgment as to whether to allow such infringement. By contrast,
following the September 11, 2001, terrorist attacks on the World
Trade Center and the Pentagon, such due process rights have been
notably weakened in the United States in the name of thwarting
terrorism (e.g., Herman 2011). Such erosions, we can note, are
further coherent with the shifts we have seen in "Western" understandings of privacy and private life – namely, away from strongly
individual conceptions towards more group or shared conceptions; again, these shifts in part appear to correlate with changing
emphases in our notions of selfhood and identity – precisely from
more strongly individual conceptions towards more relational conceptions. Such notions of relational selfhood and group or family
privacy are striking similar to earlier "Eastern" notions – and thus
coherent with only negative conceptions of individual privacy and
correlative comfort with more hierarchical regimes enforcing
community harmony.

In sum, while "Westerners" thus head in what was a more
"Easterly" direction in terms of selfhood, privacy, and law,
"Easterners" appear to be heading in what was a more "Westerly"
direction in those same terms. The resulting pattern thus suggests a strong convergence towards basic conceptions of selfhood
(as both individual and relational), privacy (as individual but also
group), and, perhaps, the laws defining privacy and its protections.

Privacy and private life:
cultural differences and ethical pluralism

Such convergences do not necessarily mean, however, complete agreement on identical conceptions of individual privacy and privacy protections. Rather, foundational cultural differences are likely to remain in play for generations to come. However much convergence we may see between "Eastern" and "Western" societies, insofar as such differences remain, they force us to confront the obvious ethical question: who's right?

We can usefully explore this question – and primary ethical responses to it – by way of an example provided by Soraj Hongladarom, a Thai Buddhist philosopher. To begin with, Hongladarom (2007) points out that, while earlier cross-cultural discussions of privacy tended to emphasize these sorts of contrasts, there are also important similarities between, say, Western and Buddhist views. To begin with, Buddhism must emphasize at least a relative role and place for the individual: while, from an ultimate or enlightened standpoint, the individual is a pernicious illusion, the individual remains squarely responsible for his or her realization of enlightenment. For its part, Western thought – both in pre-modern traditions such as that of Aristotle and in modern philosophical streams such as that of Hegel – includes emphasis on the community, not simply the individual. From this perspective, Hongladarom has argued for a Thai conception of individual privacy – one that ultimately disagrees with Western assumptions regarding the individual as an absolute reality, but nonetheless retains a sufficiently strong role and place for the individual. Such a Buddhist individual, again, is the agent of its own enlightenment but also serves as a citizen of a fledgling democratic state in Thailand. In this way, Hongladarom argues, there are strong philosophical grounds for granting such an individual privacy rights similar to those enjoyed by Westerners – even if, by comparison, these rights will be more limited in light of the greater role of the state and greater importance (on both Buddhist and Confucian grounds) of the community.

In ethical terms, Hongladarom hereby articulates for us an

important ethical pluralism regarding the nature of privacy. Such a pluralism, as we will explore more fully in chapter 6, stands in the middle ground between ethical relativism and ethical absolutism. Most briefly, the important point is that, in such pluralism, it is possible to hold together both shared norms and values – in this case, privacy – while these norms and values are understood, interpreted, and/or applied in diverse ways – i.e., in ways that reflect the distinctive values and norms of diverse cultures. In this way, pluralism allows for a shared global ethics, on the one hand, while avoiding, on the other hand, a kind of homogenizing ethics that ignores or obliterates all important cultural differences. And so, ethical pluralism provides the possibility of a global ethics made up of shared norms and values while preserving the essential differences that define diverse cultural identities.

In the case of "privacy," these cross-cultural comparisons can thus be understood to constitute an example of such an ethical pluralism. This is to say: US-style conceptions of "privacy" as strongly individual and (earlier) Thai notions of "privacy" as primarily familial privacy thus present us with strongly different ideas of "privacy." For the ethical relativist, these differences would be one more example arguing that there are no universal values or norms: the validity of ethical norms and values is solely relative to a given culture and time. In this instance, the US notion of individual privacy as a positive good is legitimate – but only if you're a member of the US culture; and the (earlier) Thai emphasis on familial privacy alone as ethically suspect is also legitimate if you were born and raised in Thai culture in those days. This is fine – at least as long as people from both cultures have nothing to do with one another and thus require no shared norms or values.

For the ethical monist, we can establish a shared norm or value rather simply: one of these values or norms must be true – absolutely, finally, and universally – and hence any different value or norm can only be false. Again, if we had nothing to do with one another, this might be a workable solution: but in today's world it is more or less impossible to live in such splendid isolation. And so, if the ethical monist has his way, we must choose which norm or value is right and which is thereby wrong. This approach seems to condemn us to intolerance and conflict – not very useful either for genuine understanding of the Other as Other[3] or for efforts to avoid cultural imperialism, much less warfare.

The ethical pluralist, finally, hopes to avoid such intolerance and conflict by way of arguing that both cultures share a notion of "privacy," but this notion is understood and practiced in different ways – ways that are directly shaped by each culture's distinctive traditions and assumptions. Ethical pluralism thus argues for a middle ground between relativism and monism. Yes, norms and values vary from culture to culture – but, contra monism, this does not necessarily mean that only one cultural norm can be right and the other wrong: both can be correct as instances of different interpretations of a shared norm. Contra relativism: because varying cultural norms may thus instantiate a shared norm, cultural variations of this sort do not necessarily mean that there are no universally legitimate values or norms. On the contrary, the pluralist can argue that in this way privacy – however widely understood and practiced in diverse cultures and times – indeed appears to be a human universal. (See Soraj Hongladarom [2007: 110f.] for discussion of the work of James Moor [2000] and Adam D. Moore [2003] on this point.)

To be sure, not all of our ethical differences will be resolved through pluralism. But given that ethical pluralism works in at least some cases, including the case of privacy, whenever we encounter strong differences in cultural norms and practices, we cannot simply assume that our options for dealing with them are either ethical relativism or ethical monism.

---

3 The phrase "Other as Other" is intended to suggest that we recognize the Other as fully equal, fully human, while simultaneously irreducibly different from us. This draws from Levinas's analysis of "the Other as Other," as a positive "alterity" (e.g., Levinas 1987). By contrast, I use "other" – i.e., without a capital – to signal a viewpoint or perspective on the "other" whose difference from ourselves at least initially inspires suspicion, fear, and/or contempt for the other seen as inferior, etc. This interpretation of *difference* between "us" and "them" is familiar as the viewpoint of ethnocentrism and related perspectives of racism, sexism, etc.

Philosophical and sociological considerations: new selves, new "privacies"?

These dramatic changes in our conceptions of selfhood, privacy, and privacy law are but part of a much larger discussion. Not surprisingly, there is considerable debate among philosophers in information and computing ethics regarding the nature of privacy, its possible justifications, justifications for its protection, etc. (see, e.g., Floridi 2006; Tavani 2008; Tavani 2013: ch. 5, 131–73). Herman Tavani helpfully summarizes three basic kinds of privacy. The first of these is accessibility privacy (freedom from unwarranted intrusion). This notion of privacy, also formulated as the right to "being let alone" or "being free from intrusion," was defended in a landmark paper in 1890 by Samuel Warren and Louis Brandeis – who thereby made the first explicit claim in the United States that privacy exists as a legal right (Tavani 2013: 135). Second, decisional privacy is defined as a freedom from the interference from others in "one's personal choices, plans, and decisions" (ibid.: 135f.). Such privacy, Tavani points out, has been crucial in the US context in defending freedom of choice regarding contraception, abortion, and euthanasia. Finally, informational privacy is a matter of our having the ability to control information about us that we consider to be personal (ibid.: 136).

Tavani goes on to point out that both James Moor (2000) and Helen Nissenbaum (2010) have developed accounts of privacy that seek to include these three forms (Tavani 2013: 136–8). Moreover, from my perspective, what is most helpful about both Moor's and Nissenbaum's accounts is that they move us away from earlier, more spatial and static conceptions of "privacy" and foreground instead the relational dimensions of privacy and private life – namely, the intuitions developed above that our senses of "privacy" in "Western" societies are shifting towards notions of "partial privacy" and "group privacy." Again, what we think/feel needs protection are those aspects of our close relationships, as increasingly mediated through (analogue) digital media, that increasingly define our sense of selfhood as more relational than individual. In particular, Nissenbaum's account emphasizes that what is at stake in our privacy concerns is first of all precisely the context in which specific relationships play out that involve some sort of information exchange. These contexts or "spheres of life" include education, the marketplace, political life, etc. (Tavani 2013: 138). Each of these contexts entails, first, its own "norms of appropriateness" that "determine whether a given type of personal information is either appropriate or inappropriate to divulge within a particular context" (ibid.). At the same time, each context is further accompanied by its own "norms of distribution [that] restrict or limit the flow of information within and across contexts" (ibid.). As Federica Fornaciari emphasizes, both sets of norms "are often implicit, variable, and incomplete" (2012). On this view, what we think of as violation of privacy is more precisely a violation of the appropriateness and/or distribution norms defining a given context. As Fornaciari continues, most such violations occur "because the information is *somewhat* available in a *somewhat* public forum" (ibid.). Moreover, we can add that this dynamic ambiguity (my term) of the multiple contexts of our relationships is further subject to constant renegotiation and reformulation. This happens, for example, when one or more of the persons constituting a communicative cohort feels his or her "privacy" or private life has somehow been breached by disclosures others have made. So Stine Lomborg (2012: 428) has analyzed the communicative interactions of a prominent Danish blogger and her audience, noting that these interactions taken together constitute a "public personal space" that is neither individually private nor simply public. In such conversational spaces, "both author and readers balance a fine line between, on the one hand, pressure to reveal personal issues as a preamble for developing relationships among participants and, on the other hand, a norm of non-intrusiveness to protect each other's [individual] privacy" (ibid.: 432). On occasion, either the blogger or one of her readers may reveal something that is received as rather too personal, too individually private. This occasions a renegotiation process that, in response to the violation of the contextual norms of the blog (to use Nissenbaum's term), more articulately redefines the "line between what is appropriate to share and what is too private" (ibid.: 429).

Lomborg's analysis is especially relevant here as it relies on the sociologist Georg Simmel's account of "the sociable self," a version of the relational self that is "attuned to the norms and practices within the network of affiliation" (Lomborg 2012: 432). Such attunement of relational selves should remind us of my Japanese student's account of the communicative expectations of such selves in her context – namely, the expectation among (highly) relational selves to "read the atmosphere" in order to avoid acts or utterances that would disrupt the harmony of the group. At the same time, Simmel's sociable self and the correlative emphasis on relationality further resonate with Erving Goffman's (1959) conception of the self as defined by its multiple social roles or relationships, and thereby centrally engaged with "impression management" that seeks to tune one's self-presentation to the expectations and norms of a given role. Goffman's account of selfhood is central to an extensive array of analyses of online behaviors – among them that of boyd and Marwick, who point out that such relationality includes our (familiar) capacity to grant one another some form of "privacy" by pretending not to listen – e.g., in a crowded restaurant, a behavior that Goffman called "civil inattention" (1966; cited in boyd and Marwick 2011: 25). More broadly, as their extensive use in numerous analyses of online interactions suggests (e.g., Baym 2011), these sociological conceptions of selfhood, as they emphasize our primary attention to the relationships that define us, seem especially well suited to understanding ourselves and our interactions with one another as these reflect an increasing emphasis in "Western" societies on relationality rather than solely the individual. This growing sense of relational self, coupled with online venues as "public personal spaces" (so Lomborg), as "publicly private" and "privately public" (Lange 2007), hence require the more fluid, dynamic, contextually oriented understandings of "privacy" and private life that we see beginning to emerge in the work of Moor and Nissenbaum.

At the same time, just as our technologies continue to change rapidly, so our senses of selfhood and identity and correlative understandings and expectations of "privacy" and private are likewise in flux. All of this is thus continuously under further development and refinement. Nonetheless, to paraphrase Socrates: whether we find ourselves in a swimming pool or the ocean, we must start swimming nonetheless. Happy swimming!

REFLECTION/DISCUSSION/WRITING QUESTIONS

1. How would you define "privacy" and/or private life? It may be helpful here to think of what sort of "things" – acts, events, behaviors, internal notions, imaginations, "information flows" (what kinds?), etc. – you think of as:

- "private" in a strongly individual way,
- "publicly private"/"privately public" (e.g., as shared in what Lomborg characterizes as "public personal spaces"), and
- "public."

It may be further helpful to review this selection from the EU Data Privacy Directives, as a detailed listing of what sorts of "things" are considered private and thus as protected information:

> it is forbidden to process personal data revealing racial or ethnic origin, political opinions, religious or philosophical beliefs, trade-union membership, and the processing of data concerning health or sex life.

That is, would you agree with or want to modify this list – if so, how?

2. Discuss as clearly and precisely as possible:

(a) What kind(s) of privacy (and private life) do you believe to be most important – especially in terms of the three sorts of privacy described by Tavani?

(b) Given your account of privacy, do you want to justify privacy as an intrinsic and/or an extrinsic good? If extrinsic, then what is privacy "good for" – that is, for what other (and, ultimately, intrinsic goods) does it serve as a means?

(c) What additional sorts of justification(s) can you provide for privacy as you have defined it?

3. Discuss as clearly and precisely as possible how far your understanding of privacy and private life seems to be dependent on

- more individual notions of selfhood and/or more relational notions?
- more static conceptions of (individual or familiar) spaces and/or more dynamic conceptions (such as Nissenbaum's) of "privacy" as contextual – i.e., referring to specific "personal spaces" constituted by a given set of communicative engagements between a (relatively defined) set of (relational) persons?

4. Can you discern how far your approach to privacy is shaped by utilitarian arguments (such as those at work especially in the US context) and/or by deontological arguments (as more characteristic of EU approaches, for example?)

5. We have seen that Soraj Hongladarom argues for a Thai notion of privacy that rests on especially Buddhist understandings of the self. As we might expect, Hongladarom goes on further to argue for correlative data privacy protections – protections that might seem limited as compared with contemporary Western (especially EU) laws, but are nonetheless recognizable as protections justified for the sake of participating in democratic governance, for example.

But Hongladarom goes still further. He draws on the Buddhist analysis of human discontent as rooted in the ego-illusion to point out:

> Violating privacy is motivated by what Buddhists call mental defilements (*kleshas*), of which there are three – greed, anger, and delusion. Since violating privacy normally brings about unfair material benefits, it is in the category of greed. In any case, the antidote is to cultivate love and compassion. Problems in the social domain, according to Buddhists, arise because of these mental defilements, and the ultimate antidote to social problems lies within the individuals themselves and their states of mind. (Hongladarom 2007: 120)

In other words, from a Buddhist perspective, if we want to enjoy privacy protections, then we must go beyond (negative) laws that largely tell us what not to do (most simply, don't violate others' rights to privacy) to important positive ethical injunctions that tell us what to do – namely, to pursue enlightenment (in the form of overcoming the ego-illusion), in part through cultivating love and compassion for others.

As we will explore more fully in chapter 6, this recommendation is characteristic not simply of Buddhism but of virtue ethics in the Western tradition. (It further resonates, of course, with "the Golden Rule" – in Christian formulation: do unto others as you would have them do unto you. But, of course, the Golden Rule is central to the three Abrahamic faiths of Judaism, Christianity, and Islam – and, indeed, some argue, is found throughout the world, beginning with Confucian traditions.) At the same time, this recommendation reflects a Buddhist understanding of identity as primarily relational. As with the Japanese injunction to attune our acts towards the harmony of the group, the approach here resolves privacy issues first by having us (re)shape ourselves to harmonize better with others by reducing greed and increasing compassion and love.

(A) How persuasive (or not) do you find Hongladarom's arguments and recommendations regarding privacy – including the positive injunction to minimize greed and maximize compassion? Be as clear as you can about your arguments/ evidence/reasons and/or other grounds for your response(s).

(B) As we have seen, the national and cultural traditions surrounding us have a significant influence on our conception of selfhood (more individual, more relational?) and thereby on our ethical values and approaches to ethical decision-making. How far can you trace your (dis)agreements with Hongladarom to the cultural and national traditions that have shaped your ethical views and sense of selfhood?

That is, if you agree with Hongladarom, is this solely because you likewise have grown up in a culture more shaped by relational emphases of selfhood and/or because you are already convinced of the truths of Buddhism? And/or: if you disagree with Hongladarom, is this solely because you have grown up in a culture shaped by more individual emphases of selfhood and/or remain convinced of the truths of other traditions?

And/or: can you find other reasons/grounds/evidence, etc., for your (dis)agreement(s) with Hongladarom beyond those reasons, etc., that may hold legitimacy primarily in one culture but not in another?

ADDITIONAL RESOURCES AND QUESTIONS FOR REFLECTION/
DISCUSSION/WRITING

1. The Electronic Freedom Foundation (EFF) is, in my view and experience, a critical resource in attempting to keep track of events and issues surrounding privacy, copyright, and so on. At the time of this writing, the EFF has documented the legal and technical processes that led to the resignation of General David Petraeus, now former director of the US Central Intelligence Agency (https://www.eff.org/deeplinks/2012/11/when-will-our-email-betray-us-email-privacy-primer-light-petraeus-saga, accessed November 17, 2012). Review these processes, along with the recommendations included here for how US citizens can better protect their privacy and anonymity online, e.g., by using many of the software packages and add-ons discussed at the opening of this chapter.

A) In the US approach, as we have seen, IP addresses are not considered to be personal and sensitive information that, under EU law, would be protected by default. Do you think General Petraeus's rights to privacy were violated in this case – either because they were inadequately protected by US law to begin with and/or because you think privacy rights should include keeping IP addresses anonymous?

B) US citizens, as this article recommends, can build in more privacy and anonymity protections that, in effect, bring them closer to (and in some ways surpass) current EU data privacy protections. But these require (i) a somewhat sophisticated awareness of the risks to privacy when sending emails or browsing the Web and (ii) undertaking positive actions such as installing and learning how to use various forms of security software.

Should protecting privacy and private life be so hard? More carefully:

(i) Where such effort is likely to be beyond what most casual users will have time, interest, and/or ability to pursue, should privacy and anonymity require such effort? And/or: should individual privacy, anonymity, and/or private life be better protected through more stringent regulation, including those under consideration in the current draft revisions of the EU guidelines? BEFORE ANSWERING . . .

(ii) We have seen that Google has argued that introducing such proactive steps, beginning with users being asked to give consent to a website to track their IP address – a step that NoScript, for example, also requires – would "break the Internet" (Gapper 2012). At the very least, these stronger protections would reduce to some degree or another the ease and convenience of visiting and using such websites. As is often the case, then, there is a trade-off between convenience and securing one's rights.

Taking these two questions together: given your views on what counts as privacy and private life, and their relative importance, are the current regulations in the country in which you find yourself adequate for protecting what you take to be your rights to privacy and private life? Or should there be stronger protections of anonymity and privacy – whether by governments and/or individuals – even at the cost of (some) ease of use and convenience?

2. Perhaps the most foundational – but thereby, also the most difficult – philosophical considerations cluster about the nature and qualities of human identity and selfhood. As we have started to see above, our understanding of selfhood – beginning with whether we emphasize the more individual or more relational aspects of our identity – determines in large measure what we think of

"privacy" or private life, whether individual privacy is a positive or negative good, and so forth. Attending to our sense of selfhood in a digital age thereby also opens up two further critical philosophical and sociological discussions:

A) Is human identity primarily singular (and thereby relatively constant and enduring through time) and/or primarily multiple (and thereby fluid and ephemeral)? As many readers will recognize, these are debates that were opened up early on in the intersections between then emerging postmodern conceptions of identity (as multiple, fluid, and ephemeral) and MUDs and MOOs as then new venues for computer-mediated interactions with others in various role-playing games initially inspired by "Dungeons and Dragons." The pioneering work of Sherry Turkle (1985, 1995) showed how players in such environments realized postmodern notions of multiple and fluid identities: this became the dominant paradigm in the first decade or so of what we can now call Internet studies (from the mid-1980s to the late 1990s). Subsequently, however, as "the Internet" rapidly diffused throughout societies and around the globe, and thereby became increasingly ubiquitous and taken for granted, our uses and interactions shifted to those more seamlessly interwoven with our everyday lives (including shopping, banking transactions, and constant accessibility via social media and smartphones, for example). Correlatively, Internet studies over the past decade or so has rather foregrounded the continuities between our online and offline lives, and thereby a greater coherency between our sense of identity and selfhood offline and online (Ess and Consalvo, 2011; cf. Ess 2012). In many ways, it appears that there is a renewed stress on identity as continuous and singular: we do not change our basic identities on an SNS, for example, and certainly our banks would not be happy if we insisted on changing identity on a frequent basis.

B) In what we will call high modernity (following Anthony Giddens [1991]), ethical thought focused on the self as a single autonomy – one that was thereby the primary agent of its acts, and thereby the agent that bore primary or exclusive *responsibility* for those acts. Postmodern challenges to these conceptions may have receded slightly, but early on in this century notions of the self as a "networked individual" (Wellman and Haythornthwaite 2002; Papacharissi 2012) became increasingly prominent. The term refers to the social and technical reality that, as our lives are increasingly suffused with (analogue) digital technologies, we are thus ever more interconnected with ever growing networks of both human and artificial agents ("AAs," such as the programs that monitor your bank transactions to prevent payment of what appears to be a fraudulent use of your credit card). Such a "networked individual" is thus a strongly relational or sociable self, to recall Simmel and Goffman, where our various social roles and relationships are directly expressed through computer networks and networked communication technologies.

This convergence of philosophical, sociological, and technological realities thus requires us to rethink the nature of ethical responsibility. Most briefly, contemporary philosophers are exploring how we might shift from understanding ethical agency and responsibility as belonging primarily to a (relatively solitary) individual to understanding agency and responsibility as *distributed* across these networks – resulting in what Luciano Floridi (2008) first identified as "distributed morality."

QUESTIONS, SUGGESTIONS

(i) Facebook and other social networking sites are the focus of much of contemporary concern and debate over identity, privacy, and private life.

A particularly useful resource here is:

Vallor, Shannon (2012) Social Networking and Ethics, *Stanford Encyclopedia of Philosophy* (winter 2012 edn), ed. Edward N. Zalta, http://plato.stanford.edu/archives/win2012/entries/ethics-social-networking/ (accessed February 28, 2013).

As Vallor notes in her introduction, SNSs raise central ethical questions with regard not only to privacy but also to our notions of "identity and community; friendship, virtue and the good life; and democracy [and] the public sphere" (2012, 1).

We will take up the themes of democracy and the public sphere, as well as return to Vallor's analyses of friendship and virtues in chapter 4. At this point, reading through Vallor's article should help you respond to the following:

Given your own account of privacy and private life (question 1 above, pp. 78–9), does Vallor's discussion of privacy help expand or refine your account – and, if so, in what ways? That is, what specific insights, arguments, and/or evidence does she offer that help you extend and/or polish your own reflections on privacy and private life?

(ii) A recent special issue of the journal *Philosophy and Technology* focuses on the question "Who am I online?" In the introduction (Ess, 2012), I summarize the individual articles making up the special issue and describe their contributions to a number of larger philosophical discussions regarding identity. These discussions include questions of the role of *embodiment* in our sense of selfhood, mind–body dualism (still at work, for example, in conceptions of immortality in cyberspace by way of "downloading" our consciousness and memories to sophisticated computer systems), and their connections with larger philosophical frameworks such as environmental ethics, feminist ethics and ethics of care, and theological understandings of sin and sexuality.

For the philosophically minded – and/or those of you reading this chapter in the context of a philosophy class – a review of the introduction should help you develop a list of particular questions and possible responses regarding your sense of identity and selfhood that can be developed into at least brief essays and/or exam questions.

SUGGESTED RESOURCES FOR FURTHER RESEARCH/
REFLECTION/WRITING

Fuchs, Christian (2011) An Alternative View of Privacy on Facebook, *Information*, 2(1): 140–65.

Fuchs takes up a critical ethical concern, namely, how far our identities are commodified – turned into material for sale, first of all in the form of marketing information – through our use of social networking sites (SNSs) such as Facebook. Drawing on both Marxian frameworks of political economy and theorists such as Hannah Arendt and Jürgen Habermas, Fuchs's analysis is further important for connecting privacy matters with central issues of democratic governance.

Debatin, Bernhard (2011) Ethics, Privacy, and Self-Restraint in Social Networking, pp. 47–60 in S. Trepte and L. Reinecke (eds), *Privacy Online*. Berlin: Springer.

Debatin provides an excellent summary of privacy conceptions and law as background for discussing privacy matters on SNSs – again, including the importance of privacy to democratic processes, especially as influenced by the work of Habermas. His arguments for a "privacy literacy" and an "ethics of self-restraint" can be usefully compared to the approaches developed in this chapter, and especially the recommendations from virtue ethics offered by Vallor (2009, 2011) and Hongladarom (2007) explored above.

CHAPTER THREE

Copying and Distributing via Digital Media: Copyright, Copyleft, Global Perspectives

For content that is covered by intellectual property rights, like photos and videos (IP content), you specifically give us the following permission, subject to your privacy and application settings: you grant us a non-exclusive, transferable, sub-licensable, royalty-free, worldwide license to use any IP content that you post on or in connection with Facebook (IP License). This IP License ends when you delete your IP content or your account unless your content has been shared with others, and they have not deleted it.

> (Facebook Terms of Use [December 18, 2012], www.facebook.com/legal/terms)

We want fans to enjoy their iPods, CD burners, and other devices, but we want them to do so responsibly, respectfully, and within the law.

> (Recording Industry Association of America [RIAA], FAQ, www.riaa.com/faq.php)

"Free software" is a matter of liberty, not price. To understand the concept, you should think of "free" as in "free speech," not as in "free beer."

> (The Free Software Definition [Richard Stallman/GNU Operating System], www.gnu.org/philosophy/free-sw.html)

Chapter overview

We begin with "first thoughts" – a set of reflection/discussion/ writing questions intended to help gather initial thoughts and sensibilities regarding the issues and arguments surrounding matters of copying various forms of digital media. This will also introduce us to the important logical matters of analogy and questionable analogy.

I then describe the US and European approaches to copyright law and their important ethical differences, which is followed by discussion of the so-called copyleft approaches and important examples of their application in the Free/Libre/Open Source Software (FLOSS) movements. A second set of reflection/discussion/writing questions helps to practice applying these diverse approaches in conjunction with the ethical frameworks of utilitarianism and deontology.

Lastly, I highlight and expand upon the cultural backgrounds and diverse cultural traditions at work here – specifically, Confucian thought and the (Southern) African framework of *ubuntu*. We conclude with a final set of reflection/discussion/writing exercises that include attention to the ethical questions brought to the fore by this attention to culture.

INITIAL REFLECTION EXERCISES:
ILLEGAL DOWNLOADING VS. STEALING

A) A friend tells you about a new band that she really likes to listen to, and says that you'd really like them as well. The problem is that, as a university student, you don't have the money easily available required to purchase the band's new CD from a local music store. One solution: your friend knows how to disable the anti-theft tags on the CD, so the alarms should not go off as you walk out the door. Since the likelihood of getting caught is thus very low, she suggests that you can simply steal a copy of the CD from the store.

Yes, I know: you know where this is going, but bear with me for a bit. As you consider the above scenario carefully . . .

  1. What seem to be your options? That is, the scenario suggests an either/or: either you steal the CD and, presuming you don't get caught, get to enjoy some great music for free – or

you don't. These may well be your two primary options, but, in undertaking ethical analysis, it is always a good idea to see if we are clear about all the realistic options, not just the most obvious ones. (Note: after you've done this exercise, you may want to review section 4 in chapter 6 on feminist approaches to ethics and an ethics of care; see p. 229.)

2. Develop – individually, perhaps in group discussion, and/ or as a class – as fully as you can the arguments, evidence, reasons, and/or other grounds that support each of the options you describe in (1) above.

3. Given that you have likely described at least two possible options, each with reasonably strong supporting arguments, at this point, can you provide any additional arguments, evidence, reasons, and/or other grounds for a specific choice that help justify that choice as the better of the available options?

4. (Optional: You may want to review at least the first two ethical frameworks discussed in chapter 6, consequential-ism/utilitarianism and deontology. After doing so, return to the arguments, etc., that you've provided above. Do you notice whether your arguments are more consequentialist, perhaps utilitarian, and/or more deontological in some way?)

OK, hold those thoughts . . .

B) A good friend of yours is in a band that is struggling to gain recognition and an audience. All the band members are just getting by on their day jobs – the band as such doesn't make enough money to support any of the members full-time. The band has just produced a new CD, and they're hoping that it will become a major hit. Following a number of well-known bands before them, they offer on their website the possibility of downloading a sample track from their album, but, of course, hope that this will lead to sales of the full album at the going price of US$10.00. You are no stranger to downloading illegally music from the Internet. But, since you want to support the band, you've gone ahead and paid the US$10.00 for your legal copy of the full album.

1. While in this circumstance, you are willing to pay the US$10.00 required for downloading a legal copy of the album, presume that you also think that under some circumstances it's OK to download music from the Internet illegally. With regard to the later case(s), what are your arguments, evidence, reasons, and/or other grounds for justifying such illegal downloading? (Nota bene: this question assumes that a strong ethical justification is both distinct from – indeed, may override – arguments based exclusively on current law.)

2. Presuming that you've now marshaled some good arguments, etc., that justify at least some sorts of illegal downloading, what arguments, evidence, reasons, and/or other grounds come into play in the instance of your deciding not to download illegally the full album of your friend's band?

3. (Optional: Again, you may want to review at least the first two ethical frameworks discussed in chapter 6, consequentialism/ utilitarianism and deontology. After doing so, return to the arguments, etc., that you've provided above. Can you discern whether your arguments are more consequentialist, perhaps utilitarian and/or more deontological in some way?)

C) Another friend who likes the band's sample track offered for free on the Internet asks you if you'd mind making a CD of your copy of the album, so that he can either:

(i) highlight the band's music at an upcoming party where he's going to provide the music – in part, so that the album might generate a few more sales; and/or

(ii) make copies of the album to give to friends of his who are also interested in the music; and/or

(iii) put a copy of the album on his computer so that it is available to others on the Internet, using one of the current peer-to-peer file sharing networks, and/or

(iv) all of the above.

1. If you think that you might agree to (i), but not to (iii), explain as best you can:

     (a) what the relevant differences are between these two scenarios, and

     (b) what arguments, etc., you can provide that can justify your ethical position in both cases.

2. What is your response to (ii) – that is, something of a middle ground between (i) using copies of music to help the band, it is hoped, by generating sales, and (iii) making copies freely available to anyone interested on the Internet – which might well lead to a reduction of the band's sales of its new album? Again, for our purposes, whatever your response here, what is important is your analysis of the choice/action and the arguments, etc., that support it.

3. (Optional: Again, as with the optional questions above, you may want to review the arguments developed here vis-à-vis the ethical frameworks of consequentialism/utilitarianism and deontology, if only to discern which set of arguments you tend to use – so far.)

4. It is likely that at least some of your class would have responded to the scenario described in (A) – i.e., the possibility of stealing a CD from a music store – by arguing that this would not be a good idea. There are at least two likely arguments here: one consequentialist (even if the risk of getting caught is small, the consequences of getting caught are potentially catastrophic, and so it's better not to take such a chance); and a second, more deontological argument (stealing is simply wrong, even if by stealing you might gain something desirable and enjoyable).

    By contrast, there will likely be many members of the class who are perfectly happy to download, say, a song track or two from a famous (and wealthy) artist whose work is distributed by equally well-to-do multinational corporations. Here, at least in my experience, the arguments tend to be primarily consequentialist – e.g., the chances of my getting caught are extremely small, and the very modest profit that both the artist and the multinational corporation lose by my not paying for a legal copy will never be missed by either, since both are already so financially well off.

(a) Are there any additional arguments that occur to you and/or others in your group/class that work to justify not stealing in the first case, but do justify illegal downloads in the second case?

(b) Given the arguments that you uncover here, do these arguments always derive from the same framework? Again, it may be that the arguments against stealing a physical copy of a CD include deontological arguments, while arguments for illegal downloading are primarily consequentialist.

If this is the case, then the disagreement between these two cases runs beyond the first-order level of what we are to do in a particular instance – the disagreement includes a second-order or "meta-theoretical" difference as to which ethical framework(s) we are to make use of (i.e., either consequentialism and/or deontology – and/or any of the additional frameworks described in chapter 6).

(c) At this point, it may be sufficient simply to notice these differences, so far as they seem to be at work – and observe that, if our arguments do derive from different frameworks, then perhaps there is not quite the contradiction that may first appear to be the case (i.e., between disapproving of stealing a CD physically while approving of illegally downloading a virtual copy of one).

That is, if our arguments against and for (respectively) these forms of stealing derive from different frameworks, then to say that there's a contradiction here is like saying that there's a contradiction between the rules of American baseball and the rules of European soccer. This doesn't make immediate sense: it seems rather that, because these are two different games played under two different sets of rules, there can be no serious contradiction between them.

While this observation would relieve us of a first-order contradiction, it nonetheless still leaves us with a second-order question, namely: how do we justify – or, to use Aristotle's suggestion, judge (i.e., use *phronesis*) – using a specific framework in one instance and another framework in a different instance?

Thoughts?

D) As we proceed in applying familiar ethical frameworks to the ethical challenges evoked by new technologies, we inevitably proceed by way of analogy. And so, in the scenarios described above, I have suggested an analogy between physically stealing a copy of a CD from a music store and illegally downloading a copy from the Internet.

Just to make it explicit – an analogy argument based on the above scenarios might look like this:

- We agree that stealing a physical CD from a music store is wrong.
- Downloading an illegal copy of a music album is like stealing a physical CD from a music store.
- Therefore, downloading an illegal copy of a music album is also wrong.

But, as good logicians know, every analogy runs the risk of becoming faulty or questionable. Such an analogy, rather than helpfully lead us to justifiable conclusions, may instead mislead us. Happily, you don't have to be a logician to see how this is so (though it helps enormously). Rather, at least as a starting point for reflection and discussion, we can draw on the idiomatic phrase "comparing apples and oranges." That is, we sometimes recognize rather easily that a given analogy or comparison is in fact false or misleading somehow – in part because the comparison in fact holds together two radically different sorts of things (the apple and the orange).

So, especially if you disagree with the conclusion in the above argument – that illegally downloading a copy of an album on the Internet is ethically wrong – you might be able to make your case by arguing for one or more important differences between the two scenarios that are held together in the analogy argument.

So: are there important, ethically relevant differences between these two scenarios – and, if so, what are they?

The ethics of copying: is it theft, Open Source, or Confucian homage to the master?

1. Intellectual property: three (Western) approaches

As we saw in chapter 1, there are a number of characteristics of digital media that make the copying and distribution of various kinds of information – whether representing software, a text, a song or video, etc. – much easier to do than with comparable analogue media. That is, once we have access to the various components required – an access that in turn is likewise growing rapidly around the world, despite the grave difficulties of the "digital divide" – copying and distributing a file in digital format is both trivially easy and all but cost-free.

Moreover, the general rules, guidelines, and laws applicable to such copying are wide-ranging and frequently shifting. In its ongoing battle against illegal music downloading, the entertainment industry relentlessly lobbies for more stringent laws intended to stop (or at least slow down) widespread distribution of music and video files on the Internet via peer-to-peer (p2p) file-sharing networks; these industries have likewise pushed for digital rights management (DRM) and copy protection schemes also designed to prevent illegal copying or piracy – efforts backed in the United States by the Digital Millennium Copyright Act (DMCA). Critics such as the Electronic Freedom Foundation (EFF) counter that "there's no evidence that DRM" succeeds in doing so: rather, "DRM helps big business stifle innovation and competition by making it easy to quash 'unauthorized' uses of media and technology" (www.eff.org/issues/drm).

In 2011 and 2012, these battles came to a head in the US with (so far, failed) efforts to introduce SOPA (the Stop Online Piracy Act) and PIPA (the Preventing Real Online Threats to Economic Creativity and Theft of Intellectual Property Act). Whatever restrictions against copyright infringement these acts intended, SOPA and PIPA were equally significant for evoking protest in the form of a Google-sponsored petition drive, voluntary service blackouts (e.g., by the English Wikipedia), and denial-of-service (DOS) attacks – ostensibly, by Anonymous – against organizations in favour of the act. (See Tavani 2013: 260–1.)

Meanwhile, one of the most significant developments in these struggles is the establishment of the Pirate Party. Most readers will know that Pirate Bay first emerged as one of the primary sites for sharing files via peer-to-peer (P2P) networking via BitTorrent or similar file-sharing software. Despite massive legal threats and a trial that resulted in 2010 in brief prison sentences but hefty fines for four of the Bay's ostensible organizers and operators, and despite blocking efforts by several countries – including otherwise quite liberal Denmark (Mauger 2012) – at the time of this writing, the Pirate Bay website is alive and well. Along the way, the Pirate Party was founded as a political party, first in Sweden in 2006. For its part, the German Pirate Party has enjoyed varying support in opinion polls – as high as 13 percent, but recently between 4 and 5 percent – and finding its way towards becoming an electable party has been difficult. The basic principles of the party are clear: reform of copyright law, abolition of the patent system, and respect for the right to privacy (www2.piratpartiet. se/international/english). But German voters would apparently like something more – including policies regarding the economy, foreign affairs, and pensions: achieving agreement on such matters is proving elusive, at least according to prominent newspapers, such the *Frankfurter Allgemeine Zeitung* and *Süddeutsche Zeitung*, reporting on the party's 2012 congress (Wiegand 2012; Schulz 2012).

How far the Pirate Parties will manage to transform the current laws regarding copyright and patents is, of course, very much an open question. But developments along these lines are precisely – if only in part – how laws are made and changed. Stay tuned!

(a) Copyright in the United States and Europe
The polarities exemplified by the RIAA (Recording Industry Association of America) vs. the EFF and the Pirate Parties in fact

entail at least three major positions or streams of response that we can consider as ethical responses to these sorts of dilemmas.

To begin with, as Dan Burk (2007) characterizes it, intellectual property (IP) law in the United States is shaped by a utilitarian ethic (see chapter 6 for discussion), one that argues that copyright and other forms of intellectual property protection are justified as these contribute to the larger public good over the long run. That is, proponents of this view believe that authors, artists, software designers, and other creative agents will take the trouble to innovate and develop new products and services that will benefit the larger public only if those agents can themselves be assured of a significant personal reward – primarily in terms of money or other economic goods. What this means in practice, however, is that it is principally the industries that have a strong economic interest in copyright and other protections that argue and lobby for such protections. Indeed, the interests and possible benefits of the individual agent are secondary in this view. Given its utilitarian framework, "The rights of the author should at least in theory extend no further than necessary to benefit the public and conceivably could be eliminated entirely if a convincing case against public benefit could be shown" (Burk 2007: 96).

By contrast, European approaches to copyright can be characterized as deontological in character. As Burk puts it,

> copyright is justified as an intrinsic *right* of the author, a necessary recognition of the author's *identity* or *personhood*. . . . the general rationale for copyright in this tradition regards creative work as an artifact that has been invested with some measure of the author's personality or that reflects the author's individuality. Out of respect for the *autonomy* and humanity of the author, that artifact deserves legal recognition. (2007: 96; emphasis added)

As Burk goes on to point out, we are thus currently caught in an international competition between the US and the EU as to which of these approaches to copyright will prevail – with the US currently dominating, according to Burk (ibid.: 99–100).

The third ethical response to these sorts of dilemmas – namely, copyleft/FLOSS – is the subject of the following section.

(b) Copyleft/FLOSS

Third, alternatives to what are seen as excessively restrictive conditions especially on the development and use of computer software have been developed – initially under the rubric of Free and Open Source Software (FOSS). More broadly, these comparatively early notions of FOSS are now discussed in terms of a more inclusive acronym, FLOSS – Free/Libre/Open Source Software – in recognition that a great deal of the interest and work in FOSS operates in Latin-speaking countries (primarily Latin America and the francophone countries).

This rubric, in fact, conjoins two important but conflicting philosophical and ethical frameworks – those of the free software (FS) movement, affiliated with Richard Stallman and the Free Software Foundation, and those of the subsequent Open Source Initiative (OSI), begun in 1998 by Eric Raymond and others. While both share the common goal of fostering the development of software to be made freely available for others to copy, use, modify, and then redistribute, the free software movement began in largely conscious opposition to commercial development of profit-oriented proprietary software and the copyright schemes seen to protect such software. By contrast, the Open Source Initiative was driven by the goal of making free software more attractive to for-profit businesses. These differences, as we will see, are significant for us on a number of levels: we will explore them in greater detail in Resources/research question 1 (pp. 116–18 below). But, for now, we can begin to explore FLOSS by way of Stallman's basic definition of what "free" in "free software" means:

> Free software is a matter of the users' freedom to run, copy, distribute, study, change and improve the software. More precisely, it refers to four kinds of freedom, for the users of the software:
>
> • The freedom to run the program, for any purpose (freedom 0).
> • The freedom to study how the program works, and adapt it to your needs (freedom 1). Access to the source code is a precondition for this.
> • The freedom to redistribute copies so you can help your neighbor (freedom 2).

• The freedom to improve the program, and release your improvements to the public, so that the whole community benefits (freedom 3). Access to the source code is a precondition for this.

A program is free software if users have all of these freedoms. Thus, you should be free to redistribute copies, either with or without modifications, either gratis or charging a fee for distribution, to anyone anywhere. Being free to do these things means (among other things) that you do not have to ask or pay for permission.

(The Free Software Definition [Richard Stallman/GNU Operating System], partially quoted at the outset of this chapter, www.gnu.org/philosophy/free-sw.html)

Ethically, what is interesting here is the justification for such freedom in terms of benefits to the whole community. Rather than relying on copyright schemes as oriented towards either economic incentives or protecting authorial rights as the engines of creative development and distribution, the free software movement begins with a more communitarian sensibility, one that is inspired in part by a deep conviction that the potential benefits of computer software (and information more generally) should be shared as broadly and equally as possible.

To state this slightly differently, it may be helpful to understand that, by "property right" in the contemporary world, we mean first of all a right to access and use something – whether a material item (such as your pen, backpack, computer, bicycle, etc.) or something more non-material, including "intellectual property" such as an author's words or a computer programmer's code. Given that property means first of all such a right, then we can distinguish between copyright and copyleft/FLOSS approaches in terms of exclusive and inclusive property rights. Briefly, the US and European copyright approaches tend to start with and favor exclusive property rights. That is, property rights (of access and use) belong exclusively to the individual owner: the "default setting" of such exclusive rights is that the owner has the right to exclude others from use and access to his or her property. Copyleft/FLOSS approaches, by contrast, involve notions of inclusive property rights. So, in Richard Stallman's definition of free software (quoted above), the starting point is the users' freedom – i.e., a community of software users – not the individual's right to exclude others from use and access.

Similarly, the Creative Commons approach, while recognizing and protecting individual rights ("some rights reserved"), does so in a way that is inclusive – i.e., "by default" recognizes the rights of others to access and use property. So the Creative Commons "Attribution-Noncommercial-Share Alike 3.0 United States" license reads:

> You are free:
> **to Share** – to copy, distribute and transmit the work
> **to Remix** – to adopt the work
> to make commercial use of the work
>
> **Under the following conditions:**
> **Attribution** – You must attribute the work in the manner specified by the author or licensor (but not in any way that suggests that they endorse you or your use of the work).
> **With the understanding that:**
> **Waiver** – Any of the above conditions can be waived if you get permission from the copyright holder.
> **Public Domain** – Where the work or any of its elements is in the public domain under applicable law, that status is in no way affected by the license.
> **Other Rights** – In no way are any of the following rights affected by the license:
> • Your fair dealing or **fair use** rights, or other applicable copyright exceptions and limitations;
> • The author's **moral** rights;
> • Rights other persons may have either in the work itself or in how the work is used, such as **publicity** or privacy rights.
> **Notice** – For any reuse or distribution, you must make clear to others the license terms of this work. The best way to do this is with a link to this web page.
> (http://creativecommons.org/licenses/by/3.0/)

That is, individuals retain their "moral rights" – including a right to exclude others from using one's property for others' commercial advantage. At the same time, however, others' rights of access and use, such as copying, distributing, and remixing an individual's property, are likewise granted under this license: that is, the individual owner's rights are in this way inclusive rather than exclusive.

In these terms, we will see when we focus more on the cultural backgrounds at work here that a wide range of non-Western traditions and approaches to property – beginning with the initial discussion of the (Southern) African tradition of *ubuntu* (next section) – likewise stress inclusive rather than exclusive rights.

FLOSS in practice: the Linux operating system   As is well known among Linux enthusiasts especially, in the early 1990s Linus Torvalds developed a variant of the UNIX operating system[1] that was intended for free distribution from the outset – and this in the free software sense: that is, Torvalds chose to distribute his software under Stallman's GNU General Public License. Subsequently, a great deal of FLOSS work focused on the development and distribution of the Linux operating system and affiliated applications. Among the many distributions of Linux that can be freely downloaded online, the Ubuntu distribution is one of the most popular – in part, perhaps, because of its clear communitarian philosophy. Drawing directly upon the philosophical principles of the Free Software Foundation (as articulated by Stallman, above), the Ubuntu distribution website declares: "Ubuntu is created by open-source developers because we believe that everybody should have access to the best possible technologies" (www. ubuntu.com/project). Indeed, Ubuntu is driven by a specific sort of philosophy: "Ubuntu is an African concept of 'humanity towards others'. It is 'the belief in a universal bond of sharing that connects all humanity'" (https://help.ubuntu.com/10.04/about-ubuntu/C/ about-ubuntu-name.html). Consequently, Ubuntu Linux explicitly

---

1   For those of us who are not computer geeks: the operating system, or OS, is the base-level software that defines the various operations required to make your computer "work" – including reading and writing files from various media (floppy disks, CDs, DVDs, memory sticks) and through various communication channels and networks (phone lines, Ethernet connection, wireless networks), along with the many operations required to let you interact with and use that information (e.g., keyboards and mice and the computer screen). For most of us in the developed world, this means in practice some variant of Windows or the Macintosh OS X. Application software, by contrast, is software that runs, so to speak, on top of the OS: this commonly includes applications that make possible wordprocessing, email, spreadsheets, presentation, web-browsing, instant messaging, etc.

invokes the Free Software Foundation's definition of the freedoms constituting the "free" in free software, including:

The freedom to redistribute copies so you can help others. [freedom 2]
The freedom to improve the programme and release your improvements to the public, so that everyone benefits. [freedom 3]

(See "Our Philosophy," www.ubuntu.com/
project/about-ubuntu/our-philosophy)

The clear intersection between free software sensibilities and the *ubuntu* tradition, then, is the emphasis on inclusive rather than exclusive property rights – and for the sake of benefiting one's neighbors and the larger (indeed, now worldwide) community.

Ubuntu as a free software project hence directly reflects the greater emphasis on community well-being that characterizes indigenous (Southern) African cultural values. At the same time, you may remember that, in chapter 2, we saw this emphasis on the larger community as a characteristic of other cultural traditions – especially Confucian and Buddhist traditions – and its consequences for non-Western conceptions of privacy. We are now starting to see how this emphasis on community well-being has crucial consequences for our notions of property and thereby such common acts as copying and distributing via digital media. We will return to this discussion of culture and ethics in the next section, as we consider Confucian thought and copyright.

FLOSS in practice: applications and Wikipedia   The FLOSS movements have produced not only operating systems such as Linux, but also equally popular web browsers and email clients (perhaps most notably Firefox and Thunderbird, respectively, which run on Windows and Macintosh as well as on Linux machines) and even complete office suites that largely duplicate the functionalities of Microsoft's Office software (primarily, Open Office). Such software is hence not only attractive to young people and university students with limited resources; it may also play a vital role in efforts to overcome the "digital divide" and to exploit digital media for the sake of development.

But the ethical sensibilities and developed applications of

FLOSS are not limited to computer applications; in addition, they have generated other fruitful, perhaps even essential kinds of sharing online. One example is the Wikipedia encyclopedia project (www.wikipedia.org). Exploiting the famous interactivity possible on the Web – such that individuals can not simply read, but also actively write for and contribute other forms of media to a given webpage – Wikipedia has become a remarkable resource, representing the input of more than 77,000 active contributors, totaling more than 22 million articles in 285 languages (see http:// en.wikipedia.org/wiki/Wikipedia:About). In contrast to traditional copyright schemes, Wikipedia initially relied on the GNU Free Documentation License (GNU FDL, or simply GFDL), a copyleft license originally developed by the Free Software Foundation (FSF) for documentation affiliated with the GNU project. The license is designed to accomplish two goals:

> The purpose of this License is to make a manual, textbook, or other functional and useful document "free" in the sense of freedom: to assure everyone the effective freedom to copy and redistribute it, with or without modifying it, either commercially or noncommercially. Secondarily, this License preserves for the author and publisher a way to get credit for their work, while not being considered responsible for modifications made by others.
>
> (http://en.wikipedia.org/wiki/Wikipedia:
> Text_of_the_GNU_Free_Documentation_License)

Wikipedia has subsequently developed its own dual-licensing scheme, one that incorporates the GFDL (version 1.3) along with the Creative Commons Attribution-ShareAlike 3.0 Unported License (CC-BY-SA) (see http://en.wikipedia.org/wiki/ Wikipedia:Licensing_update). While Wikipedia is clear that it is not to be used as a primary resource for academic research (you have been warned!), it has nonetheless become one of the most common first stops in undertaking research: in particular, because the materials here may be updated and corrected much more quickly than printed sources, Wikipedia articles may be especially useful (at least as a starting point) for looking into current events, recent changes in a field, and so forth.

In these ways, Wikipedia – along with other "products" of the FLOSS movement – may be taken as paradigmatic fulfillments of the philosophical claims and assumptions underlying these alternative or copyleft approaches. And, as exemplifying and fulfilling some of the best promises of the FLOSS movement, these examples provide strong justification for the ethical frameworks and approaches at work in their licensing schemes. They thereby serve as important counterexamples to proponents of more traditional (either US or EU) copyright schemes, especially as such proponents might argue that FLOSS approaches are somehow utopian, excessively idealistic and impracticable, etc.

REFLECTION/DISCUSSION/WRITING QUESTIONS:
IP, ETHICS, AND SOCIAL NETWORKING

We've now seen a range of possible approaches to how intellectual property may be treated:

(i) US, property-oriented copyright law (consequentialist);
(ii) EU, copyright law, oriented towards authorial rights (deontological);
(iii) Open Source/FLOSS/"copyleft" schemes, including Creative Commons and GNU General Public (GPL) and Free Documentation (FDL) licenses.

1. Given your own country/location, which of these licensing schemes seems to be prevalent in your experience?
2. In your view, what are the most important – but especially ethically relevant – differences between these three approaches? Be careful here, and, insofar as you are now familiar with one or more of the ethical frameworks discussed in chapter 6 (beginning with utilitarianism and deontology), try to discern how far a distinctive ethical characteristic of a given licensing scheme may be seen to depend upon a given *ethical framework*.
3. Return to your responses to one or more of the scenarios introduced at the start of this chapter – e.g., stealing a CD from a music store, making an illegal copy of new music for a friend, making your music library available for others online through a p2p network, etc.

(i) Which of these three approaches to IP seems closest to your own responses to such scenarios and the ethical justifications for those responses that you have developed?

(ii) Which of these three approaches to IP most clearly contradicts your own responses and justifications?

(iii) Develop a summary of the arguments, evidence, and/or other reasons offered in support for the approaches you have identified in (i) and (ii). Now: in light of the contrasts here between the arguments, evidence, etc., can you discern additional arguments, evidence, etc., that might support one of these approaches more strongly than the other?

4. Presuming you have an account on a social networking service such as Facebook, MySpace, and/or others:

(i) When you signed up for the account, did you review the "Terms of Use" or equivalent legal/ethical agreements required of you as a user of the site and its affiliated software? If so, why? If not, why not?

(ii) Review the "Terms of Use" for your networking site – looking particularly for the important claims it makes regarding your ownership of the materials that you post on the site. (For Facebook users, the pertinent section of the "Terms of Use" is reproduced at the beginning of this chapter.)

(iii) Are there claims here that
 (a) surprise you
   and/or
 (b) upon reflection, you may not be comfortable agreeing to?

If so, identify these (both for your own reflection and, perhaps, for class discussion and further writing).

(iv) Can you discern which of the three approaches to IP that we have examined are presumed in these claims? If so, is part of your discomfort with the claims made upon you here because you have a strong ethical disagreement with the approach to IP presumed here? That is, can you argue – most easily, from a different ethical approach to IP – that the claims made upon you are somehow wrong?

(v) Social networking sites depend on acquiring as many user accounts as possible in order to make money (primarily through advertising, the sale of at least aggregated information about its users, etc.). In this way, they are at least somewhat sensitive to the interests, needs, and opinions of their users.

If you find that the "Terms of Use" of your favorite social networking site conflict with your own ethics and underlying assumptions regarding IP, it would be an interesting exercise to write the site owners (either individually and/or as a larger group) and explain your disagreements and reasons for these. If nothing else, their response(s) to your communications might provide additional material for interesting ethical analysis!

ADDITIONAL (META-ETHICAL) QUESTIONS

5. As we have seen, digital media make copying and distributing materials – whether computer software or entertainment resources such as songs, videos, etc. – much easier and quicker than previous sorts of media. Some thinkers and proponents – including Stallman, Lawrence Lessig, and others we encountered briefly above – have suggested that, because digital media are distinctive in these ways, they require either

(i) a very different sort of ethics with regard to IP – but one that still represents an extension of familiar ethical frameworks as applied to digital media, or
(ii) a radically new sort of ethics – perhaps one that we have yet to develop and articulate fully, much less apply carefully to the ethical issues of IP (as well as other ethical issues evoked by digital media).

What is your response to these sorts of claims? That is, do you think that

(a) IP issues can be fully and satisfactorily dealt with using traditional ethical frameworks, and/or

(b) IP (and other ethical issues in digital media) will require totally new ways of thinking ethically?

Try to justify your response here, perhaps by way of using a particular example from either your own experience and/or one or more of the scenarios discussed in this text.

2. Intellectual property and culture: Confucian ethics and African thought

Finally, as the example of Ubuntu and the differences between US and EU approaches to copyright suggest, our attitudes and approaches to matters of intellectual property and how far and under what circumstances such materials may be justifiably shared with others are strongly shaped by culture. (Keep in mind, of course, the sense and limitations of any generalizations we may try to make about culture: see chapter 2, Interlude, pp. 47–51.)

As a further example: US copyright law is moderately clear with regard to what counts as "fair use" for teaching and research purposes – at least as far as printed materials are concerned.[2] In particular, under most circumstances, it is illegal for me to make, say, photocopies of an entire book that I would then distribute to my students at the beginning of the semester for their use during the course. On the other hand, in general I am allowed to place original materials, such as articles or book chapters, on reserve for my students in the library; they are then free to check out these materials and make copies of them – as part of their "fair use" of these materials as students.

By contrast, European copyright law makes no equivalent provisions for "fair use." On the other hand, in Thailand I received a now highly cherished gift from some graduate students: a

---

2 The US Copyright Act of 1976 was accompanied by the development of "Guidelines for Classroom Copying in Not-for-Profit Educational Institutions with Respect to Books and Periodicals" (see, e.g., www.unc.edu/~unclng/classroom-guidelines.htm). Perhaps, by this point, readers will not be surprised to discover that an equivalent set of guidelines has yet to be established for "fair use" copying of digital materials.

nicely photocopied version of an important book in philosophy of technology, complete with a carefully crafted cover, on which the students inscribed their names. In US circumstances, this could only be seen as a crass violation of copyright law, but, in the Thai context, this copying was seen to be a mark of respect, both for the (famous and well-known) author of the text and for me as the recipient of the gift.

In the latter case, the gift from the students reflected not simply relatively limited economic resources – a (consequentialist) reason often cited as a justification for making illegal copies of materials. In addition, it reflected the influence of Confucian tradition: as Dan Burk has summarized it, Confucian tradition emphasizes emulation of revered classics – and, in this way, copying (as it was for medieval monks in the West) is an activity that expresses highest respect for the work of the author (Burk 2007: 101). By the same token, a master philosopher or thinker is motivated primarily by the desire to benefit others with his or her work – rather than, say, to profit personally through the sale of that work – and so she or he would want to see that work copied and distributed widely rather than restricted in its distribution.

In this light, the Confucian tradition and practice thus closely resemble what we have already seen of *ubuntu* as a (Southern) African cultural tradition. While they are distinct from one another in crucial ways, they share the sense that individuals are relational beings, ones centrally interdependent with the larger community for their very existence and sense of meaning as human beings. Compared with Western systems that highlight the individual and the individual's exclusive property right, both Confucian and *ubuntu* traditions downplay the importance of the individual and individual interests, stressing instead the importance of contributing to and maintaining the harmony and well-being of the larger community. (We will explore these matters more fully in chapter 6, but it is important to stress here that this emphasis on the community does not mean – as sometimes appears the case for my Western students – the complete loss of "the individual." On the contrary, individual human beings retain significance and integrity in these views, precisely as they are able to interact with others in ways that foster community harmony and well-being.)

Hence, whether it is copying an important text out of respect and gratitude and a desire to show respect and gratitude (my Thai students), or making available an operating system such as Ubuntu for free (in more than just the economic sense of being without cost), in both cases, the approach to what counts as property is inclusive: the right to access and use these materials belongs to the community, not exclusively to the individual.

In sum: we have now seen culturally variable understandings of property and the ethics of copying and distribution – initially within Western cultures (US and European copyright schemes, along with copyleft schemes affiliated with FLOSS), and now between Western and non-Western cultures and traditions. In this light, it should now be clear that the various software operating systems and applications developed under FLOSS are popular in the developing world not simply for economic reasons: that is, at least in terms of licensing arrangements (though not necessarily in terms of technical and administrative costs), FLOSS avoids the licensing fees characteristically charged by corporations such as Microsoft. In addition, we have seen what we can properly call the ethos or ethical sensibilities surrounding FLOSS: this ethos includes an explicit emphasis on one's contribution to a shared work for the sake of a larger community, and a sense that "information wants to be free" (meaning, specifically, freely copied). Moreover, this ethos resonates closely with the emphasis on community well-being that we have now seen to be characteristic of Confucian tradition and *ubuntu*, as but two examples of non-Western philosophical and ethical traditions.

And, presuming you read chapter 2 before this one, there is a larger coherency that, I hope, is also beginning to become clear: just as major cultural variations regarding our understanding of the individual vis-à-vis the community shape our conceptions of privacy and expectations regarding data privacy protection, so these major cultural variations likewise shape our understandings of property and the ethics of copying and sharing.

In particular, recall the discussion there regarding changing conceptions of selfhood in both "Western" and "Eastern" traditions. Most briefly, just as strongly individual notions of selfhood correlate with strongly individual notions of privacy – so it appears that these notions further undergird and correlate with strongly individual notions of property, including intellectual property, as primarily an exclusive right held precisely by the individual as copyright holder. And: just as more relational notions of selfhood correlate with more inclusive or shared notions of privacy – such as group privacy or familial privacy – so these notions, as manifest here especially in Confucian and *ubuntu* traditions, further correlate with shared or inclusive notions of property. In this light, the widespread and largely accepted practices – however illegal – of file-sharing, especially among younger folk, does not necessarily mean, as some are tempted to argue, that there is some sort of outbreak of unethical behavior among the more recent generations. And/or: it may be that such behavior – often under the mantra of "sharing is caring" – further reflects these foundational shifts in our basic understandings of selfhood and identity – i.e., precisely towards more relational selves for whom such sharing is directly coherent with more communitarian and inclusive notions of property.

In these lights, finally, the future of the Pirate Parties may be a most interesting index of how far these correlations are indeed taking place. That is, if the various Pirate Parties manage to gain greater acceptance for their agenda of reforming copyright law and abolishing the patent system, that acceptance might not simply indicate a lack of concern for (individual) property rights among their followers. And/or: that acceptance might further indicate a fundamental shift in our most basic understanding of our selfhood and identity in "Western" societies – i.e., precisely in the direction of more relational selves for whom property rights certainly exist, but understood in inclusive and communitarian ways.

REFLECTION/DISCUSSION/WRITING QUESTIONS:
LAW, ETHICS, CULTURE

1. *COPYING: LAW, CULTURE – ETHICS?*

Does the legality of copying music make a difference ethically? And how do our cultural attitudes towards texts, authorship, and property affect our ethical analyses of copying?

We have now seen a continuum of possible approaches to notions of intellectual property and the ethics of copying and distributing such properties. One way to schematize that continuum looks like this:

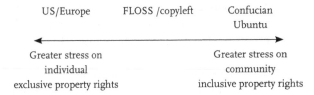

| US/Europe | FLOSS /copyleft | Confucian |
| | | Ubuntu |

Greater stress on	Greater stress on
individual	community
exclusive property rights	inclusive property rights

(Again, these generalizations about culture are starting points only.) As you review your initial arguments and responses to the questions concerning copying and distributing copyrighted materials:

A) Can you now see one or more ways in which your views, arguments, etc., rested on one or more of the assumptions underlying these three diverse approaches to intellectual property? That is, how far (if at all) do any of your views, arguments, etc., rest on
   • assumptions about the relative importance of the individual vis-à-vis the community
     and/or
   • assumptions about the nature of property rights (exclusive or inclusive)?
   If so, identify the specific assumption(s) at work in your initial arguments and views.
B) Does it appear that your relying on these assumptions is related to your culture(s) of origin and experience? That

is, do the assumptions you're making regarding either the individual/community relationship and/or the inclusive/ exclusive character of property *correlate/not correlate* with these assumptions as characterizing the larger culture(s) of your origin and experience?

C) Especially if there is a correlation between the assumption(s) underlying your views and arguments and the culture(s) of your origin and experience, what does that mean in terms of ethics? This is to say: recognizing the role of culturally variable norms, beliefs, practices, etc., in our ethical arguments characteristically leads to at least two sorts of questions:

(i) Are our ethical norms, beliefs, practices, etc., ethically relative – i.e., entirely reducible to the norms, beliefs, practices, etc. of a particular culture? If so, then we could say, for example:

for persons in a Western culture whose basic assumptions tend to support individual and exclusive notions of property and thus more restrictive copyright laws – if those persons violate more restrictive copyright laws (e.g., through illegally copying and distributing music), they thereby violate the basic ethical norms of their culture and should be condemned as wrong; but:

for persons in, say, a Confucian culture whose basic assumptions tend to support more community-oriented, inclusive notions of property and thus less restrictive copyright laws – if those persons violate the more restrictive copyright laws of Western nations, they are thereby simply following the moral norms and practices of their culture, and should not be condemned as wrong.

Consider/discuss/write: Does this approach of ethical relativism to the sorts of differences we have seen "make sense" to you as a way of how we are to understand and respond to these deep differences between cultures? If so, explain why. If not, why not?

(ii) If you do think there's something mistaken about the above scenario – and, thereby, about ethical relativism – then additional questions arise:

    (a) Do you want to shift to a posture of ethical absolutism – claiming that the norms, beliefs, and practices of country/culture X are the right ones: those countries/ cultures/individuals who hold different norms and beliefs are thereby wrong?
    and/or
    (b) Do you think it's possible – as we saw in chapter 2 on privacy – to develop an approach to matters of copying and distributing digital media that works as an ethical pluralism?

As a reminder: ethical pluralism conjoins shared norms or values with diverse interpretations/applications/understandings of those norms and values – so as thereby to reflect precisely the often very different basic assumptions and beliefs that define different cultural and ethical traditions.

Consider/discuss/write: Given what we've seen regarding the current conflicts between US and European approaches to copyright law (above, pp. 92–3), do these conflicts point towards an ethically absolutist approach on the part of the different countries engaged in these conflicts? And/or: in light of those conflicts, do you see any possibility of an ethically pluralistic solution emerging?

D) If you find that your beliefs, norms, and practices do not correlate with those underlying the culture(s) of your origin and experience, why might this be the case?

    Are we – especially in terms of our ethical sensibilities – somehow capable of discerning and establishing moral norms apart from, perhaps even against, prevailing norms and assumptions of our culture(s) of origin and experience? If so, how does that "work" in your view? That is, how do we as human beings come to develop our own ethical sensibilities? On what grounds?

2. *Copyright:*
Different Ethics for Different Countries, Cultures?

A student from a developing country justified the practice of pirating in that country – of illegal copying and selling imported music CDs – under the conditions that they were

(a) the work of well-to-do (and primarily Western) artists and
(b) distributed and sold in that country by equally well-to-do multinational corporations.

The student justified the practice of pirating in an interesting way:

(i) The widespread practice of pirating – of illegal copying and selling – imported music CDs effected an interesting change.

Originally, imported CDs cost around US$10.00. Pirated CDs were being sold for US$1.00. But, after a certain period of time, the prices of legal, imported CDs dropped to US$2.00 – thereby making them much more affordable for that country's inhabitants, and thus allowing the multinational corporation and Western artist to make at least more profit than they had before. This is to say: illegal copying and sales of CDs in effect broke a market monopoly, so that the market forces worked as they are supposed to – i.e., with free(er) competition leading to lower prices.

(Historical reference: Adam Smith, the author of the philosophical arguments that ground modern capitalism [*Wealth of Nations*, 1776], justified modern capitalism in clear utilitarian terms. Very briefly, free markets that thereby allow for competition should, if coupled with the laws of supply and demand, lead to the economic greatest good for the greatest number: the largest possible supply of goods and services made available at the lowest possible prices for the largest number of people. While Adam Smith would not countenance breaking the law, this first justification offers a utilitarian argument, insofar as it argues that the practice of pirating, in effect, helped the market function as it should, and thereby resulted in at least greater good for more people than if people had only the choice to buy legal imported CDs at US$10.00 each.)

In addition, the student pointed out that, by contrast, many students and others of limited means consciously choose to pay full price for a CD produced by a local/regional/national music group. Again, the argument is, on first blush, utilitarian:

(ii) By paying full price for CDs produced by local/regional/ national musicians, they thereby supported those who really needed it – and thereby helped boost their own economy.

In both examples, the student's arguments echo the arguments I hear from many students in the developed world. Again, in the case of nationally or internationally known musician(s), whose work is distributed by wealthy and powerful corporations, the positive benefits or consequences of illegal copying and downloading (in terms of making the music more easily available for more people) outweigh the possible negative costs (of a modest amount of lost profit to the musicians and the companies). By contrast, many will make a conscious effort to "buy local" – to pay full price for CDs produced and distributed by local bands struggling to make a start.

Responses? In particular:

(i) Does it seem to you that, say, students and others in developing countries can make a greater/stronger case for pirating and other forms of illegal copying than students and others in developed countries?

(ii) Assume that the developing country in this example is a country marked by one of the more community-oriented traditions discussed above – e.g., *ubuntu* or Confucian thought. And assume that the students in the developed world that I refer to live in the well-to-do countries such as the United States and Scandinavia – i.e., countries and traditions shaped by Western conceptions of the individual and primarily exclusive property rights.

In light of the important differences between the cultural and ethical backgrounds, how do you respond to the claim that the students in the developing country (shaped by *ubuntu* or Confucian tradition) have a stronger justification for their illegal copying than Western students?

Or would you rather argue that everyone should follow the copyright laws – no matter their location and culture?

3. COPYRIGHT AND DEONTOLOGICAL ETHICS

Deontological ethics, as emphasizing, e.g., duties to respect and protect the rights of others – whatever the costs of doing so – can be invoked in these debates as offering reasons for obeying the law. Even if the consequences of doing so may be unpleasant – e.g., not having access to music one would otherwise enjoy – doing so none-theless reflects an important duty to respect the property rights of others. Such duties, however, crucially depend on establishing that the laws in question are just laws – i.e., grounded in one or more sets of values and principles that are used to demonstrate that such laws are justified as means to higher ends.

And so, Mahatma Gandhi and Dr. Martin Luther King, Jr. (and, for that matter, the signers of the US Declaration of Independence), famously argued that, while we are morally obliged to follow just laws, we are allowed, even morally obliged, to disobey unjust laws.

The trick, of course, is demonstrating that a given law is indeed unjust.

Some arguments I've heard in the debates over illegal copying sound as if people are attempting to construct a deontological argument somewhat along the following lines:

- The laws established to "protect" the work of wealthy artists and marketed by wealthy and powerful corporations are unjust.
- They are unjust because the laws are not the result of a genu-inely democratic process, one in which the consent of those

affected plays the deciding role. Rather, they are laws that result from a legislative process controlled by the powerful – those with the money to do so. Those laws thus represent and protect the interests of the wealthy and powerful – they do not represent or protect the interests of the rest of us.

- Given that these laws are unjust, I am allowed (perhaps even obliged) to disobey them.

Perhaps with the help of your instructor and/or cohorts, review some of the important deontological sources for arguments supporting disobeying unjust laws (e.g., Ess 1998). Can you find/ develop deontological arguments along these lines that support disobeying prevailing copyright laws as unjust laws? And, if so, how closely do they parallel the sorts of arguments offered by Dr. Martin Luther King, Jr., for example? In particular, how good an analogy is there between

- the situation and context supporting King's arguments that segregation laws are unjust – and thus must be disobeyed and

- the situation and context supporting the arguments you find/develop that copyright laws are unjust and thus can or must be disobeyed?

4. COPYRIGHT AND VIRTUE ETHICS

Herman Tavani, drawing especially on the work of Michael McFarland (2004), develops a framework for analyzing intellectual property issues that rests squarely on Aristotle's virtue ethics (see chapter 6 for further discussion). On this view, information is taken to have as its ultimate purpose both personal expression and utility; this means in turn that information is best understood as a common good, something whose essential nature is to be shared – rather than treated, as it is in traditional Western copyright schemes, as an exclusive property. At the extreme, an exclusive focus on information – whether as computer software or a popular song – as a property, the right to which can be controlled by one person or corporation, would lead to the end of "the public domain" – i.e., a kind of "information commons" that benefits the whole community. (The analogy here is with the commons in pre-industrial England – i.e., a parcel of land accessible to all for the benefit of all, in contrast to individual and private property.)

Arguably, much good – both individually and communally – has come from the existence of such commons. Indeed, as Niels Ole Finneman (2005) points out, part of the Scandinavian approach to information technologies and their supporting infrastructures over the past decades is based on understanding these as common or public goods – ones that thus require and deserve the material support of the state. Direct state support of ICT infrastructure and development has thus contributed to the Scandinavian countries enjoying the highest presence and use of these technologies in their daily lives.

From the perspective of virtue ethics, then, we would pursue excellence in our abilities to develop, manipulate, and distribute information as a common good – not primarily because doing so might benefit us personally in primarily economic terms but, rather, because, in doing so, (a) we foster and improve upon important capacities and abilities as human beings, including our ability to communicate with one another and benefit one another using these new technologies; as well, (b) doing so thereby contributes to greater community harmony and benefit.

To be sure, such an approach, as Tavani emphasizes, is not opposed to individual economic gain. The ideal here would be to develop a system that could conjoin these notions of virtue ethics and the common good with a recognized need for "fair compensation" for the costs and risks individuals and companies take in developing products and making them available in the marketplace. Tavani sees the Creative Commons initiative (discussed above) as one way of institutionalizing such a virtue ethics approach to information (Tavani 2013: 252–60).

Responses? In particular:

A) Are there important virtues or habits of excellence that might come into play in either

(i) practicing obeying, e.g., copyright laws (as well as other laws), at least as long as they are just laws?

(ii) practicing disobeying such laws?

B) Are there important virtues or habits of excellence that might come into play in either

(i) practicing obeying, e.g., copyright laws (as well as other laws), even if they are unjust laws?

(ii) practicing disobeying such laws?

5. CULTURE – AGAIN

(As a reminder: the following generalizations are starting points only – ones that will be accompanied by plenty of counterexamples and that will become much more complex and nuanced as we go along.)

In addition to culture correlating with basic assumptions regarding the individual/community relationship and the nature of property rights (inclusive/exclusive), we have seen that it may further correlate with the basic ethical frameworks we have been using:

• Roughly, if you have been acculturated in a Western/ Northern country such as the US and the UK, it may be that your arguments largely emphasize utilitarian approaches.

• If you have been acculturated in a Western/Northern country such as the Germanic countries and Scandinavia, it may be that your arguments more likely include deontological approaches.

• If you have been acculturated in a non-Western country – especially one shaped by the sorts of traditions we have explored so far (*ubuntu*, Confucian thought, and Buddhist thought) that emphasize the well-being of the community, you may have a stronger likelihood of appreciating virtue ethics approaches – i.e., beginning with questions about what kinds of human beings we need to become – and thus what sorts of habits and practices of excellence must we pursue, for the sake of both our own contentment and well-being (*eudaimonia*) and that of our larger community; and/or you may have a stronger likelihood of appreciating the importance of doing what will benefit the larger community in any event, insofar as we as individuals are crucially interdependent with the other members of our community.

What role – if any, so far as you can tell – does your own culture play in shaping your attitudes, beliefs, and practices in these matters? Stated differently: can you see whether or not your own arguments have been reinforced in one or more ways by the larger cultural tradition(s) that have shaped you? And/or: do your own arguments tend to run against the prevailing ethics of the larger cultural traditions that have shaped you?

(After responding to these questions, you may want to revisit the questions regarding our meta-ethical frameworks – ethical relativism, absolutism, and pluralism – raised above in question (1)(C)(i) and (1)(C)(ii), pp. 108–9).

RESOURCES/RESEARCH

In addition to reviewing available entries, e.g., on Wikipedia, regarding "Open Source Initiative," "Eric Raymond," etc., read one or more of the following resources (moving from broad introductions to more careful foci):

Tavani, Herman (2013) Intellectual Property Disputes in Cyberspace (chapter 8), esp. "8.7.2 The Open Source Movement" (pp. 250–52), pp. 230–68 in *Ethics and Technology: Ethical Issues in an Age of Information and Communication Technology* (4th edn). Hoboken, NJ: Wiley.
An excellent overview of IP, including discussion of both FS and OSS.
Raymond, Eric (2004) The Cathedral and the Bazaar, pp. 367–96 in Richard A. Spinello and Herman T. Tavani (eds), *Readings in Cyberethics* (2nd edn). Boston: Jones & Bartlett.
Provides a classic account and justification of OSS philosophy and approaches.

Spinello, Richard A. (2008) Intellectual Property: Legal and Moral Challenges of Online File Sharing, pp. 553–69 in Kenneth Einar Himma and Herman T. Tavani (eds), *The Handbook of Information and Computer Ethics.* Hoboken, NJ: Wiley.
A fine overview, focusing on the US context, including attention to the Grokster case.
Grodzinsky, Frances S., and Wolf, Marty (2008) Ethical Interest in Free and Open Source Software, pp. 245–71 in Kenneth Einar Himma and Herman T. Tavani (eds), *The Handbook of Information and Computer Ethics.* Hoboken, NJ: Wiley.
An extensive analysis of the important philosophical differences between FS and OSS.

1.A) Given the resources you have examined, highlight what seem to be the most important philosophical differences between FS and OSS regarding intellectual property and how it is to be fairly and justly developed and shared.

   (i) Given these differences, which of the two approaches seems more defensible, in your view?

   (ii) In light of the differences, which approach seems closer to your own actual practices and behaviors regarding, e.g., music and other forms of file-sharing?

1.B) Review your responses to question 1 above (pp. 107–9). In light of the contrasts we have now seen between FS and OSS, we can subdivide the "FLOSS/copyleft" position on the continuum diagram in turn:

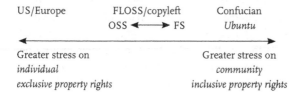

Given this more complex range of choices regarding possible philosophical positions on intellectual property, would you change any of your responses to the various questions posed in (1), especially (1)(B) (pp. 107–8, on possible correlations between your cultural background(s) and your ethics)? If so, in what ways? If not, why not?

Alternatively: are the philosophical differences between FS and OSS in fact relevant to your own cultural background and ethics? And/or: are these differences, as Benjamin Hill suggests in his review, less about philosophy and ethics and more about tactics, etc.?

2. A universal ethics of copying? (Meta-ethical issues vis-à-vis the cultural backgrounds of norms and practices of copying.)

In light of these large contrasts between how different cultures approach the ethics of copying, can there be/ought there to be a universally shared ethics of copying and thereby a universal set of laws (copyright/copyleft/other?) governing our copying and distributing the works of others?

It may be useful to review the discussion of ethical pluralism in chapter 6, along with the ethical pluralism described in chapter 2 regarding a global ethics of privacy and data privacy protection. In addition, you might want to look at

Brey, Philip (2007) Is Information Ethics Culture-Relative? *Journal of Technology and Human Interaction*, 3(3): 12–24.
Brey examines the arguments for ethical relativism in the face of the sorts of cultural differences we have examined here – and with explicit attention to Confucian, Buddhist, and African thought with regard to both privacy and intellectual property rights. As with several other philosophers in Information Ethics – or what Rafael Capurro (2005) rightly calls Intercultural Information Ethics – Brey argues for an ethical pluralism as a middle ground between ethical relativism and ethical absolutism. (Again, see chapter 6 for a fuller discussion of these meta-ethical frameworks.)

Cohen, Julie E. (2012) *Configuring the Networked Self: Law, Code, and the Play of Everyday Practice*. New Haven, CT: Yale University Press, www.juliecohen.com/page5.php (accessed December 16, 2012).

Cohen develops an important version of the relational self vis-à-vis networking technologies and explores with great care the implications of this changing notion of selfhood for core issues such as privacy (her chs. 5, 6) and copyright (her ch. 3). It would be a strong research project in its own right to compare carefully Cohen's recommendations with the spectrum of views we have explored in this chapter, specifically with regard to how more relational notions of selfhood incline in the direction of more inclusive understandings of property.

ADDITIONAL READINGS, SUGGESTED RESOURCES FOR REVIEW

Electronic Frontier Foundation (n.d.) Teaching Curriculum on "Fair Use," www.teachingcopyright.org (accessed December 18, 2012).

University of Minnesota Libraries (2010) Understanding Fair Use, https://www.lib.umn.edu/copyright/fairuse (accessed December 19, 2012).

Recording Industry Association of America, Piracy: Online and on the Street, www.riaa.com/physicalpiracy.php?content_selector=piracy_details_street (accessed December 19, 2012).

Current definitions and rationale for the RIAA's anti-piracy campaigns, plus links to related materials.

Himma, Kenneth Einar (2008) The Justification of Intellectual Property: Contemporary Philosophical Disputes, *Journal of the American Society for Information Sciences and Technology*, 59 (7): 1143–61.

Provides an exceptionally extensive and thorough discussion of major Western positions, their sources and supporting arguments – arguing, in the end, for at least limited rights over content creation and control.

CHAPTER FOUR

Friendship, Democracy, and Citizen Journalism

Online conversations played an integral part in the revolutions that toppled governments in Egypt and Tunisia.

(Howard et al. 2011: 3)

Chapter overview

We explore three aspects of life online that promise dramatic new possibilities in our personal and shared lives while also confronting us with new ethical questions and challenges. We examine first how friendship is both dramatically amplified by social networking sites (SNSs) such as Facebook and, perhaps, threatened by the affordances of SNSs, as manifest in the phenomenon of cyberbullying. In particular, their underlying assumptions regarding human identity and relationships may play a particularly important role in our ethical decision-making. We will see here that a virtue ethics approach raises some of the most serious ethical questions while also offering helpful suggestions for resolving those questions, including its suggestions for careful choices regarding our media technologies, designs, and usages.

We then turn to democracy and citizen journalism as reflecting and expressing two of the most significant transformations of our lives in a digital age. The ethics of earlier forms of journalism have been shaped by their service to democratic ends: hence one pathway into an ethics for citizen journalists is to start with important conceptions of democracy as applied to online venues. A particular focus here is on the specific ethical requirements for the sorts of dialogue and debate seen to contribute to democratic processes. We will see that early confidence in the democratizing powers of digital media has been tempered by a number of "reality checks," including the limited successes of so-called Twitter or Facebook Revolutions: in addition, online communication facilitates fragmentation and polarization that work directly against democratizing dialogue and debate. Against this large background, the potential of citizen journalism to contribute to democratization becomes all the more important – as do the ethical requirements for such journalism, where these requirements are to serve democratizing ends.

Friendship online? Initial considerations

At the time of this writing, the SNS Facebook (FB) claims that over 1 billion people – nearly one-sixth of the planet's population and around half of all those with Internet access – have FB accounts (Kiss 2012). Such staggering numbers are but one marker of the explosive growth of SNSs over the past decade or so (i.e., beginning with Friendster in 2002: see www.molglobal.net/about-us/history/). As Shannon Vallor (2012) notes, our use of these sites is "reshaping how human beings initiate and/or maintain virtually every type of ethically significant social bond or role," beginning with friendship but extending through "parent-to-child, co-worker-to-co-worker, employer-to-employee, teacher-to-student, neighbor-to-neighbor, seller-to-buyer, and doctor-to-patient" relationships – and this is simply "a partial list."

On the one hand, the boons of connecting with one another through such sites are hard to dispute. Especially in highly mobile societies such as the United States, SNSs allow friends and family who have moved apart for the sake of jobs and new opportunities to remain in touch in emotionally invaluable ways. Multiple organizations – from student groups to religious organizations – have exploited the affordances of SNSs to bring together like-minded members and attract potential new ones (e.g., Lomborg and Ess 2012). And the list goes on . . .

On the other hand: it becomes increasingly essential, for example, for young people to participate in an SNS – failure to do so threatens to isolate them from the large majority of their peers who are active on such sites (e.g., Lüders 2011). And, as we have seen, our capacity to sustain important forms of individual privacy are profoundly at risk in such sites (as well as more broadly, of course: see chapter 2, pp. 38, 39–40). As well, if you have peeked ahead to chapter 5 and the discussion of pornography*, there we explore the larger problem of self-commodification (see pp. 175–6). That is, such sites give us relatively narrow categories for self-presentation, beginning with a binary choice regarding gender – and, more generally, the strong tendency is to give users categories having to do with our preferences as consumers ("music, movies, fandom"; Livingstone 2011: 354). Finally, there are notorious cases in which "friendship" online can be used as a vehicle for cyberbullying of various forms – including forms severe enough to lead to suicide. So, in 2006, thirteen-year-old Megan Meier developed an online relationship with one Josh Evans, apparently sixteen. After some weeks of flirtation, "Josh" began insulting Megan and concluded by suggesting that the world would be better off without her. Megan committed suicide on October 15, 2006. Six weeks later, it was discovered that "Josh" was the persona of Lori Drew, mother of one of Megan's former friends; the Drew family lived four houses down the street from the Meier family. Ms. Drew apparently intended the ruse first to find out what Megan thought of her own daughter and then, allegedly, to harass her (Maag 2007). Ms. Drew was eventually convicted of three misdemeanor charges – namely, violating the MySpace terms of service by constructing a fraudulent account (Stelter 2008). Subsequent responses to such dramatic – and, fortunately, still rare – episodes range from efforts to develop new laws that better define "cyberbullying" to a multitude of educational approaches (Clifford 2009; Livingstone et al. 2011).

QUESTIONS FOR REFLECTION, DISCUSSION

1. Develop a utilitarian risk–benefit analysis of your own use of SNSs, whether Facebook, more professionally oriented sites such as LinkedIn, and/or more nationally oriented sites such as . . .

To do so:

A) Develop an informal "media log" in which you document your own uses of SNSs over some period of days – e.g., a week or a month. Try to be as careful and precise as possible in your documentation. In addition to noting, say, "I checked my SNS profile three times today," list carefully just what you did as you did so – e.g., looked at a friend's profile page, commented on a photograph or other comment, checked out a "person of interest" in your class, etc. The idea is to provide as rich and fine-grained a picture of your media use as possible with a view towards responding to the second part of this exercise, namely: as you do so – what are, for you, some of the most important benefits of your using the site(s)?

B) Have you (and/or your cohorts, friends, and/or family) ever had any negative experience(s) in using SNSs? If so, describe these with some care, being sure to explain why these experiences were negative. That is, did they result in hurt feelings, feelings of betrayal, lack of privacy, loss of trust, loss of "face" among your friends and family, serious sorts of financial cost or fraud . . .?

C) Either individually and/or in a group, line up your positive experiences (and their approximate "utils"[1]) in one column, vis-à-vis negative experiences (and their approximate utils) in an adjacent column. You can then develop a continuum of possible ethical responses to the benefits and risks – e.g., ranging from a complete abstinence from SNSs (because

---

1 A positive "util" is a proposed unit of pleasure; a negative "util" would quantify a dissatisfaction, pain, etc. The util was proposed as a unit of measurement by nineteenth-century economists inspired by utilitarianism and specifically Jeremy Bentham's "hedonic calculus" as a first effort to maximize pleasure and minimize pain in straightforwardly quantitative ways. The term is commonly used to illustrate utilitarian approaches and economic notions of utility (e.g., Baumol and Blinder 2011: 85). And if you have difficulty assigning "utils" (either positive or negatively), this is because, despite best efforts otherwise, no one has succeeded in defining such a measurement in any consistent way – first of all, because our experiences of pleasure and pain vary widely (ibid.). This difficulty in fact highlights a serious limitation of utilitarianism: see the discussion of this problem in chapter 6, pp. 203–4.

the risks of possible harms are too high) to a moderate use of SNSs (as guided by careful consideration of how to avoid known risks) to a complete embrace of SNSs (on the view that the possibilities of serious harm are very low and are outweighed by a clear set of benefits).

In light of your experiences, your columns of risks and benefits, and the continuum of possible responses you develop, which response(s) to SNSs and their possible uses would your utilitarian calculus recommend?

As always, the chief question for our purposes is, why? That is, whatever your response to this question, what reasons, arguments, grounds, feelings, intuitions, sensibilities, etc., support and provide justification for your position?

2. Deontologists would approach SNSs from the perspective of basic rights – beginning with rights to privacy, but also rights, e.g., to the intellectual property (IP – as distinct from IP [Internet Protocol] addresses) uploaded and created on a profile (e.g., a photograph).

Review the Terms of Service (ToS) and privacy policies of the SNS you use primarily. (This will take a while: they are long, long documents.) What rights do these documents indicate are in fact protected – and/or what rights seem to be only moderately protected, if at all?

In light of this review – and referring to the continuum of possible responses or uses of SNSs you developed above (1.C) – how would a strict deontologist – i.e., one insisting that basic rights to privacy and (perhaps) IP – respond to the SNS's ToS and privacy policies? That is, if the primary issue is to preserve these rights at all costs, where would a strict deontologist likely stand on the continuum of responses you have developed?

3. As we have seen, a number of researchers and ethicists raise further questions about how far our engagement with SNSs involves forms of self-commodification, of turning aspects of our identity and selfhood into commodities or saleable products in a marketplace. On a first level, the focus is on how such sites require us to present ourselves in terms of our consumer tastes such as

music preferences, etc. (Livingstone 2011). On a second level, the data we provide – both in setting up a profile and then the additional data generated by our further use of an SNS – constitute the economic bread and butter of the sites' owners: this information, when aggregated with that of many, many others, is sold to various corporations and businesses who seek to advertise their goods and services more effectively. On both levels, the design of the SNS foregrounds those aspects of our selfhood and identity that (a) can be appropriately captured in the categories of consumer preferences and thereby (b) prove valuable for marketing and advertising purposes.

Up to a point (as may be apparent in your initial utilitarian analyses), such self-commodification may be perfectly useful and benign. But deontologists would further raise the question: is there a point in these processes when our focus on self-commodification risks having us lose sight of our primary ethical identity as moral autonomies – i.e., as freedoms that cannot be reduced to commodities simply for sale in a marketplace?

Again, in light of this ethical focus – where would a strict deontologist likely stand on the continuum of possible responses you developed (1.C)?

4. Shannon Vallor notes in her article on "Social Networking and Ethics" (http://plato.stanford.edu/archives/win2012/entries/ethics-social-networking) that the ethical implications of SNSs are not "strictly interpersonal": in addition, our engagement with SNSs implicates us in a "complex web of interactions between social networking service users and their online and offline communities, social network developers, corporations, governments and other institutions."

In slightly different terms, this means that our engagement with SNSs inextricably ties us (including our ethical agency and moral choices) in with an extensive "web of relationships" that extend across the whole range of actors and agents (including artificial agents) knotted together by these networks. What this would further seem to mean is that our ethical choices and responsibilities are thereby "distributed" or likewise shared across such networks.

If you did not already take into account the distributed nature of our ethical responsibilities in your first responses to the above questions, take some time to reflect on that now. In particular:

- Does the distributed nature of ethical responsibility change any of your utilitarian calculations and/or decisions/judgments regarding what utilitarians would ethically recommend in terms of the continuum of possible engagements with SNSs (including no use at all)?
- Does the distributed nature of ethical responsibility change any of your deontological analyses and/or decisions/judgments regarding what deontologists would ethically recommend in terms of the continuum of possible engagements with SNSs (including no use at all)?

5. Finally:

A) Are there significant differences between the utilitarian and deontological responses or judgments regarding possible uses of SNSs (including no use at all)?

For example, you may find that deontologists, as concerned with privacy and IP rights, as well as insisting that human freedom must not be eliminated through commodification processes, would weigh in more on the side of moderate to no use of SNSs. Utilitarians, by contrast, might well argue more in favour of moderate use to a full embrace of SNSs.

B) If there are differences, which responses come closer to your own current use and ethical sensibilities? That is, do you find your uses and ethical judgments agreeing more with the utilitarians or more with the deontologists?

C) Either way, can you provide arguments, evidence, and/or some other form of warrant that would argue in favour of your taking up either the utilitarian or the deontological approach here?

D) Keep in mind that these preferences tend to be strongly shaped by our national and cultural backgrounds – e.g., with utilitarianism tending to be stronger in English-speaking countries, while deontologies, for example, tend to be stronger in especially Northern European countries. In this light, do your preferences for either utilitarianism or deontology "line up" with your national-cultural background?

If so, do you have additional arguments, evidence, and/ or some other form of warrant that would suggest that your preferences are not simply the result of your background and enculturation? If not, can you point to specific experiences, arguments, etc., that have encouraged you to take up an ethical framework perhaps somewhat at odds with those prevailing in your country/culture of origin?

Friendship online: additional considerations

As discussed more fully in chapter 6 (pp. 238–44), virtue ethics provides a third framework for analyzing and resolving ethical issues. For a number of reasons, virtue ethics has become increasingly significant in the digital age. To begin with, as the above exercise may suggest, neither utilitarianism nor deontology alone may always "work" to help us resolve some of the ethical issues occasioned by digital technologies and networked communications: first of all, how do we judge and resolve the conflict(s) if deontology and utilitarianism result in different, perhaps antithetical recommendations? Moreover, both utilitarianism and deontology tend to emphasize the ethical responsibilities of human beings understood as primarily individual moral agents. But, as we have seen (chapter 2, pp. 61–8), our sense of selfhood in "Western" societies appears to be shifting from more individual emphases towards more relational emphases. In both its ancient and contemporary forms, virtue ethics begins with the view that human beings are precisely such relational or social beings, not solely individual ones. Hence virtue ethics is especially well suited to serve as an ethical framework in the digital age, insofar as digital media and networked communications incline us in more sociable or relational directions. So we will see in chapter 5, for example, that virtue ethics approaches become increasingly useful in our efforts to respond to some of the ethical challenges clustering about sexually explicit materials (SEMs) online and violence in games.

By the same token, virtue ethics has emerged as a primary approach to questions of friendship online. In addition to the general considerations noted above, keep in mind the guiding questions of virtue ethics – namely, what capacities or habits must I acquire, practice, and develop with excellence in order to enjoy a life of contentment (or happiness – *eudaimonia*)? Again, for both ancient and contemporary virtue ethicists, such a life is always a relational or social one: and so our sense of contentment or well-being (*eudaimonia*) is inevitably interdependent upon our relationships with others: friendship is among the most important such relationships and is hence a primary focus of virtue ethics. In particular, and as our experiences of friendship (should) highlight for us, *eudaimonia* is not simply a personal (or "subjective") sense of well-being or contentment: in addition, it entails a more external ("objective") sense of "*actively* doing well, or *flourishing* in one's practical environment," where such active flourishing follows on our taking up the practices or virtues that help us function and act, for example, as better friends to others (Shannon Vallor, personal communication, December 14, 2012).

In these directions, the virtue ethicist Shannon Vallor (2009, 2011, 2012) has carefully examined how far SNSs may foster and/ or hinder the virtues – the capacities and habits – apparently required for developing and sustaining deep friendships. The question then becomes: how far do our engagements with SNSs incline us to acquire and foster the virtues required for friendship – and how far might the very designs of SNSs rather discourage our acquiring and fostering these virtues?

As first examples, Vallor focuses on the virtues of patience, perseverance, and empathy as requirements for deep, long-term friendships (and, we can add, long-term intimate relationships). She describes how we learned these virtues in non-digital settings – say, a visit to an elderly relative when we were young. If only out of desperation and having no possibility of escape, we gradu-ally learn how to develop points of engagement, beginning with simple conversation. But such beginning and then sustaining such engagements builds precisely the capacities or virtues of patience and perseverance. As Vallor elaborates, these virtues are essential to sustaining most human projects, including those of close relationships:

> In communication, perseverance manifests the willingness to push through conflict or misunderstanding to reconnect with one's partner on the other side of the breach. But to be effective in maintaining the intimacy of the communication, such perseverance must be coupled with patience, the habit of "riding out" moments of irritation, boredom, or incomprehension rather than tuning out or abruptly changing the subject in an attempt to force the conversation into a more satisfactory state. Indeed, the richest joys of communication often come from being patient enough to actually grasp what is being said, to finally get the joke, or to hear a challenging truth. (Vallor 2009: 165)

To be sure, acquiring such capacities and habits is not easy,

> especially in the beginning when our existing motivations and dispositions often pull us in the opposite direction. One therefore requires, in addition to our existing motives, situational opportunities that exert some pressure upon us to move in the virtuous direction, and the social strains and burdens of face-to-face conversation have historically, and across cultures, often been rich sources of such pressure. (Ibid.)

Whatever their many benefits and advantages may be (especially from a utilitarian perspective), the general question is then: how far do our engagements with one another online foster and/or hinder the development of such core virtues as patience and perseverance? Overall, Vallor's first response is not heartening:

> For today's technologies provide us with an ever-widening horizon of escape routes from any interaction that has lost its momentary appeal, and are widely celebrated by users precisely for their capacity to liberate us from the uncomfortable strains and burdens of conventional communication. I can ... click away from a friend's blog, without the price that must be paid for physically turning away from a face-to-face conversation. (Ibid.: 166)

This is to say: as SNSs are built around online engagements that are quick, short, convenient – and frequently ephemeral (how many of us archive our Twitter streams or the SNS status updates of friends and family?) – they thereby highlight communicative habits that do not immediately seem to require the sorts of perseverance and patience characteristic of at least some of our offline encounters (including, perhaps, some of our most significant ones) with one another. In particular, online communicative environments always offer the possibility of an immediate escape, as mood, desire, and/ or necessity may dictate. Nor is this necessarily problematic from an ethical standpoint. The ethical concern, rather, is with how far I am likely also to stick with the offline engagements that require virtues such as patience and perseverance – and thereby acquire and learn how to foster those virtues.

To get at this a last way (for the time being), Vallor emphasizes that in offline venues,

> The gaze of the morally significant other, which holds me respectfully in place and solicits my ongoing patience, is a critical element in my moral development; though I might for all that ignore it, it creates an important situational gradient in the virtuous direction. (2009: 166)

In online contexts, however, it is easy to escape such a gaze. The point is not that such escape is always a bad thing: sometimes it might well be beneficent and fully justified. Rather, Vallor is raising the larger question of what sorts of habits and excellences we are likely to acquire as such online environments become our predominant venues for communication with one another.

Again, acquiring such virtues is difficult at the beginning – especially, it would seem, for a young person both as a beginner in these virtues and as someone whose communicative engagements increasingly take place in online rather than offline environments. That is: if we are at the beginning stages of learning to acquire such virtues – precisely because it is challenging and difficult to do so – it is especially tempting to quit as soon as possible. (By analogy: think about how young people fight against the sorts of practice required to become competent musicians, much less excellent ones, for example.) If the vast majority of our communicative engagements with one another take place primarily in online contexts, are we likely to acquire and foster the virtues of perseverance and patience? And/or: is it more likely that, when we are forced in offline contexts to take up the difficult practices of patience and perseverance, we will rather seek to return as quickly as possible to the relative familiarity of the comparatively less demanding online environments?

There is, of course, enormous debate over how far concerns such as these need trouble us. Before we turn to those, however, time for some further responses and reflections.

ADDITIONAL QUESTIONS FOR REFLECTION, DISCUSSION

1. Take the opening question of virtue ethics seriously: what habit or capacities (as abilities that must be first learned and then practiced – as a musician must practice her scales, as an athlete must practice the moves of the game, etc.) seem necessary to you and your cohorts for a life of contentment and well-being – both for yourself and for the communities in which you are inevitably interwoven? (Keep in mind here that such contentment is not solely a matter of subjective satisfaction, but further includes a more objective sense of having the skills – as acquired and practiced virtues – that allow us to act well and flourish in our larger communities and environments.)

2. In particular, how far do you (dis)agree with Vallor's first claim that the virtues of patience and perseverance are required for developing deep and long-term friendships? If so, why? If not, why not?

3. Return to your media log developed for question 1.A in the opening set of reflection questions. Choose the online venues or environments that your log indicates you use most often.

A) Carefully reflect upon and consider your usages of these environments from a virtue ethics perspective: what habits or capabilities do these environments incline us to practice most often?

B) Given your responses to 3.A, how far do the habits or capabilities most practiced in the online environments you use the most overlap with and/or differ from (i) your own list of virtues and (ii) the virtues identified as central by Vallor, namely perseverance and patience?

C) Recall the continuum of possible responses to SNSs developed above, ranging from no use to enthusiastic embrace.
Given your responses to 3.B, as a virtue ethicist, where on
this continuum would you argue you should stand? That
is, which point on the continuum seems most likely to
help you acquire and foster the virtues you have identified as necessary for a life of contentment or well-being
(*eudaimonia*)? (Again, keep in mind here that such flourishing is dependent on virtues as skills and abilities needed
for acting well in community with others and our larger
environments.)

As always, what counts here are your arguments and evidence.

4. Now that you've developed a virtue ethics response to SNSs
and their possible uses, how do your judgments and conclusions
compare with those developed above using utilitarian and deontological frameworks?

5. Especially if virtue ethics lands you in a different place on your
continuum than either utilitarianism and/or deontology,

A) Which of these positions – utilitarianism, deontology, and/
or virtue ethics – lands you most closely to the point on
the continuum that most closely coheres with your current
actual practices and usages?
B) Given your response to 5.A – i.e., are your current practices
and usages best recommended from a utilitarian, deontological, and/or virtue ethics standpoint – is the resulting
ethical standpoint consistent with the framework(s) you have
found yourself most closely allied with above and/or in other
exercises in this book?
C) Especially if you find yourself moving between ethical frameworks, rest assured, first of all, that this is perfectly normal.
It may well be that each framework "works" better than
another in the face of a particular ethical context or challenge: indeed, part of learning about ethics is just the (hard)
work of learning how to judge which framework(s) are best
used when and where.

That said, does it appear that there might be some basic inconsistencies or incoherencies in how you approach these ethical issues? For example, is your choice of one framework in one context warranted or justified in a way you can articulate and defend – or is it possibly more the result of, say, your national/cultural background or other factors you've previously not considered?

In all events – do you start to see ways of developing a more coherent use of these frameworks and approaches? And, if so: would doing so result in any changes in your actual practices and usages of SNSs?

Friendship online: final considerations

On the one hand, Vallor (2011) has expanded and refined her own analyses. As well, arguments along these lines are part of Sherry Turkle's warnings in her *Alone Together: Why We Expect More from Technology and Less of Each Other* (2011). More specifically, a recent anthology (Wittkower 2010) helpfully provides chapters by both critics and proponents of friendship online. Reading into these resources will help you and your cohorts further develop your own perspectives, arguments, and – it may be – practices and virtues regarding your usages of SNSs.

Specifically: as we explored in chapter 1 (pp. 19–20), there is some reason to think that our choices regarding media technologies interact with our own sense of selfhood and identity. Most broadly, the shift towards an emphasis on the individual dimension of selfhood is facilitated by the rise of literacy. This includes precisely the virtue of taking care of the self (*epimelēsthai sautou*) by way of writing, as highlighted by Foucault (1988: 19). More particularly, the (high) modern emphasis on an individual sense of selfhood, first of all, as a rational autonomy appears to be closely tied to the sorts of skills – we can now say virtues – we develop in conjunction with the media of literacy and print (e.g., books of all sorts, newspapers, etc.). By contrast, our shift towards the secondary orality-textuality of electric media (beginning with radio, movies, and TV, and then extending into contemporary digital media) correlates with a greater emphasis on the more relational (and perhaps more affective) aspects of our identity. Alongside the many advantages and benefits of developing and enjoying this more relational sense of selfhood, there may also be costs – beginning with a greater dependency on our larger networks for affirmation, a sense of well-being, and thereby direction. Some of the problems we have seen emerge in the context of SNSs and other social media appear to interact with this greater sense of dependency. For example, we have seen that deontologists would be concerned with threats to individual freedoms and rights to privacy, along with correlative diminution of respect for persons and equality. These rights, respect, and equality seem immediately at risk in particular for a more relational self that, as we have seen, appears to have little choice but to commodify itself via the consumer-oriented categories of a given SNS. This risk is amplified all the more insofar as our engagements online are oriented more towards conformity and popularity than sometimes more painful and unpleasant honesty. (There's a reason, in other words, why Facebook gives us only a "like" button – no negative comments, please!)

In particular, the phenomenon of cyberbullying highlights just how far the relational self at work in SNSs can be dependent on the affirmation and assurance of others. While this is an extreme, worst-case example – insofar as such selves can be pushed towards suicide through "just words" online – we may want to give very serious thought indeed to two ultimate virtue ethics questions. First, what sort of balance between these more individual and more relational emphases of selfhood and identity ought we define for ourselves – not only for the sake of minimizing such forms of abuse online, but also, as we will see below, for the sake of sustaining democratic forms of government? Second, what choices regarding our media usages and design do we need to make in order to cultivate both individual and relational emphases in the balance we seek to draw? That is, what balance between fostering the skills and virtues of literacy and print, with a specific focus on the virtue of cultivating and fostering an individual sense of self via writing, and those of secondary orality-textuality, with a focus on the virtue of cultivating and fostering the relational dimensions of selfhood, should we undertake?

ADDITIONAL RESEARCH/WRITING

FRIENDSHIP ONLINE: ADDITIONAL RESOURCES

William Deresiewicz is one of the severest critics of our increasing use of and reliance upon online communication – both as it threatens the experiences and possibilities of solitude and as it fosters what he calls "faux friendship" (false friendship). Both articles (2009) are available online:

> http://chronicle.com/article/The-End-of-Solitude/3708
> http://chronicle.com/article/Faux-Friendship/49308/

Peel, Mark, Liz Reed, and Jim Walter (2009) The Importance of Friends: The Most Recent Past, pp. 317–55 in Barbara Caine (ed.), *Friendship: A History*. London: Equinox.

Wittkower, Dylan E. (ed.) (2010) *Facebook and Philosophy: What's on your Mind?* Chicago: Open Court Press.

The Wittkower volume includes a number of very helpful essays that both defend and critique FB friendship. To begin with, Mimi Marinucci's "You Can't Front on Facebook" addresses important issues of anonymity and disinhibition online by way of Plato's example of Gyges' ring (as granting invisibility). Echoing Shannon Vallor's comment cited above (p. 130), Mariam Thalos uses Sartre's notion of the Gaze to consider what online communication may fail to carry over from face-to-face communication. She further raises the issue we have begun to pursue here and will explore more fully in the next chapter – namely, how far our use of SNSs and digital media more broadly risks self-commodification processes that entrap us in the power structures of capitalist economy, rather than liberating us. (Along these lines, see also "Spectacle 2.0?," by Rune Vejby and the volume editor, and Adam Briggle's untitled chapter, structured as a break-up letter to FB. Briggle's use of Ivan Illich's concept of conviviality provides one of the strongest critiques of what is amiss for many of us in FB.

Especially useful in our context are the essays that focus on friendship through the lens of virtue ethics, beginning with that by Thalos. Tamara Wandel and Anthony Beavers defend FB friendship in their "Playing Around with Identity," for example. Additional critiques and defenses draw on such virtue ethicists as Aristotle and Cicero (Craig Condella, Maurice Hamington, Chris Bloor) as well as the care ethics of Nel Noddings (Maurice Hamington).

Marturano, Antonio (ed.) (2011) Ethics of Online Social Networks, *International Review of Information Ethics*, 16, December, www.i-r-i-e.net/issue16.htm [articles available in PDF format]. Included in this special issue are three articles particularly useful for evaluating the ethical dimensions of privacy and SNSs – beginning with Richard A. Spinello's "Privacy and Social Networking Technology." Spinello, a prominent information ethicist, analyzes recent FB privacy policies and finds them to be inadequate – in part because individual privacy is at odds with FB's commercial interests.

Two additional articles provide important cross-cultural comparisons: "Interrogating Privacy in the Digital Society: Media Narratives after 2 Cases," by Caroline Rizza, Paula Curvelo, Ines Crespo, Michel Chiaramello, Alessia Ghezzi, and Angela Guimaraes Pereira. The authors attend to US and EU law seeking to protect privacy online and argue that "the values we once cherished in a non-digital society" are at risk.

"Emerging Social Norms in the UK and Japan on Privacy and Revelation in SNS," by Andrew A. Adams, Kiyoshi Murata, Yohko Orito, and Pat Parslow, offers cross-cultural comparisons based on semi-structured interviews – including interesting suggestions that the UK respondents take a strongly individual view of responsibility for what happens online in contrast to Japanese respondents, who rather reflect the "group assumption of [shared] blame and consequences" (2011: 24).

These and additional articles should be helpful for suggesting further research and writing projects, including those for Spanish-language students (i.e., "Herramientas para el análisis y monitoreo en Redes Sociales," by Juan José Prieto Gutiérrez).

1. CYBERBULLYING

At the other end of the spectrum from our efforts at friendship are the various forms of cyberbullying – including the most notorious examples, such as the case of Megan Meier discussed at the beginning of this chapter – and, more recently, the case of Amanda Todd, mentioned in chapter 1. Thankfully, such episodes are quite rare: according to the recent EU *Kids Online* study, for example, around 6 percent of respondents report that they have been bullied online – while far more (19 percent) have been bullied offline (Livingstone et al. 2011: 24). Still, as the Meier and Todd cases make clear, such tragic outcomes are real consequences for some who go online, however few they may be in terms of percentage points.

The phenomenon of cyberbullying thus suggests the following sorts of research and reflection questions:

A) What are the statistics concerning cyberbullying in your country/culture of origin? (As the EU *Kids Online* study notes, bullying is more prevalent in some countries [Livingstone et al. 2011: 24]. This is not ethically to excuse or justify such behavior – it is to say that it may well be a culturally variable one.)

B) Given those statistics, analyze the problem of cyberbullying from our three ethical perspectives – utilitarianism, deontology, and virtue ethics.

A utilitarian might counsel, for example, that, because such episodes, however regrettable and painful for the families involved, are quite rare, they are offset by the much larger number of positive experiences made possible by online communication venues. A deontologist would likely insist more strongly on individuals' rights not to be harmed or harassed, as a violation of one's freedom and dignity as a person: protecting such rights, moreover, is all the more important for the more vulnerable persons in a given population – which certainly includes children and adolescents.

Given your exploration of these three perspectives, which comes closest to your own sense of (a) what's wrong with cyberbullying and (b) how we should respond to it?

C) The problem of cyberbullying continues to evoke efforts to develop laws that might help reduce such behaviors by criminalizing them and thereby making it possible to prosecute and punish at least more extreme forms in a court of law.

   i) What is the current status of such efforts in your country/culture of origin?

   ii) How do you respond to these ethically? That is, do you find these efforts to be (a) ethically justified and, if so, (b) consistent and appropriate uses of the legal system to address the problem?

Keep in mind here, for example, that virtue ethicists emphasize not only the importance of regulatory responses to such problems but also precisely efforts to identify and cultivate the virtues – e.g., empathy, respect for Others as equals and as persons, etc. – that would work against our performing such behaviors in the first place. Such an approach is exemplified, for example, in recent efforts by the (South) Korean Internet & Security Agency (KISA) to offset illegal downloading and online defamation (an especially serious problem in cultures emphasizing the value of "face"), with the goal of restoring "the broken trust, and [to] create a beautiful internet world" (KISA, "Creating a Beautiful Internet World," www.kisa.or.kr/eng/activities/internetpromotion.jsp, accessed December 11, 2012). To do so, KISA has developed the "Netizen Code of Conduct," a series of ethical injunctions:

• Users will respect the rights and privacy of other users.
• Users will provide healthy information and materials.
• Users will not knowingly access, upload, download, store, display, distribute or publish any information that is inappropriate and unlawful.
• Users will protect information belonging to any person and manage [their] own information.
• Users will not use inappropriate and/or abusive language or conduct.

- Users will take responsibilities for [their] own online activities.
- Users will not copy, download, install or run viruses or other inappropriate or unauthorized behaviors.
- Users will respect copyright laws and licensing agreements.
- Users will participate in monitoring any intended inappropriate internet behaviors and attempt to protect the rights and safety of all internet users.
- Users will practice the Netizen Code of Conduct and create a healthy netizen culture.

(From: Keumjoo Kwak (Seoul National University), Internet Ethics Issues and Action: Psychological analysis of Cyber Deviance, International Symposium on Internet Ethics, Seoul, South Korea, September 12, 2012)

Many of these injunctions can be summarized as encouragements for individual Internet users to behave virtuously – i.e., to practice the usages and habits that will thus contribute to the larger harmony of the community, and thus to the (ostensibly) shared venture of creating "a Beautiful Internet World" that is marked first of all by the (restored) virtue of trust. Thereby – and as perfectly appropriate to its cultural context – this Netizen code of ethics relies on a strongly relational sense of selfhood coupled with a Confucian (and Buddhist) virtue ethics approach to such problems. Most broadly, that is, as relational selves inextricably interwoven with one another in a larger community, each of us is responsible for developing and cultivating the practices (virtues) that will contribute to the harmony and beauty of the larger community.

These diverse responses to the phenomenon of cyberbullying thus present us with a wide range of possible ethical analyses and correlative approaches to dealing with the problem. On the one hand, we can take a more utilitarian or deontological approach. Alongside their important differences, keep in mind that both of these emphasize primarily the individual side of our identity and thus moral agency. By contrast, virtue ethics approaches emphasize the relational side of our identity and, perhaps, a more distributed sense of ethical responsibility. At the same time, we have seen that virtue ethics thereby highlights the importance of our cultivating a set of skills and habits – virtues such as patience, perseverance, and empathy – that would likely help minimize such problems in the first place.

Finally, our initial choices of these frameworks may well be culturally variable. At the same time, however, our senses of selfhood in "Western" societies and cultures appears to be shifting towards greater emphasis on the relational side of our identities. To be sure, for contemporary "Westerners" – including many "Western" virtue ethicists – the South Korean example of a Netizen code of ethics may go too far in terms of subordinating individual freedom of choice, for example, to what is required for the harmony (if not the beauty) of the larger community. But the South Korean example is thereby useful as drawing a further point on the continuum of possible ethical responses – i.e., as one that strongly foregrounds relational selfhood and virtue ethics.

Referring to the continuum of possible responses to the phenomenon of cyberbullying that thus emerges here, develop your own list of proposals for how digital media users in your country/culture can best deal with the problem of cyberbullying (and/or related ones, such as defamation).

(An additional resource that might be useful for such a project is: Robin Mansell and Marc Raboy (eds), *The Handbook of Global Media and Communication Policy* (Oxford: Wiley-Blackwell, 2011). The volume provides a helpful overview of the challenges of building regulatory approaches to such problems, especially for a global Internet.)

2. CAN WE (RE)DESIGN FOR (BETTER) FRIENDSHIP ONLINE?

As noted above, our behaviors in online environments, including SNSs, are strongly constrained by their design and affordances – where these in turn are focused more or less exclusively on the primary goal of such sites to turn a profit, in part by way of commodifying the identities and consumer choices of their users. Hence there are a range of tensions between, say, friendship as analysed from a virtue ethics perspective – i.e., one oriented towards the goals of human excellence, harmony, and flourishing – and the friendship behaviors facilitated in online environments.

On occasion, users and designers attempt to "hack" these environments in ways that might allow them to serve such more humane goals more effectively. Perhaps most ambitiously, an Open Source project called Diaspora has worked to offer the advantages of SNSs along with much greater user control of privacy and ownership of posted content (http://diasporaproject.org/).

Such efforts make clear that we are not condemned simply to accept them "as is": it is possible to (re)design these technologies and their affordances – indeed, in the face of strong conflicts between our ethical norms and goals and the behaviors facilitated within a given SNS, there is an ethical imperative to undertake such (re)design if we have compelling reasons to preserve the norms and behaviors not well served or reinforced by current designs and implementations.

The literatures of design methods and proposed alternatives to current implementations of ICTs, including SNSs, are beyond the scope of this text. But we can point in these directions with the following general questions and resources.

In 2009, French programmer Thomas Moquet offered a "dislike" button for Facebook as an extension of the Mozilla Firefox browser (https: // addons . mozilla . org / en - US / firefox / addon / facebook - dislike/). While not overly successful in its own right – and not to be confused with a subsequent scam on Facebook (Richmond 2010) – such a button at least begins to expand the repertoire of emotions easily expressible on the SNS.

Taking one or two of the ethical frameworks we have worked with as starting points:

A) What would seem to be ethical advantages and/or disadvantages of adding a design feature such as a "dislike" button?

B) More broadly, how would you (re)design an SNS platform in ways that would easily facilitate the sorts of ethical behaviors endorsed primarily by a utilitarian (maximizing pleasure), a deontologist (emphasizing rights, including respect, privacy, and equality), and/or a virtue ethicist (what virtues and practices will contribute to *eudaimonia*)?

(My very great thanks to Shannon Vallor for suggestions along these lines.)

ADDITIONAL RESOURCES

A broad perspective on the ethics of design is developed by Maja van der Velden in "Undesigning culture: A Brief Reflection on design as ethical practice" (2010, www.globalagenda.org/file/25).

The Swedish designer Johan Redström has pursued an approach to interaction design called "slow technology." Such slowness, he explains, is "a consequence of a techno-aesthetical design philosophy that focuses on reflective and conscious use of the technology as such" (http://redstrom.se/johan/slowtechnology/project/index.html). Redström's website (http://redstrom.se/johan/slowtechnology/) provides a number of resources that elaborate on this design philosophy and its concrete expression in several projects. His suggestions for designing technologies to facilitate extended attention and unhurried time – prerequisites for acquiring and practicing such virtues essential to friendship (and other human endeavors) as patience and perseverance – are particularly useful.

See also: Daniel Skog (2011) Ethical Aspects of Managing a Social Network Site: A Disclosive Analysis, *International Review of Information Ethics*, 16(12): 27–32.

Digital media, democratization and citizen journalism

As with more or less every other aspect of our lives, digital media – most especially as interconnected via the Internet and the Web – have dramatically transformed the practices of journalism and news distribution. For our purposes, one of the most significant dimensions of this transformation is the increasingly prominent phenomenon of citizen journalism. Most briefly, in the days of "one-to-many" broadcast and mass media such as national and corporate TV networks and newspapers, journalism – and thereby journalistic practices and ethics – was almost exclusively the concern of journalists themselves and the institutions that employed them. These days, by contrast, what counts as news – most especially as distributed online – is much more diffuse. Many of us get our "news" more consistently from Jon Stewart's *Daily Show* than from a traditional newspaper or TV broadcast, for example. And serious news hounds depend on Twitter and favorite bloggers, especially as news is becoming news – that is, as a fast-breaking event unfolds such as a demonstration or, at the time of this writing, yet one more school shooting in the US. Moreover, the news we see and hear offline and online almost inevitably includes both content (such as pictures or video) and commentary from "the rest of us" – i.e., ordinary citizens and passers-by who participate or get caught up in what is deemed a news event. Culling comments from SNSs and Twitter, for example, seems essential to a news story, and readers or viewers of a story online are often invited to comment and perhaps contribute in other ways – e.g., if they happen to have additional photographs or other material.

But this means that those of us with access to digital media technologies – including the cameras in our phones – are no longer simply consumers of "news." Rather, whether by intention (e.g., by writing a politically oriented blog) or by accident (as a passer-by who ends up documenting an important moment), digital media allow "the rest of us" to take up the roles previously accorded to professional journalists. This means, in turn: insofar as "the rest of us" begin to play those roles, we need to begin to think through the ethical consequences of these transformations. Most briefly: what are our ethical rights, responsibilities, and (perhaps) virtues as citizen journalists?

To respond to this question, however, requires attention to a central context for such journalism – namely, its role in fostering democratization. That is, these transformations of journalistic practices, production, and distribution are often hailed – and with good reason – as ways in which digital media help introduce and expand democracy, especially in those parts of the world where democratic processes and regimes have not gained much of a foothold as yet. For example, central elements in these transformations are precisely the videos taken of persons harmed or killed at the hands of government forces. From the 2009 Iranian election protests to the Arab Spring of 2011 (and beyond), such citizen contributions have inspired civil movements that, in some cases, have moved governments and regimes in more democratic directions, even if they have not fully "revolutionized" a country and its structures of power.

This connection between democratization and journalistic practices – whether professional or citizen – is indeed an essential one. Historically, journalism and, most especially, the freedom of expression granted to it have been justified and protected in democratic societies by arguments that journalism, as exposing corruption and abuse and as fostering a diversity of viewpoints and debate, thereby makes essential contributions to democratic processes and regimes. Most simply, this means that the ethics of journalism have been shaped primarily by its service to democracy. In light of this larger context, then, our initial question becomes: what are our ethical rights, responsibilities, and (perhaps) virtues as citizen journalists whose work and expression are justified by their service to democracy?

As a last complication: just as our understandings and practices of journalism are transforming, so our notions of democracy are in flux – again, in good measure thanks to the multiple affordances, possibilities, and impacts of digital media. In order for us to begin to think about the ethics of a citizen journalism, then, we must first spend some time clarifying our understandings and assumptions of what "democracy" entails in a digital age, and why it is ethically justified.

Democracy and democratization online: first considerations

In the early 1990s, the emerging Internet and then the World Wide Web were frequently accompanied by fervent hopes and claims that these technologies would – perhaps inevitably – lead to greater democracy around the globe. This optimism – if not utopianism – reflected the national culture of the Internet's origins. As James Carey (1989) has noted, the *Federalist Papers* (1787, 1788), in debating the proper role of the hoped-for United States federal government, argue that one of the responsibilities of such a government is to subsidize canals and roads – precisely for the sake of democratic polity. That is, a core process of democracy is dialogue and debate among citizens. But, beginning with Plato, there have been arguments that democracy would thus be "naturally" limited. Very simply, in pre-literate days, such debate and dialogue would require face-to-face presence – and such presence in turn is limited by available transportation, either on foot or by animal. To make democratic dialogue and debate possible within a new nation spanning the original thirteen colonies would thus require more advanced transportation technologies – precisely the roads and canals under discussion – in order to overcome the otherwise quite modest "natural" limits of democracy. Carey argues that this understanding of communication technologies as undergirding democratic values and aspirations became a definitive strand of US culture. Hence, it was not surprising to see the rationales for globally expanding the Internet – as almost exclusively "born and raised" in the USA. – to include at the forefront this characteristic US optimism that communication technologies more or less inevitably improve the processes of democracy.

A first problem with these early claims, however, is: what do we mean by "democracy"? For many early proponents of electronic or online democracy the presumption was that the Internet would facilitate some form of direct or plebiscitory democracy – e.g., through instantaneous polling or votes. Such plebiscite arrangements, however, have long been criticized for their capacity quickly to turn anti-democratic as they are prey to the problem of "the tyranny of the majority." In contemporary terms, the wisdom of the crowd can quickly turn into the madness of the mob. Moreover, as Jean Beth Elshtain warned vis-à-vis television voting experiments in the 1980s, such voting lets us confuse "simply performing as the responding 'end' of a prefabricated system of external stimuli" with democratic participation (1982: 108; in Rheingold 1993: 287). Especially as new media and digital media are increasingly driven by the frameworks and assumptions of consumption and entertainment, political theorists Marcel Henaff and Tracy Strong go so far as to claim that "the main public space of our time is that of consumption; hence the political is subjected to its logic and has come to be assessed by the criterion of the image" (2001: 26). But consumer choice, as relentlessly assaulted by ubiquitous advertising appealing to our individual tastes, desires for convenience, and so forth, is not entirely the same as democratic choices ostensibly influenced by reasoned debate and with at least some view towards the larger good, not simply one's own. In such consumer-oriented models of decision-making, then,

> Democracy thus loses its rationality. Images displace arguments. Debates are turned into games. The show never stops. All games become interchangeable; the political stage tends to be no more than one among others. (Henaff and Strong 2001: 26f.)

Worst case, as Elshtain warns, "plebiscitism is compatible with authoritarian politics carried out under the guise of, or with the connivance of, majority views. That opinion can be registered by easily manipulated, ritualistic plebiscites, so there is no need for debate on substantive questions" (Elshtain 1982: 108; in Rheingold 1993: 287).

Responding to critiques of these sorts, scholars and theorists interested in the democratization potentials of computer-mediated communication frequently turned to the theories of Jürgen Habermas. Habermas's account of democratic forms of debate and dialogue focus on an "ideal speech situation" that would ensure equal voice to all participants in the decision-making that directly affected them. While highly contested, some version of Habermasian deliberative democracy has remained an important theoretical alternative to more plebiscite notions of democracy. In particular, Habermas's early emphasis on exclusively rational (if not simply masculine) forms of debate was effectively criticized and amplified by a number of feminists. So Seyla Benhabib (1986) and Iris Marion Young (2000), for example, affirm from feminist perspectives and experience the core intuition that democracy involves free and equal debate that should shape the decisions that affect us. But they go on to argue that such equality requires precisely the inclusion of the voices that an excessively rational (if not bluntly masculine) model of debate has historically excluded, namely the voices of women and children. Part of Habermas's response to early critiques along these lines was to emphasize solidarity and (empathic) perspective-taking as necessary conditions for (ideal) democratic discourse – the practice of attempting empathically to understand and take on board not only the (largely) rational arguments but also (sometimes more affective or emotional) experiences of those with whom we engage in dialogue. Such (empathic) perspective-taking then serves as a bridge leading to more forthrightly feminist insistence that our notions of democratic debate must conjoin (often more affective) narrative with (often more rational) argument. Finally, as with earlier, more plebiscite visions, proponents of these more Habermasian and feminist understandings of participatory dialogue likewise hope that these ideals of egalitarian dialogue and debate can be more fully realized by exploiting the multiple forms of communication and interactivity made possible through networked digital media. In particular, May Thorseth (2006, 2011) helpfully documents how these more inclusive understandings of what is required for fair and equal dialogue are taken up in contemporary notions of deliberative democracy and a number of important efforts to realize such ideal speech situations and deliberative process in online environments. (See also the more severe critiques of Habermasian notions of a public sphere in a digital age in Papacharissi 2010.)

The upshot is that, when we speak about "democracy" as a political ideal in a digital age, we need first to define with some care what we mean by it. This will be the work of our first exercise, below.

Whatever we might mean by "democracy," it remains a commonplace that the Internet and the Web "democratize." This claim seems especially persuasive when we think of the iconic example of citizen journalism as made possible by digital media – a mobile phone video of repressive violence that quickly becomes viewed globally and included in mainstream news reports. At the same time, however, the hope that digital media can lead to greater democratization around the globe is often overstated. To be sure, as Howard and his colleagues (2011) articulate at the opening of this chapter, SNSs and micro-blogs such as Twitter have played important roles in contemporary political uprisings. At the same time, however, phrases such as a "Facebook Revolution" or "Twitter Revolution" indicate that we risk focusing more on the technologies involved than on the persons who are making use of them. (This is, among other things, a form of technological determinism that should be carefully avoided.) Moreover, as the failure of the 2009 protests in Iran suggest (unfortunately), there is more to democratic revolution than successful organization of protesters through social media such as Facebook and Twitter. By the same token, how far the Arab Spring of 2011 will indeed issue in more democratic regimes across the countries that witnessed dramatic protests and sometimes profound changes (e.g., Tunisia, Algeria, Morocco, Yemen, and Egypt – but not, say, Bahrain or, so far, Syria) remains to be seen. More broadly, the record for democratizing by way of online venues is mixed. On the one hand, a recent summary study highlighted the importance of blogs and other forms of social media as opening up new venues that allow new voices to be heard. At the same time, however, the increase in voices also means the increase of noise – of too much information for one person to collect and make sense of. The upshot is often just the opposite of democratic dialogue, as we retreat to the cozy nests of those who agree with us and whose views we already endorse. Cass Sunstein identified this as the problem of "The Daily Me": as the Internet and the Web allow me to filter and choose only those contents I prefer to consume, the result is both fragmentation (a retreat from dialogue) and polarization (the end of dialogue) (Sunstein 2001: 65). More broadly, "the powers that be" – both well-entrenched political parties and their (oftentimes wealthy) supporters – are quick to learn how to use new media in ways that reinforce their own place and power, *contra* democratizing efforts that might challenge those (Stromer-Galley and Wichowski 2011; Howard et al. 2011; cf. Ess 1996: 198–212).

The view of technological determinists would argue, for

example, that the Internet and the Web are somehow inherently democratizing technologies, and their worldwide diffusions means the inevitable spread of democracy in turn. As is demonstrated, however, by the examples of Iran, Egypt, and a number of other countries, such as China, repressive regimes can be quite adept at controlling and channeling online communication media in ways that preserve rather than challenge their power. Whatever the inherent democratizing potentials of these media may be, it seems at least as important to focus on how we use such media. In particular, citizen journalism, among other practices, may help offset the online phenomena such as fragmentation and polarization that work against democratization.

To do so, however, citizen journalism would need to be more carefully defined and shaped as an ethical practice, one whose ethics derive at least in part from the goal of supporting democratizing communication. But, in order to set an ethical framework for citizen journalism, we first need to clarify what we mean by democracy. In particular, what kinds of communication and debate are required by such democracy? Once we are clearer about these points, we can better discern the role of citizen journalism in contributing to such democracy – and then determine at least some first responses to ethical issues raised by and for citizen journalists.

FIRST REFLECTION, DISCUSSION, WRITING:
DEMOCRACY AND DEMOCRATIZING ETHICS IN A DIGITAL AGE?

1. *WHAT DO WE MEAN BY "DEMOCRACY"?*

We have seen that there are at least two distinctive conceptions of "democracy," beginning with a once prevalent libertarian view that emphasized plebiscite forms of democracy, vis-à-vis feminist and Habermasian accounts that emphasize, rather, the importance of dialogue and debate shaped by rational argument, diverse narratives, and ethical commitments to equality, freedom, solidarity, and perspective-taking. (Depending on how far you and your class care to go in these directions, you can also explore a third alternative – communitarian democracy – which stresses service to the common or public good: see Abramson et al. 1988: 22–5 for an early account.)

Given these two poles as a starting point,

A) articulate as best you can what you see as the best and most desirable form(s) of democratic polity and processes – especially as these might be facilitated by digital media and networked communication.

B) identify where your notion of democracy lies on a continuum between the two poles of more libertarian or more feminist/ Habermasian forms of democracy.

C) Can you offer arguments, evidence, and/or other forms of warrant that would support and justify your choices? These can come in at least two forms: arguments, etc., for your own choices and/or arguments, etc., criticizing the alternative(s).

2. *THE ETHICAL REQUIREMENTS OF DEMOCRACY?*

In an early effort to apply Habermas and feminist thought to the topic of online democracy, I concluded by observing that

> the discourse ethic requires the ability to engage in critical discourse and the moral commitment to practicing the ability to take others' perspectives and thus seek solidarity with others in a plurality of democratic discourse communities. (Ess 1996: 220)

In the ethical frameworks we have examined here, we can rephrase this to include two ethical components:

- a deontological insistence on respecting the arguments and experiences of others as equals in a shared discourse community, and
- a virtue ethics argument that the correlative perspective-taking required for a free and equal dialogue and debate is an ability that must be practiced – i.e., such perspective-taking stands as a habit of excellence or virtue that requires practice if it is to be acquired and exercised well.

Given your definitions and affiliated requirements for "democracy" as you have outlined above, how far are either of these ethical dimensions necessary for fostering democracy – whether online or offline – as you understand it?

3. THE ETHICAL REQUIREMENTS OF DEMOCRACY AND THE ETHICS OF JOURNALISM

As we have started to see, much of journalistic practice and ethics turns on the core service of journalism to democratic processes, beginning with fostering more open, better informed, and diverse debate and dialogue.

Especially in light of your analysis of the ethical requirements of democracy (if any), what do these imply (if anything) for an ethics for citizen journalists? For example, if you endorse some sort of free and equal debate as central to democratic processes, this would imply that journalists are obliged to remain (relatively) neutral (or "objective") in their reporting, to seek to ensure that as many different voices and views are represented in their reporting, and so forth. We further assume that good news reporting is as truthful as possible: we do not want to build our views and arguments on falsehoods of any sort.

But would there be similar requirements for a citizen journalist? For example, should we hold citizen journalists to strict standards of truth, and/or grant them greater latitude in their compilation of photographs and videos, in their accompanying commentary, etc.? Similarly, does it make sense to require citizen journalists to hold to some criterion of objectivity – of seeking to ensure that what they contribute to a news and information stream is not (overly) one-sided, perhaps misrepresentative, etc.?

As you may have begun to recognize, you are entering relatively fresh ethical territory. Comparatively very little has been written (so far) by ethicists in these directions. In the above exercise, we made a first effort towards developing an ethics for citizen journalists by drawing on theories of democracy and their possible implications for such journalists. A second approach is more from "the ground up" – in this instance, from an important example of where citizen journalism, precisely intended to foster democratization, went awry. The case should help us move a bit further in identifying at least two components of an ethics for citizen journalists.

CASE-STUDY: CITIZEN JOURNALISM?

In 2009, Iranian President Mahmoud Ahmadinejad was re-elected to office in what many alleged to be an illegitimate election process. On June 20, 2009, a young Iranian philosophy student – Neda Agha Soltan – was shot in the chest during clashes between anti-government demonstrators and government security forces. The shooting and her death were captured on video, quickly uploaded to YouTube, and, as the phrase goes, went viral – helped in part by attention to the shooting through the Twitter hashtag #neda. *Time* magazine commented that it was "probably the most widely witnessed death in human history" (Mahr 2009).

Neda was quickly lifted up as a martyr in the cause of the opposition to the Iranian regime. Anti-government protesters carried photographs of her in subsequent demonstrations, and her name and memory are invoked in current Tweets concerning the 2012 Iranian elections. (At the time of this writing, the video has logged over 1,283,000 views on YouTube: https://www.youtube.com/watch?v=76W-oGVjNEc&bpctr=1355383619.)

Most unfortunately for university English professor Neda Soltani, however, several Western news outlets – including Fox News and CNN – pulled her Facebook profile picture to use in their coverage of the event. This led to an explosion of requests to friend her on FB – as well as arrest and detention by the Iranian government, which wanted her to help in their efforts to smear the video as a hoax. When she refused, she was accused of spying for the West. With the help of friends, she escaped Iran and is now struggling to rebuild her life.

In his commentary on this episode, BBC picture editor Phil Coomes (2012) notes that, in earlier times, news organizations would have gathered pictures of such victims from their families: "But this takes time and today we consume, and demand, stories and photographs faster than ever before, which means news organisations will dig for those pictures on social media sites." He adds that there are certainly issues of copyright and verification – as well as "the ethical angle: whether the media has the right to take a photograph from one context and use it in another, away from the audience it was intended for." For Coomes, there are apparently some circumstances that would justify what many of us would see as a profoundly problematic misuse of someone else's face and photograph: he concludes his response by noting that "There is no simple answer as the situation varies from story to story."

QUESTIONS FOR REFLECTION, DISCUSSION, WRITING

1. Imagine that you are someone – whether in Iran or beyond its borders – deeply sympathetic to the protesters' opposition to the Iranian regime and an election process widely seen to have been manipulated, etc. Among your first impulses, when seeing the video of Neda Agha Soltan's shooting and death, would almost certainly be to tweet about it, re-post it in some fashion or another – in short, to use all available social media at your command to spread the word, and thereby the outrage and continued opposition.

Are there any ethical considerations that would guide you in deciding whether or not to re-post, retweet, etc.? For example, can you be certain that the video is real – and not, as the Iranian government worked hard to demonstrate later, a fake of some sort? As well, especially utilitarians will want to consider: given the subsequent misuse of Neda Soltani's FB profile picture, how far would such re-posting on your part achieve your desired ends (of highlighting an unjustified killing, of fostering support for anti-regime efforts, etc.), and how far might such re-posting only compound Neda Soltani's problems – and perhaps yours if you are somehow within the reach of the Iranian regime?

Most broadly, can you demonstrate that such re-posting, retweeting, etc., indeed contributes to and thus is ethically justified by democratizing processes – including, perhaps, those entailed by feminist and Habermasian understandings of free and equal dialogue, accompanied by empathic perspective-taking, etc.?

2. Imagine now that you are a more distant observer, someone who stumbles across the story of Neda Agha Soltan's death, perhaps as a casual reader of the news accounts that bubble up almost immediately following the uploading of the video onto YouTube. Are there any ethical requirements that might apply to you, simply as a consumer of news in a (we will presume) democratic society? This might seem to be a strange question. But consider: especially if you are likewise tempted to re-post, retweet, and/or redistribute the story in some way through your own networks and channels, do you have an obligation first of all to determine how far the story might be accurate, including its use of photographs allegedly portraying the face of Neda Agha Soltan? To state this slightly differently, especially if your goal is to contribute to democratizing discourse and dialogue, do you have an ethical obligation to be critical, first of all, in how you gather, interpret, and decide to redistribute news and information?

In these directions – again, your responses here will depend in some measure upon how you have defined "democracy" and thus the role of journalism in contributing to democratizing dialogue and discourse. For example, if you take a more libertarian view – and, perhaps, a more utilitarian view – you may trust that the truth will emerge precisely through the contest of diverse claims and opinions, as it seems to have done, arguably, as the uncovering of the misuse of Neda Soltani's FB profile picture suggests. By contrast, a more deontological or virtue ethics approach might endorse precisely the practice of critical reading and evaluation. For example, a deontological emphasis on respecting basic rights would argue that Neda Soltani has a right not to have her photograph misused in these ways, most especially as they lead to such severe harms – and utilitarians might agree. And a virtue ethics approach would emphasize the practices of critical reading and careful judgments as to what in fact will contribute, alongside other virtues such as empathic perspective-taking, to democratizing discourses and dialogues.

3. (Optional). Consider Phil Coomes's response to the Neda Soltani affair. For him, to begin with, it is apparently justifiable, especially under the time pressures created precisely by digital and

networked media, sometimes to lift someone else's photograph for an important news story: again, "There is no simple answer as the situation varies from story to story" (Coomes 2012).

Coomes's response can be interpreted to mean one of two things. On the one hand, he is perhaps an ethical pluralist – someone who would recognize that, alongside our agreement on larger and shared norms, beginning with truth-telling, we might interpret what counts as "truth" as differing from context to context. For example, it is not uncommon, precisely in order to protect potentially vulnerable persons' identities (e.g., women who have been victims of domestic violence), to build a composite account of a given group of people. Such a composite account is in a narrow sense fictional, as it does not perfectly or literally refer to a single real or given person. But it can be perfectly true in the sense that it conveys critical points about a given group of persons' experiences, feelings, insights, etc.

Alternatively, Coomes's response may reflect the position of ethical relativism: there are no right or wrong answers that hold universally – because there are no universal rights or wrongs.

Either way:

A) Does the knowledge that even premier and profoundly trusted news outlets such as the BBC may be open to the sorts of practices at work in the Neda Soltani affair have any ethical implications for you as a reader – and possible re-poster – of news and information from such a source? If so, what are these? Try to identify how far these derive from primarily utilitarian, deontological, and/or virtue ethics positions.

B) Phil Coomes further notes that "we consume, and demand, stories and photographs faster than ever before, which means news organisations will dig for those pictures on social media sites." Recall the warning from Henaff and Strong that consumption paradigms, if taken to their extreme, mean the end of democratic deliberation and decision-making (above, p. 146). Indeed, a primary justification for citizen journalism is just that, as a more participatory practice, it helps offset the tendencies of mass media to reduce us simply to consumers making relatively passive choices. Might citizen journalism – along with affiliated injunctions that we become more critical readers – also mean that time and speed are ethical matters? That is, might one component of critical reading and citizen journalism be the ethical injunction to slow down and take the time needed for careful investigation, double-checking, etc.?

ADVANCED RESOURCES AND TOPICS FOR REFLECTION, DISCUSSION, WRITING

In his book, *Ethics and the Media: An Introduction* (2011), Stephen J. Ward offers a complete re-evaluation of journalism ethics in light of the sorts of transformations we have begun to explore here. A brief overview of some of his central arguments is available online ("Digital Media Ethics," http://ethics.journalism.wisc. edu/resources/digital-media-ethics/; this resource can further be helpfully complemented by the companion piece "Global Media Ethics," http://ethics.journalism.wisc.edu/resources/global-media-ethics/).

In the section "Difficult questions for digital media ethics," Ward addresses some of the questions we have begun to raise here, starting with "Who is a journalist?" and "What is journalism?" in the age of digital media. He goes on to consider, for example, how anonymity in online fora may be ethically more justifiable than in the age of newspapers and TV broadcasting, as well as the issues of "Speed, rumor and corrections." It would be useful, for example, to juxtapose this latter section with some of the observations and comments we have seen above from Phil Coomes.

Moreover, Ward takes up the problem of traditional commitments to impartiality and avoiding conflicts of interest vis-à-vis partisan journalism – i.e., precisely the sort of reporting that would highlight unjust violence as a way of supporting a larger political movement. Finally, Ward discusses "Citizen journalists and using citizen content" and the specific "Ethics of images."

Each of these sections suggests initial questions for reflection and further research, accompanied by a list of further readings.

CHAPTER FIVE

Still More Ethical Issues: Digital Sex and Games

The plethora of available online pornographies guarantees that virtually any stance on porn can be backed up with multiple examples supporting one's argument.

(Paasonen 2011: 432)

I'm not saying video games make you a killer. But if you're a psychopath, video games help you get in the mode to do the killing.

Pat Brown (CNN 2012)

Chapter overview

We begin with pornography*[1] as an ethical problem – depending first of all on how we may define it: such definitions differ dramatically from culture to culture. As is also true with violence in games, a central question is how far production and consumption of these materials – increasingly common and easy in the age of Web 2.0 – has any connection with our real-world attitudes and behaviors. We examine basic philosophical and religious frameworks that shape contemporary reflections on sexuality and identity and then explore central ethical issues here in terms of utilitarianism, deontology, feminist ethics/ethics of care, and virtue ethics. (If you have

---

1 Borrowing from a convention suggested by Grodzinsky et al. (2008), I use "pornography*" – i.e., with an appended asterisk – as a way of signaling to the reader that this term is intrinsically ambiguous and open to a wide range of interpretations. The intention of the asterisk is thereby consistently to remind the reader of the need to specify further (or, in a fancier term, disambiguate) what one means more precisely when speaking of pornography*, rather than uncritically assuming that the term holds a straightforward and unambiguous meaning.

not already reviewed these frameworks for ethical decision-making in chapter 6, you should do so before moving into this chapter.). We return to the central question of how far computer-based gaming experiences of violence and rape may influence our offline behaviors and attitudes – and again explore the ethical significance (and/or lack thereof) especially vis-à-vis utilitarianism, deontology, and virtue ethics.

Introduction: is pornography* an ethical problem – and, if so, what kind(s)?

There is no doubt but that the Internet is awash with pornography* of every imaginable stripe and genre. The production and diffusion of "sexually explicit materials" (SEMs), to use the ethically more neutral term (Livingstone et al. 2011), is aided and abetted by the increasing diffusion of Internet-connected digital media: more or less anyone who cares to do so can produce and distribute such materials with ease. At the same time, the complex interplays between digital media and the larger spheres of our lives (or "lifeworlds," to use the concept from phenomenology) means that pornography, however it is to be defined, is so diffused throughout contemporary societies that it has become "the wallpaper" of our lives (David Amsden, in Wolf, 2003). Indeed, at a time when "mommy porn," as a description of the wildly popular novel *Fifty Shades of Grey* and its competitors in the genre, enjoys mainstream media attention (including, for example, a rating system using "whips" and "penises" as categories; Daily Mail Reporter 2012), the boundaries between our offline and online lives seem more or less blurred, if not irrelevant.

At the same time, however, these complex interplays have been amplified over the past several years by so-called Web 2.0 technologies and communication venues: these include social networking sites, micro-blogs (think of Facebook status updates and Twitter), and "produsage" sites such as YouTube which allow just about anyone with a digital camera and/or simply a smartphone to record still images and videos and then upload them for all of the Internet world – currently more than one-third of the planet's population

– to see. These facilities and capacities thereby both continue and dramatically expand earlier forms of amateur pornography, for example, while simultaneously enabling new forms of SEMs such as Netporn:

> Netporn entails the blurred boundaries of porn producers and consumers, the proliferation of independent and alternative pornographies, as well as the expansion of technological possibilities brought forth by digital tools, platforms and networked communications. Ultimately, what is at stake is no less than a redefinition of pornography as a cultural object in terms of esthetics, politics, media economy, technology and desire. (Paasonen 2010: 1298)

Such redefinition, in particular, occurs within the subgenre of alt porn, defined in part by "its exhibition of non-standard subcultural styles, community features and interaction possibilities" (ibid.: 1299).

All of this profoundly complicates the ethical issues surrounding pornography and SEMs in at least three significant ways. One, as the Internet and digital media have facilitated such an explosion of the production and diffusion of SEMs, they have thereby made the difficulties of defining pornography* that much more complex. Two, this mediatization of sex and sexuality thereby intersects with the larger patterns of mediatization – meaning the various ways in which we use digital (and analogue) media to represent ourselves and our lives, both to ourselves and to others: as digital media continue to diffuse into every corner and wrinkle of our lives, so more and more of our lives are experienced through and with these media. As we saw in chapter 2, for example, the pocketfilm *Porte de Choisy*, which otherwise violates earlier notions of bedroom and bathroom privacies, can be understood as simply an extension of our increasing ability to record and present ourselves via digital technologies. Re-presenting ourselves through the resulting artifacts – whether in the form of a text-based blog, an online photo album, or a home-made video – is not only a way of communicating with one another in enhanced ways, ways that are more enjoyable because they are quick, convenient, engage more of our communicative senses (sound and vision, not simply reading), and globally accessible. In addition, as Anna Reading (and others) argue, as *we* are the ones who take charge of and direct these media productions, we thereby (re)gain agency and control over our media self-representations. Such mediatized self-revelation, then, can be experienced as a form of empowerment and liberation in an age of surveillance, for example. When it comes to sexuality and gender, similar comments hold, at least in part: an especially strong argument in favor of online SEMs and their amateur production is just that these allow persons to explore otherwise marginalized sexualities (including, to use the acronym GLBTq, gay, lesbian, bisexual, transgendered, and/or queer) and sexual "tastes" (including bondage, discipline, dominance, submission, sadism and/or masochism – S&M for short [Thorn and Dibbell 2012]) – and thereby to determine for themselves their own sexual identities and preferences. In this direction, pornography* may serve nothing less than the (high) modern values of emancipation, autonomy, agency, and equality (cf. Bromseth and Sundén 2011; McElroy 1995). To be sure, this line of argument directly contradicts ethical objections to pornography* and SEMs as objectifying women and children (and, in some instances, men): such objectification obscures, if it does not eliminate, their agency and autonomy, allowing us to see women, children, and/or men as "just meat" (Adams 1996). And without agency and autonomy, there is no person "there" to be emancipated or regarded as an equal.

Finally, all of this is – yet again – made even more complex when taken up from a cross-cultural perspective. No one should be surprised to learn that judgments and attitudes regarding bodies and sexuality vary dramatically from culture to culture. In India, for example, material that merely implies sex, such as beauty pageants, counts as pornography* (Ghosh 2006); in Indonesia, the term is bound up with laws regulating women's clothing and demeanor, including public displays of affection (Lim 2006, both cited in Paasonen et al. 2007: 16). On the other hand, it is not an accident that, in 1969, Denmark was the first Western nation to legalize pornography* (Time 1969). That is, in Denmark and Scandinavia more broadly, bodies and sexuality – inclusive of the sexuality of children and adolescents – are widely regarded as simply positive aspects of human nature and experience. These judgments and attitudes can be seen, for example, in respected Danish newspapers such as *Jyllands-Posten* and *Politiken* routinely publishing photographs that involve full frontal nudity – e.g., depicting the "naked run" that is part of the spring student festival at Aarhus University (Pedersen 2011) and, more famously, the annual Roskilde Music Festival (Politiken 2012), much less a Jeff Koons painting of himself and his wife (former porn-star Cicciolina) delicately titled *Ice – Jeff on Top Pulling Out* (Hornung 2010). What counts in this context as pornography* gets difficult to determine: indeed, a recent book argues that pornography is simply part of Danish culture (Nordstrøm 2012). In any event, in these cultural contexts, there is less concern with pornography* as a possible problem, especially for young people (Haddon and Stald 2009). Indeed, in European countries, children are concerned more with the problem of cyberbullying than with unwanted exposure to SEMs (Livingstone et al. 2011: 25). It may also be of interest to note that an extensive survey (some 5,490 respondents) in the UK showed that "The peak age for extreme and high importance for viewing porn is 26–35, while the age at which it has the lowest importance is 18–25" (Smith et al. 2012: 3).

Part of the difficulty here is that, as compared with Europe – and especially Scandinavia – attitudes and judgments regarding bodies, sexuality, and thus pornography* in the United States are considerably more restrictive. This likely has to do with the Puritan influences in early American life, and most certainly has to do with contemporary religious attitudes and commitments: around 78 percent of Americans describe themselves as Christian (Pew Forum 2008), and the great majority of these subscribe to traditions that, as shaped by Augustine and his doctrine of Original Sin, identify women and sexuality as primary ethical problems (to put it politely).[2] Of course, Americans are free to believe as they choose,

---

2 The doctrine of Original Sin is historically associated with patriarchal control of women: as the doctrine lays the responsibility for the introduction of sin and death into the world upon Eve, it thereby works to demonize women, the body, and sexuality. This interpretation of the second Genesis creation story (Genesis 2.4–3.2), while orthodox in Western Roman Catholicism and subsequently

but for us the difficulty is that, until the last decade or so, much of the discussion regarding pornography and digital media largely arose in and has been dominated by both popular and scholarly voices based in the United States (Paasonen et al. 2007; Paasonen 2011: 427).[3] This is not to say that a US-based scholar or view is automatically suspect: it is to say that such views – as views from any other cultural domain – tend strongly to be shaped by a specific set of cultural backgrounds. The first point is to be aware of these backgrounds – and how they vary from European, Scandinavian, Asian, African, indigenous, and other traditions – in order to avoid inadvertent dominance of one view and, simultaneously, to raise our awareness of the role of our own cultural backgrounds in shaping our own judgments and attitudes. (In turn, the point is not to fall into an ethical relativism but, rather, to point towards an ethical pluralism that can make room for a diversity of views and judgments.)

INITIAL REFLECTION/DISCUSSION/WRITING EXERCISE:
GENDER, SEXUALITY, CULTURE, AND PORNOGRAPHY*

1. In light of these initial comments and first ethical arguments,

A) How would you characterize the prevailing attitudes and judgments, both positive and/or negative, towards bodies, women, and sexuality in the country/culture you count most as your own?

B) Insofar as your own judgments and attitudes regarding bodies and sexuality may be different from the prevailing

---

among some Protestant reformers, is directly contrary to earlier Christian and Jewish readings of the text, which emphasize rather the positive nature of Eve's choice: acquiring "the knowledge of good and evil" is specifically understood as the attainment of the distinctively human capacities of moral understanding and free choice – capacities that, in turn, early Enlightenment thinkers such as John Locke see as foundational to arguments for democratic polity – i.e., the political arrangements of human beings capable of rational self-rule.

3 It may be helpful to remember here that, as late as 1998, over 84 percent of those using the Internet were located in North America (GVU 1998). While regrettable from the standpoint of pluralism, the dominance of US perspectives in these early debates is at least understandable in light of the Internet demographics at the time.

ones around you, can you characterize these (at least for yourself, if not for your sister and fellow students and/or instructors just now)?

C) How would you define pornography*? Be careful here: given the considerable diversity of SEMs "out there" (both online and offline), you will want to start building a continuum of materials that would either count or not count, in your view, as pornography – and then what is for you ethically objectionable pornography.

For example, child pornography is all but universally condemned and criminalized. But what about SEMs involving violence or torture – at the extreme, "snuff films" that appear to depict the death of the (usually female) object of sexual violence and torture? At the other end of the continuum might be sexually explicit material that, in your view, counts more as erotic art, not pornography. All fine and good: but where on the continuum is a line crossed into pornography – and then ethically objectionable pornography?

D) Given your definition of "pornography," what are your personal responses to it – including any ethical ones?

E) Equally importantly: can you identify how far your own responses to pornography are (in)consistent with the prevailing judgments and attitudes regarding bodies and sexuality you describe above?

2. Given your responses to pornography (1.D, above), what arguments, evidence, experiences, and/or other grounds can you offer to support those responses? For example, you may want to argue that exposure to pornography may be harmful for children and adolescents, as it might foster both less than respectful attitudes towards young girls and women and understandings of sexuality that emphasize power and exploitation rather than respect, equality, and mutual intimacy.

These sorts of arguments are common consequentialist or utilitarian arguments, and are frequently invoked in debates surrounding pornography and its regulation. But you may well have other arguments, etc., to offer.

3. Review the first two arguments sketched out above regarding pornography and SEMs as

A) ethically objectionable because these materials objectify persons as "just meat" and thereby deny them agency, autonomy, and equality, vis-à-vis
B) ethically defensible because these materials may contribute to the (high) modern values of emancipation, autonomy, agency, and equality, especially for those persons whose sexual identities and preferences do not align with the preferences and identities dominant in their culture.
   Which of these two arguments do you find more persuasive – and why?

4. Both of the arguments in 3 above are exemplars of deontological arguments. That is, as Kant argued, human beings are primarily autonomous, and thereby capable of rational self-rule. This means that, far from being seen and treated as "just meat," free human beings must be allowed to determine their own ends or goals, rather than serve as the means ("just meat") to ends and goals imposed by others. On this line of reasoning, free human beings thus have (near) absolute rights, beginning with the right to respect from others and the right to be treated as equals.

The debate here, then, is whether or not – and, if so, how and in what ways – SEMs serve to enhance or degrade this core human autonomy. In this light, one's judgments and attitudes towards bodies and sexuality become especially critical to the debate. A Scandinavian feminist, for example, as someone who is inclined to regard sexuality as normal and natural, may be more open to the view that SEMs can work to enhance human autonomy. A US Christian, by contrast, may be persuaded that bodies and sexuality are implicated in Original Sin and are thereby to be enshrouded in privacy, if not shame, and so she or he is far more likely to view SEMs as only reinforcing already such strongly negative views towards women and sexuality. From this perspective, it is hard to see how they could thus work for equality and the emancipation of women.

In this light:

A) given that you endorse a deontological emphasis on human beings as primarily free agents who must be respected and not treated as "just meat," how far do you find SEMs to be more likely to work (i) against emancipation and equality and/or (ii) for emancipation and equality?

B) especially if you find yourself coming down strongly on the side of either A(i) or A(ii), can you tell if your response is consistent with your personal and/or cultural judgments and attitudes towards bodies, women, and sexuality?

Pornography: (more) ethical debates and analyses

These three major difficulties facing any ethical discussion of pornography* underline Susanna Paasonen's warning at the opening of this chapter: "The plethora of available online pornographies guarantees that virtually any stance on porn can be backed up with multiple examples supporting one's argument" (2011: 432). To say this somewhat differently, the dramatic explosion of diverse forms and genres of SEMs online thus makes it difficult to move forward with any sort of ethical analysis and arguments without first defining a focus: that is, which (relatively) specific form(s) of pornography* do we have in mind?

One extensive survey conducted in the UK shows that the largest number of both women and men visit first of all so-called tube sites – i.e., the porn equivalents of YouTube such as porntube.com (Smith et al. 2012: 5). These sites appear to emphasize SEMs designed primarily to arouse heterosexual males through a focus on women as both the targets and active agents of male sexual pleasure. With this genre of pornography* as a starting point, we'll now turn to three different analyses and arguments that I hope will be useful both in their own right and as providing examples and models for approaching other forms of SEMs.

Pornography* online: a utilitarian analysis

At least in the English-speaking world, approaches to pornography* online often follow utilitarian lines of argument. As a start, classical liberals, beginning with John Stuart Mill, defend freedom of speech and object to censorship on straightforwardly utilitarian grounds. First, freedom of speech is defended as leading to such positive goods as individual happiness and a flourishing society. By contrast, censorship is rejected because of its many negative consequences, including inadvertent suppression of what may be grains of truth in an otherwise suspect claim or view (Warburton 2009: 22–31.).[4] We can add to these considerations common objections to proposed Internet regulation as being too costly, as imposing unneeded costs and inconveniences on governments, the corporations responsible for maintaining the Internet infrastructure, and users/consumers. On the other hand, critics of pornography* argue that the production and consumption of such materials is harmful to women. Indeed, for all of the debate regarding the difficulty of demonstrating causality between consumption, on the one hand, and attitudes and actions, on the other, at least one significant meta-study has shown "an overall significant positive association between pornography use and attitudes supporting violence against women in non-experimental, as well as experimental, settings" (Haid et al. 2010; West 2012).

Putting aside for the moment the critical questions concerning the validity of such claims, the upshot is a simple utilitarian calculus: do the possible costs and other negative consequences of some sorts of restrictions on consuming pornography* outweigh the possible benefits of such restrictions – namely, reducing avoidable harms to women?

Part of our response here depends first of all on determining just what the possible costs would be – in utilitarian terms, how

---

4 As Warburton points out, Mill's arguments are directed to freedom of expression and freedom of speech. For pornography* to be defended on these grounds, however, it must first be established to be a form of speech or expression. For arguments pro and con on this point, see Warburton 2009: 60–4.

many negative utils would be generated by efforts at censorship or regulation? This would depend in turn, of course, on just what sorts of efforts we have in mind. For example, there has been deliberation in the UK regarding an approach to filtering SEMs called "active choice-plus." This would require Internet service providers to impose a default setting on their systems that automatically blocks SEMs: users would then have the option of changing this setting if they wanted "access to sites promoting pornography, violence and other adult-only themes" (BBC News 2012a). As might be imagined, the ISPs involved will complain of the expense of installing and maintaining such filters, along with affiliated costs of developing services for allowing customers to opt in to such sites. At least some number of customers will also find the proposed necessity of taking time and action to opt in to cost at least a few negative utils – multiplied in turn by however many such customers there may be who would want to opt in.

On the other hand: how many positive utils might be gained by a potentially significant reduction in harms against women? For example, if MP Ann Coffey is correct, there has been a "surge" of sexual groping and manhandling of young girls in the UK: around one-third of sixth-form girls have been targets. Coffey, moreover, squarely blames this rise of sexual aggression against young girls on Internet pornography* fostering "distorted" sexual attitudes among teenage boys (Martin 2012). So: how many positive utils can we assign – presumably a very large number – to the young girls who would no longer be victimized in this way should stronger blocks be placed on access to Internet pornography*?

As discussed in chapter 6 (pp. 203–6), this example brings forward three of the critical reasons why applying a utilitarian cost–benefit analysis in practice is so difficult. The first question is: how far can we be confident of our predictions of the outcomes of our possible choices? That is, can we be confident of the predictions on either side – whether of high negative and/or of high positive consequences of imposing new controls on access to online SEMs? Second: even if we could predict these outcomes with some degree of certainty, how do we quantify costs and benefits beyond the monetary costs involved? That is, how many negative utils should we assign to a customer being required to take the time and trouble to opt in to access currently available by default? How many positive utils can we assign to a predicted reduction in sexual aggression against young women? While the utilitarian approach forces us to weigh the negatives and positives against one another, it seems clear that at least some aspects of human experience, including a sense of security against unwanted and unjustified aggression, defy straightforward quantification. Hence weighing pros and cons becomes a very murky business indeed.

Finally, let's return to the debate over the causal linkages claimed to exist between consumption of online SEMs and aggressive attitudes towards women. Again, there are complex and ongoing controversies here over how experimentally to confirm or disconfirm such a causal linkage. It may be that new experimental approaches may be devised in five or ten (or fifty) years down the road that would provide us with more reliable evidence one way or another; it may also be that little to no progress along these lines will be made.

In the meantime, however, we have to make judgments and decisions one way or another. The best we can do (so far) is to judge and decide based on the best evidence we have (so far), but this still leaves us facing the first two problems attending any utilitarian approach – namely, uncertainty about predicting outcomes and the very great difficulty of attempting to quantify outcomes in order to balance them against one another in a cost–benefit analysis.

As we see in chapter 6, these sorts of limitations mean that utilitarianism doesn't always bring us very far in our efforts to grapple with complex moral issues. And, precisely because of these sorts of limitations, many ethicists argue we must expand our ethical decision-making frameworks to include deontology and, perhaps, virtue ethics. This turn is exemplified in the next analysis.

"Complete sex" – a feminist/phenomenological perspective

In her article "Better Sex" (1975), Sara Ruddick offers an account of sexual experiences that begins with phenomenological analyses – most simply, analyses based in carefully disciplined attention to human experience as primarily embodied beings – to critique otherwise prevailing understandings that focus on sex and sexuality as something involving only bodies.

These understandings can derive from at least two sources. The first is a kind of dualism – whether religious or philosophical – that makes a strong separation between the person as a soul or mental agent, on the one hand, and their body, including their sexuality, on the other. These dualisms have predominated in Western traditions since at least the time of Augustine, and are carried through into modern philosophical thought in the profoundly influential work of René Descartes ([1637] 1972). For better or for worse, these sorts of dualisms predominated 1980s and 1990s understandings of "cyberspace" and virtual worlds as radically different from our more ordinary, offline worlds – beginning with William Gibson's novel *Neuromancer*, which invented the term "cyberspace" and defined it as opposed to the world of "meat" (1984: 6; see Ess 2011). The second source is simple materialism – the view that holds that human beings are fully reducible to the workings of their solely material bodies, as described by and predictable through the various natural laws of biochemistry, neurology, simple physics, and so forth. On this view, there is no free human agent – only the illusion of freedom. We really are "just meat" – no different in any significant way from, say, dolphins, other hominids, or cows. For many in the contemporary world, especially those raised in highly secular societies in Northern and Eastern Europe, particularly Scandinavia, and some parts of Asia, this view may seem common sense and unproblematic. Be aware, however, that this view is rejected by most contemporary philosophers, who opt instead for a position called "compatibilism." This view holds that "free will is compatible with [material] determinism" (McKenna 2009). The trick here is to be a compatibilist without being a dualist; it is not necessarily easy, but it can be done.

For Ruddick, such dualistic understandings are problematic for two reasons. The first is that they result in an account of sexuality that radically separates a given individual's sense of unique identity and distinctive selfhood from sex as something that takes place solely between (more or less interchangeable) bodies. The second is that, in doing so, such understandings seem inevitably to lead to an ethically problematic account of sexuality – namely, one in which individuals can use one another's bodies only as the means to satisfy their own desires. Ruddick does not think that such understandings of sexuality are necessarily mistaken. But she first argues that, from a phenomenological perspective, they are incomplete. As we know from some of our most intense experiences – such as playing sports – we do not feel or experience some sort of mind–body dualism: on the contrary, one of the reasons we enjoy such experiences so profoundly and completely is just because they involve an immediate sense of unity between our selves (as unique and distinctive selves or agents) and our bodies. (The German phenomenologist Barbara Becker [2001] later suggested the term "body-subject" [*LeibSubjekt*] to refer to this experience of being in the world as an individual in both mind and body.) Ruddick does not intend to argue with this that all our sexual experiences must involve such direct unity. Rather, she maintains that those that do are morally preferable first of all because our own personhood and autonomy cannot be separated from our bodies in such experiences. Specifically, to approach sexuality as embodied beings, as individuals and moral agents who *are* our bodies, especially as they are diffused with sexual desire, issues in what Ruddick calls "complete sex" – a sexual engagement marked precisely by mutuality and reciprocal care and concern for each other. Such "complete sex," as inextricably interwoven and suffused with the distinctive identities of the persons involved, thereby literally embodies the felt uniqueness of the relationship with each other, along with other feelings such as pride and gratitude – all of which reinforce the status of the Other as a person, not a thing.

In contrast to, say, "cookbook sex," that treats any given body as a more or less interchangeable component of a given recipe, complete sex thereby fosters the Kantian duty of respect for the Other as a person – i.e., precisely as an autonomous and unique person deserving fundamental respect. In Kantian language, this means a person we must always treat as an end in itself, never as a means only – i.e., as "just meat." Indeed, Ruddick's analysis helpfully points towards what many of us find most important in such experiences – namely, the sense of being loved fully and completely, precisely as the unique body-subject that we experience ourselves to be much of the time. Ruddick goes on to argue that complete sex fosters two additional virtues – namely, the norm of equality and the virtue of loving (Ruddick 1975: 98ff.).

Many of my US students, especially those who are not particularly religious, find Ruddick's account valuable because it helps them make sense of one of their primary moral intuitions about their sexuality and intimate relationships. That is, most of my US students – and, so far as I can gather, most of my European ones as well – are "serial monogamists." In contrast with an earlier sexual ethic that would limit sex to a single partner over a lifetime, serial monogamists are happy to have sexuality as part of some sort of close, intimate, and exclusive relationship that will endure for some length of time, whether a few weeks, months, or years. Once a given relationship is over, of course, then the serial monogamist is perfectly free to take up a sexual relationship with another person or persons over time. But generally, within a given relationship, the intuition is that, if one's partner "has sex" with someone else, it amounts to some form of cheating or infidelity.

A dualist – someone who strongly separates body and sexuality from personal identity and thus the ethical commitments and norms associated with respect for persons as unique individuals – has difficulty, however, making sense of serial monogamy. Rather, the consistent dualist would regard sexual activity as simply one more activity of bodies as radically distinct from their "owners" as individuals. So how can sexuality have any connection with some sort of personal commitment to a romantic relationship with another as somehow unique, distinctive, and thus excluding sex with other bodies? Why should "sex," if it's simply a matter of actions between two more or less interchangeable bodies, be any more personal or exclusive than, say, shaking hands?

By contrast, many of my students find in Ruddick's analysis a way of accurately describing first of all their own experiences of being a "body-subject" in at least their better experiences of sexuality in a (serially) monogamous relationship. This experientially oriented, phenomenological account hence provides them with a way of making ethical sense of their moral intuitions that, as serial monogamists, there's something ethically problematic about sex with someone else besides their current partner – but without having to appeal to either religious or philosophical frameworks they otherwise reject.

In short, Ruddick's account brings forward:

1) a deontological emphasis on treating one another as free and unique persons, where the recognition of such autonomy requires fundamental respect for another as equals, and
2) a virtue ethics emphasis on loving – i.e., as the practice of learning to treat one another as individuals worthwhile in themselves.

Both of these directly challenge experiences of sex and sexuality that rather present a person as just body, as "just meat" – i.e., as an object that (not who) exists solely as a means to our own ends and desires.

Ruddick does not directly mention pornography, but she does comment that "Obscenity, or repeated public exposure to sexual acts, might impair our capacity for pleasure or for response to desire" (1975: 102). This at least raises the question as to whether our enjoyment of the sorts of pornographic materials described above – i.e., ones that consistently depict women and children (and sometimes men) as exclusively the targets and agents of fulfilling male pleasure and desire – reinforce and/or incline us towards adopting a dualistic attitude towards body and sexuality that sees the sexual other as "just meat."

Insofar as our answer to this question is "yes," then we would have reason to be cautious – perhaps very cautious – regarding consumption of pornography of these sorts.

SECOND REFLECTION/DISCUSSION/WRITING EXERCISE:
ACCESS TO PORNOGRAPHY* ONLINE

1. We've now seen three approaches to some of the ethical issues evoked by easy access to online pornography*. Using the concrete

proposal discussed above – of implementing an "active choice-plus" policy that would block access to online pornography* (as well as sites promoting violence) by default, such that customers desiring access to such materials would have to opt in for such access:

A) What is your recommendation? That is, do you oppose or support the implementation of such a proposal?
B) Whatever your recommendation, what arguments, evidence, and so forth, can you offer in support of your view?
C) Given the arguments and evidence you offer, how far do these follow primarily utilitarian, deontological, and/or virtue ethics lines of argument?
D) Perspective-taking: take up one of the ethical decision-making frameworks you did not use. For example, if you found yourself arguing primarily along utilitarian lines, shift your perspective to that of a deontologist and/or virtue ethicist.

   As Ruddick's analysis exemplifies, just because you take up different ethical frameworks does not mean that you will land with different ethical conclusions. Rather, she shows how both deontological ethics and virtue ethics raise important questions about how far consumption of pornography* is an ethical good. In any case, by taking up an alternative ethical framework and applying it to the proposed "active choice-plus" policy, do you find yourself landing with a conclusion that is the same as or different from your own conclusions?
E) Especially if you should find that the alternative framework leads you to a different conclusion, you can now confront a still more difficult meta-ethical question: what arguments, evidence, and/or other kinds of warrant (including, for example, strongly positive and/or strongly negative experiences and emotions) can you offer in support of the ethical framework you prefer?

2. As we saw in the shift from the utilitarian approach to deontology and virtue ethics, a key factor in such shifts is that a given

ethical framework or analysis simply doesn't help us actually form reliable judgments and/or choose in the face of a difficult decision.

Especially if you are not satisfied with any of the approaches and outcomes that we have seen thus far – that is, they fail to capture your own ethical intuitions and approaches in one or more ways – can you articulate just what is missing and/or what is lacking here? (You may find, after this reflection, that at least some of what you consider to be missing is taken up in the next exercises.)

ADVANCED REFLECTION/DISCUSSION/WRITING EXERCISES

1. If we expand our definition of pornography* to include the forms and genres characterized as "alt porn" or "indie porn" (see Paasonen's definition, above, p. 159), again, the ethical issues become ever more complex. On the one hand, there seems to be plenty of good warrant for the view that these alternative forms of SEMs serve laudatory values and goals, including freedom of expression, creativity, exploration of potential/new forms of sexuality and sexual identities, and so on (McElroy 1995; Bromseth and Sundén 2011). At least some number of married moms find "mommy porn" – including overtly sado-masochistic novels such as *Fifty Shades of Grey* – important precisely because they find it validating sexual tastes and preferences otherwise marginalized by those around them (Mora 2012). More broadly, there is no shortage of voices in contemporary (third-wave) feminism strongly defending diverse forms of pornography* that include fine-grained details of BDSM: see, for example, "Violet Blue" and her blog titled "Tinynibbles: Open Source Sex" (www.tinynibbles.com/).

Presuming you, your cohorts, and/or your instructor are comfortable doing so, identify an example of alt porn or indie porn that would seem to work as a strong instance of how these materials, especially as they go beyond the relatively narrow genres of "tube" sites such as those discussed above, indeed serve ethically important and defensible values and norms such as creativity, freedom of expression, diversity of sexual identity and tastes, and so forth. Given this example:

A) Does it provide strong warrant not simply for the pursuit of alt porn or indie porn as, e.g., important vehicles of self-expression, exploration, and development of sexual identities and tastes, but thereby for unrestricted access to such materials online? That is: you may think that such materials are fine for adults (defined as . . .?). Are they fine for children as well?

B) If you think that some sort of restrictions might be justified regarding access to these (as well as more "mainstream" sorts of pornography*), what are your arguments, evidence, etc., for such restrictions?

C) Given the arguments and evidence you offer, how far do these follow primarily utilitarian, deontological, and/or virtue ethics lines of argument?

D) Perspective-taking: take up one of the ethical decision-making frameworks you did not use. Does this alternative framework land you with any different conclusion(s) from the one(s) you initially present and defend?

E) Especially if you should find that the alternative framework leads you to a different conclusion – again, you can now confront a still more difficult meta-ethical question: what arguments, evidence, and/or other kinds of warrant (including, for example, strongly positive and/or strongly negative experiences and emotions) can you offer in support of the ethical framework you prefer?

2. On the other hand: Susanna Paasonen (2011: 429) has noted an important ethical concern brought forward, for example, as profiles on dating sites may mimic self-presentations characteristic of various genres of pornography* – namely, the problem of self-commodification. We can put this problem this way. To begin with, how far do the models of sexually attractive bodies and actions dominating (pun intended) those genres begin to influence and perhaps dominate what "the rest of us" think and believe to be primary ways of being attractive, especially sexually attractive, to others? Insofar as this kind of influence takes place, how far are we reshaping ourselves in the image of commodities, of (more or less) interchangeable bodies to be bought and sold at market?

The (third-wave) American feminist Naomi Wolf, for example, has noted that the young women in her gym have adopted the pornography* fashion of shaving and trimming their pubic hair. Wolf argues that the upshot is a sense of sexuality among males that judges real women as less and less "porn-worthy," and a sense of sex as literally stripped of any sense of romance or mystery – i.e., the sort of reduction or impairment that Ruddick worried about (http://nymag.com/nymetro/news/trends/n_9437/, accessed December 1, 2012).

If there is a problem here, it is not one unique to self-representation on dating sites, in gyms, or in bedrooms. In addition, a number of scholars and researchers have pointed to ways in which SNSs more generally incline us to such self-commodification. Sonia Livingstone, for example, observes:

> Not only are advertisements commonly placed at the top or centre of home-pages, blogs, chat rooms and social networking sites, but also the user is encouraged to define their identity through consumer preferences (music, movies, fandom). Indeed, the user is themselves commodified insofar as a social networking profile in particular can be neatly managed, exchanged or organized in various ways by others precisely because it is fixed, formatted, and context-free. (2011: 354; cf. Fuchs and Dyer-Witheford 2012).

Echoing earlier feminist debates over pornography* as reinforcing patriarchal subordination of women and/or providing new pathways of liberation from patriarchy, beginning with the presumed norms of heterosexual sexuality – so we can inquire whether or not alt porn, indie porn, and/or other forms of pornography* online serve primarily the (high modern) ends of new forms of liberation and equality and/or encourage an ultimate form of bondage (pun intended) – that of being reduced to meat for sale in a (highly competitive) marketplace.

Given these considerations:

A) How far does it seem to you that we are increasingly pressured to "commodify" ourselves, to present a public face, profile, and/or body image and set of sexual tastes that are shaped by contemporary popular tastes and images, for the sake of selling ourselves in a competitive marketplace –

whether on a dating site, an SNS such as Facebook, and/or our real-world engagements with one another?

B) Insofar as such self-commodification is specifically influenced by online SEMs, so it would seem, as Wolf suggests, that more and more of us will think about ourselves, our bodies, and our sexualities in terms of how far they are "porn-worthy."

    i) How far does this seem to be true? That is, in your experience, does it seem that you encounter more and more examples of self-representation online that reflect some degree of effort to portray ourselves as sexually attractive in ways defined within pornographic genres – including those of alt porn or indie porn?

    ii) Especially in light of how you respond to "i)," does our self-commodification seem to you to contribute more to the (high modern) goals of equality and liberation and/or to our further being reduced to meat for sale in a (highly competitive) marketplace?

To help you reflect on this question, here are some initial responses to consider.

A supporter of alt or indie porn might argue that, insofar as such self-commodification fosters autonomy, it offers at least some people new opportunities to explore sexualities and sexual tastes otherwise marginalized in a society. This self-commodification thereby has a kind of liberatory effect. Such an argument could be bolstered with a *utilitarian* one: insofar as self-commodification along these lines leads to greater pleasure (both quantitatively – i.e., more people having more sex than they might otherwise – and qualitatively – i.e., more people having sex in ways that are more in tune with their own preferences and identity), then such self-commodification would be preferable to its absence.

By contrast, a deontologist might object that such self-commodification is rather the abdication of autonomy: as we commodify ourselves according to either mainstream or alt/indie forms of pornography, our "choices" are simply determined for us by the majority of either a mainstream or an alternative set of tastes and preferences.

Finally, a virtue ethicist would first ask how far the habits and practices we acquire and cultivate through such self-commodification represent our own judgments (*phronesis*) and thereby contribute to the cultivation of the larger set of virtues (e.g., empathy, patience, perseverance, etc.) that lead to contentment (*eudaimonia*) and community harmony. Specifically, following Ruddick, a virtue ethicist would want to know how far such self-commodification, especially along lines suggested by various pornographies, fosters our ability to regard our sexual partner (and ourselves) as an Other in the strong sense – i.e., as a unique, autonomous individual whose identity is fully interwoven with his or her body and sexuality, and so always to be treated as a complete equal and, in Kantian language, as an end-in-itself. Perhaps it goes without saying at this point, but it seems hard to square the practice of these forms of these virtues of respect for the Other as autonomous equal with the practice of seeing the other as "just meat." Insofar as the latter practice is encouraged by mainstream and/or alt or indie forms of pornographies, most especially of the BSDM sort, a virtue ethicist is likely to be highly critical of such pornographies. (See the discussion of Ruddick above, pp. 168–72, and Strikwerda's application of Ruddick to the issue of virtual child pornography, below, pp. 190–3).

C) Perspective-taking: take up one of the ethical decision-making frameworks you did not use in "B.ii". Does this alternative framework land you with any different conclusion(s) from the one(s) you initially present and defend?

D) Especially if you should find that the alternative framework leads you to a different conclusion, again, you can now confront a still more difficult meta-ethical question: what arguments, evidence, and/or other kinds of warrant (including, for example, strongly positive and/or strongly negative experiences and emotions) can you offer in support of the ethical framework you prefer?

Now: what about games?

As with the development and diffusion of all sorts of pornographies via digital media, so computer-based games have likewise dramatically evolved and developed over the past two decades. The range of games is staggering: while popular press reports (still) tend to focus because of their intense violence on so-called first-person shooter (FPS) games and massively multiplayer online role-playing games (MMORPGs) such as "World of Warcraft" – the world of computer-based games runs the gamut from dance and exercise games (especially as facilitated through the Wii and Microsoft's Kinect technologies) to serious or educational games designed to achieve specific learning outcomes. Indeed, one of the most striking applications of "gamification" – of presenting tasks and challenges within the structures, genres, and tropes of a game – was "Foldit": problems of protein folding that had defied solution for over a decade were "crowdsourced" through the game – made available globally through the Internet for a collective of interested players to take up – and solved within a day (Khatib et al. 2011). The diffusion of games, as with the diffusion of pornography*, has of course followed the diffusion of digital devices, most especially mobile phones and mobile tablets. Whether playing games such as "Farmville" or "Scrabble" with friends through Facebook, or amusing ourselves with "Angry Birds" and its thousand cousins on our mobile devices while waiting on friends or commuting, the omnipresence of computer-based games attests certainly to their increasing cultural importance. This importance should perhaps not surprise us: game scholars and researchers often hark back to the work of Johan Huizinga, who famously named us *Homo ludens* – "[hu]man the player" ([1938] 1955).

Along the way, of course, there have been casualties – or so at least critics claim. Whether fairly or not, the Columbine (Colorado) killings in 1999 were linked with the killers' affection for violent video games. Subsequent school shootings, both in the US (e.g., the Virginia Tech killings in 2007) and in Europe (Emsdetten, Germany, 2006; Jokela High School, Tuusula, Finland, 2007), were likewise linked to heavy use of violent games. More recently,

in the event many Norwegians refer to simply as "22 July," Anders
Behring Breivik killed 74 people and wounded 242 others, including 69 young people simply shot down on the island of Utøya.
Breivik acknowledged playing games such as "Modern Warfare
2" and "World of Warcraft," in part as "training" (e.g., Daily Mail
Reporter 2012). By the same token, James Holmes, dressed as the
Joker, killed twelve people and injured over sixty others during the
premiere of a new Batman movie in Colorado: media reports were
quick to allege the role of video games – even if in a somewhat
qualified fashion, as the quotation from Pat Brown at the beginning of the chapter exemplifies (CNN 2012). Not surprisingly,
these claimed linkages are hotly contested – and not without some
reason – by those who want to defend such games against media
tendencies to scapegoat both games and gamers. The issues we've
examined above – specifically, how to determine causal linkages
between consumption and use of such materials, and just what
harms and/or liberations they may foster (if any) – thus emerge
here as well.

At the same time, just as with the transformations of pornography*, the range of ethical issues affiliated with computer-based
games and the sophistication with which those issues are taken up
have likewise expanded in remarkable ways over just the last five
years. One of the most notable contributions here is the work of
Miguel Sicart, whose 2009 volume *The Ethics of Computer Games*
develops an extensive and careful analysis of the game-player as
an ethical subject. Sicart draws on phenomenology (including
the work of Barbara Becker and her notion of the body-subject
[*LeibSubjekt*], discussed above, p. 170) and virtue ethics to argue that
game-playing requires game-players to "reflect critically on what we
do in a game world during a game experience, and it is this capacity
that can turn the ethical concerns traditionally raised by computer
games into interesting, meaningful tools for creative expression, a
new means for cultural richness" (2009: 63). Contrary, then, to the
usual "moral panics" evoked by games such as "Super Columbine
Massacre RPG!" (which, as the title should indicate, puts the player
in the role of Eric Harris and Dylan Klebold, the students who
killed twelve of their classmates and a teacher before killing them-

selves at Columbine High School in 1999), Sicart sees in them critical sites for the development of ethical judgment – Aristotle's primary virtue of *phronesis* – since "players present moral reasoning, a capacity for applying ethical thinking to their actions within a game, not only to take the most appropriate action within the game in order to preserve the game experience, but also to reflect on what kind of actions and choices she is presented with, and how her player-subject relates to them" (ibid.: 101). The kind of game being played must also be taken into account: so Subrahmanyam and Šmahel summarize some research showing that "the violent aspects of MMORPGs are counterbalanced by their group-based, cooperative culture" (2011: 190). At the same time, all of this would seem to depend clearly on the particular psychology and development of the individual involved: some youth appear to be "more susceptible to aggressive content in media," and hence playing such games may put them (and the rest of us) at risk (ibid.).

Finally, there are of course multiple national and international efforts to control and regulate games somehow. These efforts vary widely, beginning with the Entertainment Software Rating Board (ESRB) in the US, which "assigns the age and content ratings for video games and mobile apps, enforces advertising and marketing guidelines for the video game industry, and helps companies implement responsible online privacy practices" (www.esrb.org/index-js.jsp). As with pornography*, video games are vociferously defended on First Amendment grounds – i.e., as invoking rights to free speech. So, for example, a California law banning the sale of violent video games to children was struck down by the US Supreme Court: such games, the Court ruled, are "subject to full First Amendment protection" (Liptak 2011). Instead, the US tends to rely on such "self-regulating" approaches – approaches that we have seen also pursued in the issue of privacy. By contrast, South Korea recognizes "game addiction" as a psychological problem, unlike the American Psychological Association, for example (Hsu et al. 2009; cf. Subrahmanyam and Šmahel 2011: 157–78). Game addiction is also taken seriously in Germany, where at least one prominent psychology professor notes that the country has the strictest regulations of games in the world as part of its approach to "youth media protection" (*Jugendmedienschutz*) (Lukesch 2012a, 2012b). Japan, as a last example, is both famous for the diverse aesthetics brought to game design and (in)famous for games such as "RapeLay" that, as the title suggests, focus on sexual violence against women.

All of this should suggest that the ethics of games deserves its own chapter (if not another book). Here, however, we will take up only a small set of the central issues – specifically those that parallel the debates we have explored surrounding pornography*. But first . . .

INITIAL REFLECTION/DISCUSSION/WRITING QUESTIONS: DON'T GET VIOLENT?

1. If you are a game-player, describe the game(s) you are familiar with and play most frequently. If you a not a gamer, describe one or more games you've watched others play regularly. Either way, what sorts of habits or excellences are required in order to play these games successfully? That is, what sorts of skills and abilities do they require and foster?

2. Given the habits, skills, etc., that you identify above, can you use one or more of the ethical frameworks we have explored to develop arguments for the playing of such games? For example, you might argue from a utilitarian framework that playing the game leads to a clear set of benefits (e.g., relaxation, harmless pleasure, improvement of certain skills, etc.) at a modest to negligible cost (e.g., the cost of the game and required equipment, one's time, etc.). Similarly, can you use one or more of the ethical frameworks we have explored to develop arguments against the playing of such games?

3. Once you've established – individually and/or as a group or class – a set of arguments pro and con, how do you respond to the debate here? That is, can you develop additional arguments, evidence, reasons, etc., that would incline the debate towards one side or another?

4. In the face of these diverse responses and perspectives on the ethical dimensions of computer games, how do you respond?

In particular, do you respond to these contrasting claims and perspectives as:

- an ethical relativist
- an ethical absolutist
- and/or an ethical pluralist?

Explain, and, more importantly, justify your response. That is, what additional reasons, evidence, grounds, etc., can you give in support of your meta-theoretical response to the first-level debates regarding computer games?

Sex and violence in games

As in the discussions concerning pornography*, there is ongoing debate as to whether or not what one does in a game – e.g., including violent and/or ethically questionable sexual acts – has any effect on one's real-world attitudes and actions. For every new study that claims to show some sort of causal linkage between game-play and players' real-world acts and attitudes, there are vociferous attacks by defenders of games and gaming – justified at least in part, as we saw in the case of pornography*, because of the extensive difficulties of demonstrating such causal linkages (e.g., Talmadge 2008).

These and related defenses of what otherwise seem to be excessive violence and violent sex in games can be captured in the phrase "it's only a game." Such defences argue, that is, that there are clear and more or less impermeable boundaries between what happens in an online and/or virtual game environment and what gamers do in the rest of their largely quite ordinary lives.

In addition, the debates we explored above regarding how far especially alt porn or indie porn serve emancipatory and/or patriarchal ends get replayed in the game context as well. In particular, as suggested by the example of the Japanese game "RapeLay," rape in computer-based games is apparently as old as the games themselves, beginning with the venerable "Dungeons and Dragons" role-playing games first instantiated on computers in the 1970s and especially popular in the MUDs and MOOs of the 1980s and 1990s. Julian Dibbell's famous "A Rape in Cyberspace" (1993) not only documented such sexual violence – but further made clear that the presumed boundary between the real and the virtual was not as solid or impermeable as some wanted to think. Rather, while the sexual assaults targeted against two of the avatars in the MOO (LambdaMOO) played out simply as textual descriptions unfolding across the screens of the avatars' real-world owners (along with those of other members of the community looking on, as it were), the sense of violation experienced by the real persons behind the assaulted avatars was sufficiently strong to evoke real tears. This, as Dibbell points out, is the flip side of more consensual forms of virtual sex: contrary to initial intuitions, he explains, virtual sex, despite its restrictions to 900 lines of text, can be as intense as any real-world encounters – perhaps even more so, "given the combined power of anonymity and textual suggestiveness to unshackle deep-seated fantasies" (Dibbell [1993] 2012: 30).

Imagine how much more powerful such experiences might be in more contemporary sound- and audio-enriched virtual worlds. For Clarisse Thorn, in fact, one of the great advantages of contemporary games is just that they can allow women – most especially those who consider themselves feminists, as she does – to explore their fantasies and alternative tastes. Specifically, Thorn points to some evidence that around one-third of women report rape fantasies, and so she argues that games and virtual worlds are valuable places for feminists interested in BDSM to hang out and explore (Thorn and Dibbell 2012).

On the other hand, Maria Bäcke's interviews with "submissives" – women who role-play as slaves to men as masters in the Second Life community of Gor – suggest that such explorations may affect the women in undesired ways (Bäcke 2011). Lastly, in her review of the game "RapeLay," Leigh Alexander states simply: "RapeLay relies on the horrendous, wildly sexist fantasy that rape victims enjoy being attacked" (2009).

SECOND REFLECTION/DISCUSSION/WRITING EXERCISE:
IT'S ONLY A GAME?

Let's begin by presuming that there is a clear line (at least for most players) between our gaming experiences and our ordinary, day-to-day lives.

1. Are there any ethical considerations that you can offer in either support or critique of the experiences of violence and (violent) sex in games such as "Grand Theft Auto"? Try to be clear here how far your considerations draw consequentialist-utilitarian, deontological, and/or virtue ethics perspectives.

2. Given some of the differences we've seen in cultural and national backgrounds as affecting prevailing attitudes towards sexuality and, now, the possible dangers as well as benefits of computer-based games, are any of your responses above in keeping and/or in tension with your own cultural/national background?

Especially if your responses are different from what we might expect or anticipate for someone with your specific cultural/national background, can you offer any reflection, set of experiences, etc., that seem to you to have played an important role in shaping your views as different from those surrounding you?

3. We've now seen – in the domain of both pornography* and computer-based games – a central debate (primarily) within feminist circles regarding whether exploration of diverse sexualities and sexual tastes and preferences (including BDSM) serve

- to help emancipate especially women from gender roles and prescribed notions of sexuality that subordinate them to the power and preferences of men, e.g., as such materials and experiences help women explore and determine for themselves their sexual identities and preferences,
  and/or
- simply to reinforce their subordination and inequality, e.g., by endorsing claims that women enjoy rape as sexist fantasies that portray them as not simply "just meat," but as enjoying such a status.

Again, both arguments agree on a central ethical norm – the especially deontological emphasis on (near) absolute respect for the autonomy of persons. The debate is, in part at least, how far the sorts of narratives found in alt porn or games such as "RapeLay" serve the autonomy especially of women.

A) Do you have (a) strong thought(s)/feeling(s)/intuition(s) regarding this debate – i.e., if forced to choose, which side you might take? If so, can you offer specific reasons, evidence (including your own experiences, both positive and negative, if you're comfortable doing so), and/or other warrants that might support your views on this debate?

B) Given your views, do they support some sorts of restrictions on such materials – e.g., filtering software intended to prevent children from accessing alt porn (and pornography* sites more generally), national legislation and enforcement systems that would rate games as appropriate to specific age groups – or no restrictions whatsoever on such materials? Explain and justify your response as best you can.

C) Is there consensus or considerable diversity of opinion and viewpoint on these matters in your class? Especially if there is considerable diversity, can you and your class, perhaps with help from your instructor(s), see any way(s) of moving forward towards resolving these differences?

Recall that we've seen three sorts of meta-ethical responses to profound ethical differences: ethical relativism, ethical monism/dogmatism, and ethical pluralism. Are any of the differences articulated in this exercise resolvable via some version of ethical pluralism – if so, what would it look like? If not, then are you comfortable with the remaining choices:

- either a relativism, which would likely threaten the basic deontological claim that human autonomy requires (near) absolute respect as a primary ethical value – i.e., one that is (more or less) universal, not relative to a given culture or time

- or a monism/dogmatism, which would insist that only one view can be correct, and any diverging views must be wrong?

4. What if it turns out that the presumed boundaries between virtual game worlds and our everyday lives are not clear and solid? What happens if, as especially virtue ethics approaches argue, what we do in such game worlds does interact with our everyday lives, insofar as we learn and practice in those worlds (as Sicart emphasizes, for example) specific habits and, perhaps, attitudes?

Presume now – if only from a virtue ethics perspective – that there are indeed crossovers between our online and/or computer-based gaming experiences and our offline lives, practices, habits, and attitudes. Given this presumption:

A) Does it change any of your responses to the questions raised above in 1–3? If so, which ones – and how?
B) In particular, especially given this presumption, where do you "draw the line" regarding which materials (whether specific forms of pornographies* and/or specific sorts of games) are generally ethically commendable (or at least ethically neutral) and which are potentially harmful, to their consumers and players and/or to those around them?

For example, Sicart points out that:

> For Aristotle, ethics and virtue are not something we have, but rather a practice – one in which we can improve. Our goal as beings trying to flourish as moral beings is to first cultivate the virtues and then develop the practical wisdom that will allow us to make virtuous choices in different situations. Similarly, playing games is a matter of maturing our capacities to create the player-subject and its moral reasoning. (2009: 103)

From this perspective, a game such as "Custer's Revenge" – which, if the player succeeds in meeting its challenges, allows him to rape a tied-up Native American woman – is to be ethically rejected. We learn nothing in playing the game, that is, that helps us flourish as moral beings – specifically, by way of cultivating specific habits and virtues, including the better practice of *phronesis* or practical wisdom. Similar arguments would seem to hold for games such as "RapeLay."

Recall that this does not mean for Sicart that all games involving violence, including rape, are necessarily beyond the pale: rather, we have seen him defend violent games such as "Grand Theft Auto" and "Super Columbine Massacre RPG!," as such games can foster the practice of *phronesis* or practical wisdom.

Using these examples as a starting point:

A) Develop with your cohorts a continuum of games familiar to you – ranging from, say "Angry Birds" and "Farmville" to games such as "Halo," "Call of Duty," etc., and games such as "RapeLay" and "Custer's Revenge."

B) Using Sicart's approach, can you identify which games indeed seem to foster the development of important habits and virtues, including the primary virtue of practical wisdom or *phronesis*, and which don't? Insofar as you can do so, you would then have a way of "drawing the line" between games that could be defended on ethical grounds, even if they include striking levels of violence and violent sex, and those that are on the other side of the line.

C) Given the line(s) that you and your cohorts draw, are you comfortable and persuaded that this/these would be useful as way(s) of offering ethically informed advice to friends and family, including younger folk, as to what games would be worth their while – and which might not? Especially if you think additional considerations need to come into play in offering such advice, articulate these as best you can.

D) Insofar as you have managed to develop what appears to be an ethically defensible set of lines regarding commendable and non-commendable games, are you comfortable and persuaded that these would further be useful as ways of developing legal guidelines for, say, age-appropriate ratings of games and/or other forms of legislation and regulation (including voluntary codes) on a national level (meaning, first of all, your country and culture of origin) and/or at an international level?

ADDITIONAL CASE STUDIES FOR REFLECTION, RESEARCH, WRITING

CASE-STUDY 1: VIRTUAL SEX?

A number of futurists have predicted the realization of a more or less complete "telepresence" within the next decade or two. This would involve a diaphanous body-suit equipped with both micro-sensors and micro-stimulators that would allow for an experience of virtual sex online. That is, the suit would both send and receive information about the movement and response of the body as represented in an online virtual world as an avatar, and as one's avatar interacted with other such avatars likewise representing online the real bodies of others. (For additional readings, see Barber 2004; Stuart 2008.)

Especially if one takes a consequentialist approach to ethics, such virtual sex could, on first blush (pun intended), dramatically change the ethics of sexuality. Specifically, if the major arguments against sex outside of marriage include warnings about the possible consequences – ranging from STDs to unwanted pregnancy – then most (but perhaps not all) such arguments evaporate with regard to virtual sex.

On the other hand, if one takes a more deontological approach – including attention, say, to promises of sexual fidelity made and thereby needing to be kept – such virtual sex would remain ethically problematic. In particular, as deontological ethics emphasizes the intentions of one's actions, the very thought of infidelity is ethically sanctioned. (So Jesus declared in his Sermon on the Mount: "'You have heard that it was said, 'You shall not commit adultery.' But I say to you that everyone who looks at a woman with lust has already committed adultery with her in his heart.'" Matthew 6.27–8, New Revised Standard Translation.)

Similarly, virtue ethics, ethics of care, and ethical frameworks that emphasize the importance of who we are in terms of the relationships we have and maintain with others might find strong reasons to condemn, say, virtual sex between strangers or multiple partners. By contrast, virtual sex between a married couple whose work and obligations keep them apart for long periods of time might be an important way of reinforcing psychological intimacy with at least a close version of physical intimacy – and hence ethically unproblematic.

REFLECTION QUESTIONS

In light of these possibilities, and/or others not elaborated here but which may be important for your ethical reflections:

1. Articulate your beliefs and values regarding sexuality – specifically, when (if ever) sexual intercourse with another person is ethically justifiable. As you do so, provide the best arguments, evidence, and/or other supporting grounds or reasons for your views that you can.

2. Consider the possibility of having a virtual sexual encounter with another person via your avatars as shared through a future, very high bandwidth connection.

(a) Offhand, under what circumstances (if any) might you consider such an encounter ethically justifiable?
(b) Under what circumstances (if any) might you consider such an encounter as ethically unjustifiable?

Again, what arguments, evidence, and/or other supporting grounds or reasons can you offer for your views?

CASE-STUDY 2: VIRTUAL CHILD PORNOGRAPHY?

As noted above, child pornography appears to stand as one of the few "bright lines" in contemporary ethical discussion. That is, such materials are criminalized more or less everywhere, as pointed out by Litska Strikwerda (2011: 141f.) But what about "virtual" child pornography – materials that are produced not with real children but with digital representations of them? Are there any ethical reasons to be critical of such materials? If so, are there strong reasons for making such materials illegal?

To explore these questions, Strikwerda examines three possible ethical and legal frameworks. She begins with John Stuart Mill's harm principle – a principle based solidly in his utilitarianism. Simply put, acts that result in more harm than pleasure thus counter utilitarian aims towards maximizing pleasure, and thus are wrong. This means, for example, that "victimless crimes," such as prostitution, cannot in fact be categorized as criminal – at least if the result is no real bodily harm, but only pleasure. By analogy (always tricky! – be careful!), if producing virtual child pornography results in pleasure for those who consume (and perhaps produce) it, but in no direct bodily harm to real children, then we have no ethical justification for criminalizing such materials (Strikwerda 2011: 144ff.).

Strikwerda then takes up paternalism – the view that society has an interest in prohibiting acts that may lead to harm of others, if not to oneself. Smokers, for example, are free to damage their own bodies and perhaps cause their own deaths through cancer, emphysema, etc., but can society prevent them from smoking in public places? Yes, insofar as their secondhand smoke, it is now demonstrated, can harm others. By analogy: what if the production, distribution, and/or consumption of virtual child pornography demonstrably leads to real-world harm – e.g., by helping pedophiles in encouraging real children to engage in sexual acts after viewing such materials, as it suggests that such acts are normal? These would be reasons to criminalize such materials, Strikwerda argues, but she goes on to point out that available evidence fails to show such a clear link between production and consumption of these materials and real-world sexual acts involving children (cf. Politiken 2012). Hence, paternalism will not justify a ban on virtual child pornography (Strikwerda 2011: 146–51).

Finally, Strikwerda draws on the analyses of Sara Ruddick and her account of "complete sex" that we examined above (Ruddick 1975) As we saw, Ruddick criticizes dualistic accounts of sexuality, ones that see "sex" as something taking place solely between bodies as somehow divorced from their "owners'" sense of unique selfhood and identity. Instead, "complete sex" is marked by a felt unity of self and body (Becker's BodySubject [*LeibSubjekt*]) and thereby fosters a (deontological) respect for the Other as a moral autonomy – followed by the virtues of equality and loving (Ruddick 1975: 98ff.).

On this view, Strikwerda argues, "it is not necessary to prove a causal link between virtual child pornographic images and actual instances of abuse to consider them as harmful" (Strikwerda 2011: 151). Rather, she finds that there is strong evidence showing that the production, distribution, and consumption of virtual child pornography are affiliated with a view of children (and women) as inferior objects to be dominated. In her phrase, these materials thus eroticize inequality (ibid.: 155). If we agree with deontological emphases on the (near) absolute rights of human beings as rational autonomies and the correlative norm of equality between persons as a virtue – i.e., one that must be practiced in our attitudes and behaviors towards others – then the production, distribution, and/or consumption of virtual child pornography appears to violate these emphases and the equality norm/virtue. For Strikwerda, such a violation justifies criminalizing virtual child pornography alongside child pornography involving real children (ibid.: 155–8).

<small>REFLECTION QUESTIONS</small>

1. In the exercise on games, above (4, p. 187), you were asked to consider if there were any sorts of games and/or pornographies* that you would argue as being "over the line." Whether you considered child pornography, much less virtual child pornography, as a candidate for consideration – on the basis of your preferred ethical framework (utilitarianism, deontology, and/or virtue ethics) – what is your first response to such materials? That is,

   (a) Do you agree that they stand on the other side of an ethical bright line, as material that must be criminalized? If so, what are your primary arguments?
   (b) If not, why not? And what are your primary arguments?

2. After reviewing this summary of three approaches to virtual child pornography,

(a) Which of these approaches prevails in your own country and culture of origin?

(b) If you believe a different approach prevails – i.e., something other than a harm principle, paternalism, and/or virtue ethics – what is that approach? How would you characterize it as an ethical framework? Does it lead to different attitudes and/or law or regulations regarding any of the materials discussed in this chapter, whether various forms of pornographies* and/or computer-based games?

3. Stuart (2008), among others, argues that, as our technologies continue to develop, we will continue to experience a blurring of what may otherwise seem to be strong boundaries between the virtual and the real. Such a blurring complicates first of all defenses of sexual violence and violence in games as "only a game." More broadly, such a blurring may mean that we will have thoroughly to rethink our ethical frameworks – especially if our primary starting points are utilitarian. That is, as the boundary between real-world harms and pleasures becomes increasingly blurred with our virtual pleasures and harms, utilitarians will have to come up with new ways of evaluating such virtual pleasures and harms, whether or not they can be shown to have any direct causal link to real-world acts.

Still more broadly, as these examples suggest, it may be that virtue ethics will become increasingly important, as it allows us to address matters of attitude and intention, at least as they intersect with virtues and habits that appear to be essential to a good life of individual contentment and community harmony. In this light, can you think of any contemporary ethical issues occasioned by our usage of digital media that you can analyze along the lines developed in this chapter? If so, which one(s)?

ADDITIONAL RESOURCES, RESEARCH SUGGESTIONS

Games and games studies have emerged over the past decade (or longer) as a separate academic discipline, one marked by an explosive growth in research topics and relevant literatures. T. L. Taylor offers an excellent overview of the field, what now amount to classic references, and future research directions:

Taylor, T. L. (2011) Internet and Games, pp. 369–83 in Mia Consalvo and Charles Ess (eds), *The Handbook of Internet Studies*. Oxford: Wiley-Blackwell.

The Games Research Network listserv (GAMESNETWORK@ uta.fi) is a primary resource in the community of researchers for posting new publications, conferences, etc. Both students and their instructors will find excellent suggestions and at least a starting list of relevant literature for research projects. Not surprisingly, the list is overwhelmingly "pro-games."

For a very dark account of the misogynist side of "gamer culture", see

Consalvo, Mia (2012) Confronting Toxic Gamer Culture: A Challenge for Feminist Game Studies Scholars, A*da: Journal of Gender, New Media and Technology*, no. 1, http://adanewmedia. org/2012/11/issue1-consalvo/ (accessed December 5, 2012).

Consalvo documents in depressing detail a hostility towards women gamers at conferences and in the online environment. After describing several examples of harassment (and worse) in the experiences of women gamers, she argues that these document "a pattern of a misogynistic gamer culture and patriarchal privilege attempting to (re)assert its position." Insofar as Consalvo is correct, it seems less than likely that games designed within such a culture would directly contribute to gender equality and women's emancipation – but this is precisely a central topic for discussion and further research. See also:

Sundén, J., and M. Sveningsson (2011) *Gender and Sexuality in Online Game Cultures: Passionate Play*. New York. Routledge.

"Gender and Computer Games," on T. L. Taylor's website, http://tltaylor.com/teaching/gender-computer-games-litera ture/, which lists additional useful resources.

MORE ON GAMES

Consalvo, Mia (2007) *Cheating: Gaining Advantage in Videogames*. Cambridge, MA: MIT Press.

Fromme, Johannes, and Alexander Unger (eds) (2012) *Computer Games and New Media Cultures: A Handbook of Digital Games Studies.* Dordrecht: Springer.

Wonderly, Monique (2008) A Humean Approach to Assessing the Moral Significance of Ultra-Violent Video Games, *Ethics and Information Technology*, 10(1): 1–10.

PORNOGRAPHY AND ALL THAT . . .

Herring, Susan C., and Anna M. Martinson (2003) Representational Bias on SexTracker, paper presented at Internet Research 4.0, Toronto, Canada, October 18.

In this pioneering analysis of the website sextracker.com, the authors use computer-mediated discourse analysis (CMDA) to examine the site vis-à-vis what they characterize as "feminist libertarian" arguments that online pornographies* could serve emancipatory ends by presenting a range of sexualities and giving users choice in their consumption of materials. What they found, however, was a "dulling sameness" of materials, overwhelmingly directed to straight male consumers, and in an environment that worked to channel users towards pay sites, rather than affording the exploratory freedoms required by the feminist libertarian arguments.

Herring and Martinson's findings are thus consistent with more recent research, beginning with Smith, Attwood, and Barker's pointing toward "tube sites" as the most popular among both men and women (2012: 5), where such sites appear to fit rather precisely the description first demarcated by Herring and Martinson.

Mowlabocus, Sharif (2007) Gay Men and the Pornification of Everyday Life, pp. 61–71 in Susanna Paasonen, Kaarina Nikunen, and Laura Saarenmaa (eds), *Pornification: Sex and Sexuality in Media Culture. Oxford and New York*: Berg.

A study of a UK gay website which finds that, contrary to their potential to expand the possibilities of sexual identity, online venues and pornography rather work to reinforce a relatively narrow sexual ideal.

Nikunen, Kaarina (2007) Cosmo Girls Talk: Blurring Boundaries of Porn and Sex, pp. 73–85 in Susanna Paasonen, Kaarina Nikunen, and Laura Saarenmaa (eds), *Pornification: Sex and Sexuality in Media Culture*. Oxford and New York: Berg.
An exploration of how far pornography shapes young girls' understandings of sexuality, etc., based on an analysis of a discussion board affiliated with *Cosmopolitan* magazine.
Smith, Clarissa (2010) Pornographication: A Discourse for All Seasons, *International Journal of Media and Cultural Politics*, 6(1): 103–8, doi: 10.1386/macp.6.1.103/3.
Smith – the lead researcher of the Porn Project referred to above (Smith et al. 2012) – offers a critical analysis of how the notions of pornification or pornographication (as in "the pornification of society" as a sometimes prominent way of attempting to discuss the impacts of pornographies* on the larger world) are used in quite diverse ways. The article thereby functions as a useful introduction to the relevant literature on the topic, as well as reinforcing the difficulty of defining "pornography" in the first place.
Stuart, Susan (2008) From Agency to Apperception: Through Kinaesthesia to Cognition and Creation, *Ethics and Information Technology*, 10(4): 255–64.
Drawing in part from cognitive psychology and neuroscience, Stuart provides an important overview of contemporary understandings of the role of the body in how we know the world and navigate through it – thereby countering a number of 1990s claims about the possibility and desirability of migrating effortlessly into cyberspace. With this as background, she introduces the possibility of a "virtual reality adultery suit" to highlight the ethical issues evoked by a blurring of traditional boundaries between the virtual and the real.

CHAPTER SIX

Digital Media Ethics: Overview, Frameworks, Resources

> Morally as well as physically, there is only one world, and we all
> have to live in it.
>
> (Midgley [1981] 1996: 119)

Chapter overview

This chapter is intended to provide especially new students of ethics
with an overview of some of the most commonly used theoretical
frameworks for ethical analysis and decision-making. We begin
with discussion (and writing exercises) regarding (1) utilitarianism
and (2) deontology. Before turning to additional theoretical frameworks, we then explore (3) important meta-theoretical frameworks
– frameworks for thinking about the theoretical frameworks. The
diversity of theoretical frameworks naturally raises questions such
as: which ones – if any – are right? And, can more than one be right?
These sorts of questions are thus the focus of the meta-theoretical
frameworks of ethical relativism, ethical absolutism [monism],
and ethical pluralism. With these meta-theoretical frameworks
in hand, we then return to additional theoretical frameworks: (4)
feminist ethics and ethics of care, (5) virtue ethics, (6) Confucian
ethics, and (7) additional perspectives – African.

Taken together, these theoretical and meta-theoretical frameworks constitute a kind of "ethical toolkit" – a collection of
important but diverse ways of analyzing and attempting to resolve
ethical problems. As we will see, part of our work as ethicists is not
simply to learn how to apply a given theoretical framework to a specific issue; given the diversity of possible theoretical frameworks,
we must also make (it is hoped, informed and well-reasoned)

choices regarding which frameworks are best suited for confronting and resolving our ethical issues – choices guided in turn by
the meta-theoretical frameworks of relativism, absolutism, and
pluralism.

A synopsis of digital media ethics

Not surprisingly, much of the ethical reflection on digital media
– most especially, on the ethical dimensions of information and
communication technologies (ICTs) – arose alongside the technologies themselves. But this means that, until the past decade or so,
most of the discussion and reflection on digital media ethics took
place primarily within Western countries, and thereby brought
into play primarily Western ethical traditions and ways of thinking.

So, for example, Terrell Ward Bynum (2000) points out that the
first book on computer ethics was written by Norbert Wiener in
1950 (*The Human Use of Human Beings: Cybernetics and Society*).
For over two decades, "computer ethics" was the concern of a very
small group of professionals – principally computer scientists and
a few philosophers. "Computer ethics" as its own term, in fact,
emerged only in the 1970s, mainly through the work of Walter
Maner but also manifest, for example, in the first professional
code of computer ethics as established by the Association for
Computing Machinery in 1973 (and subsequently revised – most
recently, in 1999). The introduction of the personal computer
(PC) in 1982, however, began a dramatic expansion of the role of
computers and computer networks into the lives of "the rest of us"
– i.e., those of us who are not computer scientists or other sorts of
information professionals such as librarians (see Buchanan and
Henderson 2008). Following the emergence of the Internet and
World Wide Web in the lives and awareness of most people in the
developed world in the early 1990s, a number of savvy observers
began (rightly) to predict that, by the beginning of the twenty-first
century, information and computing ethics (ICE) would become
a global ethics – i.e., a domain of ethical issues, debate, and possible resolution of concern to more and more people representing
an increasingly global diversity of cultural norms and ethical and

religious traditions (see Paterson 2007: 153). And in fact, in the domain of ICE, what is called "intercultural computing ethics" has been underway since the 1990s (Capurro 2005, 2008; Carbo and Smith 2008; Ess 2005).

Along the way, an important meta-ethical debate has emerged. As we have seen, digital media present us with at least three sorts of ethical challenge. First, they raise for us ethical problems already familiar from our use of more traditional media – e.g., whether or not illegally to copy a song for one's own personal use. But, second, these familiar difficulties are now sometimes accompanied by new wrinkles – e.g., the ease with which such copies can be (perfectly) made, cheaply stored, and rapidly distributed makes such copying all the more tempting than in the days of vinyl records and reel-to-reel tape machines. Third, new media may present us with distinctively new ethical problems. Perhaps most dramatically, as persons in important ways are ever more dependent on information about them (including personal identification records, banking and other financial transactions, etc.), it is by no means clear that "privacy" as understood in the modern but pre-digital era can be meaningfully sustained.

Hence a debate emerged in computer ethics as to whether or not ICE, especially as it becomes globalized, will represent (a) largely a continuation of traditional ethics, but now applied to new problems, or (b) a radical transformation of ethical thinking, as ICTs introduce us to radically new possibilities of interaction with one another, such that the ethical difficulties affiliated with these new technologies can no longer be resolved using traditional ethical frameworks and approaches (see Bynum 2000; Tavani 2013: 9–12).

For our purposes, the important point is to be aware of this larger meta-ethical question and debate as we go along. Our reflections and responses to this question will affect (and be affected by) our ethical reflections regarding other digital media.

Basic ethical frameworks

As we have seen in the opening chapter, "doing ethics" involves much more than simply picking a set of principles, values, etc., and then applying these in a largely deductive, algorithmic manner to a problem at hand. Rather, our central ethical difficulties are difficult in large measure because they require us first to determine which principles, values, frameworks, etc., in fact apply to a given problem – a determination that Aristotle famously associated with the capacity for practical judgment, or *phronesis*. Developing such judgment requires nothing less than an ongoing effort to analyze and reflect on both familiar and new experiences and problems. The good news is that our ethical judgments – at least, if we consciously seek to develop them in these ways – generally do get better over time. The somewhat daunting news is that developing such judgment is a lifetime's work, one that is in some important sense never complete or final.

Nonetheless, we must start somewhere. (As we've seen Socrates say in *The Republic*, whether we are in a swimming pool or an ocean, we must start swimming all the same.) The following material is intended to introduce you to some of the most basic and widely used frameworks for ethical reflection – beginning with characteristically Western ones, but then moving on to non-Western ones as well.

REFLECTION/DISCUSSION EXERCISE: A STUDENT DILEMMA

It's Wednesday evening, and you're packing up some books and notes to take over to a friend's apartment. You have different majors, but you are both in the same section of a required course – and tomorrow is one of two exams given during the semester; your grade on the exam will count towards 40 percent of your final grade in the course.

For you, the course is not so hard, but your friend is really struggling. You've promised to help her study this evening; you both need to get a good grade on the exam and in the course to keep your grade point average at the level required for your scholarships.

Just as you're walking out the door to go to your friend's apartment, a good friend calls you up and says that he and some of your buddies are at the local pizza place, having dinner and some beers. They'd really like you to come on over, in part because you owe them a round or two of drinks from the last time you got together. What do you do?

1. Utilitarianism

Most students in my experience approach this sort of problem in a consequentialist – perhaps even a utilitarian – way. That is, they will begin to figure out the costs and benefits of (1) turning down their buddies for pizza and beer vs. the costs and benefits of (2) fulfilling the promise to help a friend study. One of the chief advantages of this approach is that we can set up a handy table to help us keep track of the positives and negatives. An initial analysis of our choices might look like the table on p. 202.

But, of course, there are additional positive and negative consequences of our choices that may seem relevant to our decision: e.g., if I help my friend, she will do better on her exam (and, most likely, so will I); if I go have pizza and beer, I will certainly have a good time this evening but probably not do so well tomorrow on the exam. If we think further down the road, it may be that doing well on this exam will turn out to be a "make-or-break" event with regard to our success in the course: that is, should we both do well, we might subsequently end up with a better grade in the course; but, if we don't, then we might end up with less of a grade than we need in order to maintain our grade point averages for our scholarships, etc. The possible consequences even further down the road might be enormous – ranging from doing well in school more generally, moving on to a good job, etc., to (worst-case scenario) losing needed scholarships, thereby being unable to complete school, thereby failing to be able to find a good and satisfying job, etc.

You get the point. For the consequentialist, the game of ethics is about trying to think through possible good and bad consequences of possible acts, and then weighing them against one another to determine which act will generate the more positive outcome(s).

Consequentialist analysis	Possible actions	
	Fulfill promise – study with friend	Break promise – enjoy pizza and beer
Costs (negatives)	Will miss a nice evening with friends	Will disappoint a friend who's counting on your help . . . . . .
Benefits (positives)	Will be able to help a friend in an important way	Will enjoy a nice evening with friends . . . . . .

Strengths and limits

Consequentialism is certainly a tried-and-true approach to ethics: it's at least as old as Crito's efforts in the dialogue named after him to persuade Socrates to break out of jail and thereby avoid execution by the Athenians. And especially in its utilitarian form – i.e., as developed in the modern era by Jeremy Bentham and further elaborated by John Stuart Mill, both of whom argued that we must pursue those acts that bring about the greatest positive consequences (pleasure) for the greatest number – the consequentialist approach has come to dominate ethical decision-making, especially in the United States and the United Kingdom (or so some analysis suggests). Certainly, there are many cases in which consequentialism will do what we want an ethical theory to do – i.e., to help us determine which is the better choice of two (or more) possible actions.

But as this example also suggests, consequentialist approaches face serious limitations. (We will also see this to be true of every other theory we examine: after we have reviewed all the theories under discussion here, one of our questions will be to see if we can discern which theory – or, perhaps, which combination of theories – seems more sound, useful, justifiable, etc., than its competitors.) In my view, there are three important such limitations.

(a) How do we evaluate (e-valuate = place value on) the possible consequences of our acts? In simple cases, this is not a problem. Either I go get a new bus pass or I face walking to school on a cold winter day. Either I pay my phone bill or I find myself out of touch with friends and family trying to call me and send me text-messages, etc.

But the hard cases are hard in part as it's not always clear how we are to weigh the possible outcomes of one act against another.

Bentham famously thought that all possible consequences, as some form of pleasure or pain, could be evaluated in terms of their intensity and duration – for example, as part of a "hedonic calculus" (Sinnott-Armstrong 2012). Several nineteenth-century economists attempted to develop this calculus into a strictly quantitative one by introducing the notion of a "util" as a unit for measuring pleasure or pain (Baumol and Blinder 2011; Sigot 2002). Ethical decision-making would then be a strictly arithmetic matter of adding up positive and negative utils.

But what if everything cannot be measured solely in terms of pleasure or pain? What number of utils do we assign to an evening with friends, enhanced by the pleasures of food and drink? What number of utils do we assign to breaking a promise to a friend, coupled with the knowledge that our breaking that promise may lead to further, perhaps very serious consequences (= negative utils) for our friend?

As we have seen, it appears to be impossible to establish in practice a relatively standard or quasi-objective scale of pleasure and pain – physical and/or psychological – that we can thus neatly quantify in terms of utils for such a hedonic calculus. Moreover, as we will see shortly, deontologists believe that there are some aspects of human existence that cannot be assigned quantitative values. Hence both consequentialist approaches in general and utilitarianism in particular have no ethical legs to stand on: without a universal and consistent schema of positive and negative utils with which to make our calculations, the calculations at the heart of consequentialism cannot proceed. Moreover, in this case, for the deontologist, a promise is a promise; it thereby has an absolute (or near absolute) quality that means that, to break a promise, even though the promise-breaker might get great pleasure as a result of doing so (i.e., because doing so will open the door to pizza and beer), is still wrong.

But we don't have to be deontologists to recognize that there's a problem here: everything turns in consequentialism on assigning relative weights or values to given consequences, and it's simply not always clear how we are to do this.

(b) How far into the future must we consider? Ethicists helpfully distinguish between short-term and long-term consequentialists. In this example, a (really) short-term consequentialist would consider only the consequences of his or her acts over the next few hours. For most of us – at least, if we're not allergic to gluten and if our religion or physiology does not forbid alcohol – pizza and beer with friends would generate more positive utils than studying for an exam (presuming, that is, that you really do not like the subject, etc.). By contrast, extending our timeframe by 24 hours might radically change our decision: whatever the positive utils of pizza and beer, they might well not outweigh the negative utils of letting down a friend and then watching as both of us do poorly on an important exam.

And so on. It's not inconceivable that in twenty or thirty years you and your friend might look back on this exam as a key moment in your lives – one that led (in the best of circumstances) to further academic and thereby vocational success or (perish the thought) to academic failure and a lifetime of mediocre and unsatisfying jobs. The difficulty is: consequentialists and utilitarians do not appear to have a satisfying justification for telling us where in time to draw the line – the point after which we no longer need worry about the outcomes of our choices. But depending on where we draw this line can make all the difference in our calculations.

As this last point suggests, there's actually a second difficulty wrapped up in the question of how far into the future must we attempt to consider: pretty clearly, the further into the future we seek to predict, the less reliable our predictions can be. And yet, some of those future consequences may be some of the most important for us in our lives. Worst case: the chances of realizing what may potentially be the most decisive consequences of our acts become increasingly (perhaps vanishingly) small the further into the future we seek to predict those consequences. (In my experience, much of the anguish we face in ethical decisions turns on our effort to approach them in a consequentialist fashion – only to realize that we cannot be very certain at all about some of the most important possible outcomes of our actions.)

(c) For whom are the consequences that we must consider? The pizza and beer example takes into account only a small number of people. Bentham and Mill, by contrast, were far more ambitious, thinking that consequentialism would work as applied to whole societies. Up to a point, at least, this seems to be plausible. Especially in wartime, for example, generals and political leaders think in clearly consequentialist terms. Deciding to drop the atomic bombs on Hiroshima and Nagasaki, for example, were relatively easy decisions for the Allied commanders. Dropping these bombs immediately cost something like 200,000 Japanese deaths – but, as hoped, it put an end to the war. A conventional land invasion was estimated to result in around 500,000 Allied soldiers' deaths (and at least as many Japanese soldiers). At a simple assignment of one positive util per life:

- to use atomic weapons: $500,000+ / 200,000 -= 300,000 +$ utils
- not to use atomic weapons: $200,000+ / 500,000 -= 300,000 -$ utils

But what about the impact of using these weapons on those who continued to live (and die) in areas contaminated by radioactive fallout? What about the impact of using these weapons on the larger ecosystem? On future generations?

Attempting to take these possible consequences into account clearly makes the calculation much, much more complicated. Again, part of the problem is attempting to determine how far into the future we must predict relevant consequences. But the further problem is: where do I draw the line with regard to consequences affecting what group of persons/living beings/non-animate entities? As I hope is clear, depending on where I draw that line can make an enormous difference in the possible consequences of an act – and, thereby, how I decide which of two (or more) competing choices I should pursue.

In particular, as digital media radically extend the range of the possible consequences of our actions (as dramatically illustrated in the example of the cartoons of the Prophet Muhammad; Debatin 2007), the question of "consequences for whom" becomes central. Unlike commanders in war, we cannot simply assume that the consequences of our actions are limited to the citizens of a given nation-state.

In the face of these sorts of difficulties and limitations, many people find that they cannot rely on consequentialism alone. They may want to retain consequentialist approaches for certain sorts of decisions – e.g., when it is possible to make reasonably reliable predictions about the possible outcomes of our choices or when it is reasonably clear who will be affected, and within a specified timeframe. But especially when this sort of insight and information are not available, they may turn to one or more of the following ethical frameworks.

2. Deontology

For deontologists, what stands out in our opening example is that you have made a promise. And, for deontologists, promises – along with, say, notions of basic rights and duties – have an absolute quality to them, one that means that they cannot be overridden by such considerations as to how much pleasure (or pain) might be gained (or avoided) by violating them.

Religiously grounded forms of deontology are perhaps most immediately familiar to contemporary Westerners. For example, if I am a Jew, Christian, or Muslim, I believe that God has given us specific commandments and laws which define right and wrong for me – no matter the consequences. So, negatively, I am commanded not to murder, not to lie, not to covet my neighbor's property, not to commit adultery, etc. Positively, I am commanded to love God and neighbor; indeed, the Golden Rule is a commandment found in every major religious tradition around the world. Hence, a religiously grounded deontologist would believe that it is wrong to lie – even if, by lying, he or she might be able to gain significant material reward.

As a still stronger example: religious pacifists – whether rooted in Judaism and Christianity or, for example, in some forms of Buddhism – take the sacredness of life (all life for the Buddhist, not just human life) as an absolute. Hence, for pacifists, killing other human beings (and, for many Buddhists, any living thing) is always wrong – no matter the consequences. Such pacifists would not only reject the consequentialist thinking, for example, behind the decision to use atomic weapons in World War II; they would further reject the use of violence against others even in self-defense. This is to say: for the religious pacifist, killing another is always wrong, no matter the consequences – including the possible consequence of losing one's own life.

(Such pacifism, we can note, can also be supported by consequentialist considerations. Socrates, for example, argues in Plato's *Republic* and *Crito* that doing violence or harm to another has ultimately unacceptable consequences. Such harm is understood as working contrary to the central ability of reason to discern the good and the ability of judgment (*phronesis*) to determine how to enact the good properly in specific contexts and circumstances. To work contrary to these functions of reason and judgment in turn runs the risk of degrading – perhaps ultimately paralyzing or destroying – these central abilities. And, if we degrade or destroy our ability to discern the good and judge what it means, we will thereby lose our ability to make the judgments needed to pursue a genuinely good life of contentment (*eudaimonia*) and harmony. Failure to achieve these, finally, makes our lives no longer worth living. Hence, the just or good person will never harm another, no matter what sorts of other gains such harm might bring, because to do so risks making life no longer worth living (e.g., *Republic* 335b–335e).[1] However we ethically understand the pacifism of Jesus and the early Christian communities, Gandhi and Martin Luther King, Jr., famously built on these Socratic and Christian roots (and for Gandhi, at least, the Buddhist virtue of *ahimsa*, nonviolence) to argue and practice nonviolent protest against unjust laws. Such nonviolence was intended not only to prevent harm to the selves or souls of its practitioners (one consequence) but also to awaken the conscience of the larger community (a second consequence), in hopes that the larger community would come to see the injustice of its behaviors, laws, etc. (consequence 3) and then replace these with more just ones (consequence 4).)

But there are also rationalist deontologies – perhaps most importantly, the deontological ethics articulated in the modern era by Immanuel Kant (1724–1804). Kant is famous for developing what he called the Categorical Imperative – which we can think of as a kind of procedural way of determining what actions are right. Briefly (and, probably, too simply), the first formulation of the Categorical Imperative states: "So act that the maxim of your will could always hold at the same time as a principle establishing universal law" (Kant [1788] 1956: 31). We can see what this means in an initial way by using one of Kant's own examples from the *Foundations of the Metaphysics of Morals* ([1785] 1959). Consider the possibility of needing to borrow money, knowing full well, however, that you will not be able to repay the loan. You also know that, in order to get the loan, you have to promise to repay it, of course. Question: can you make what you know to be a false promise in order to secure the loan? For Kant, the maxim of this action would be: "When I believe myself to be in need of money, I will borrow money and promise to repay it, although I know I shall never do so." But the Categorical Imperative requires that we ask: "How would it be if my maxim became a universal law?" (ibid.: 40).

---

1 Plato references are to the Stephanus volume and page number.

This is perhaps recognizably close to your parents asking you in high school: what if everyone did that? But, for Kant, what is at stake in this question is whether or not the larger social order that would result from everyone following the maxim of "make a false promise when it is convenient to do so" would be coherent – or logically contradictory. On Kant's analysis, attempting to universalize this maxim would become self-contradictory in a critical way:

> For the universality of a law which says that anyone who believes himself to be in need could promise what he pleased with the intention of not fulfilling it would make the promise itself and the end to be accomplished by it impossible; no one would believe what was promised to him but would only laugh at any such assertion as vain pretense. ([1785] 1959: 40)

That is, if we knew that everyone would lie when convenient (the result of universalizing the maxim of our action), then we would never know when someone was telling us the truth. But a world in which we by default cannot trust one another to make promises in good faith – i.e., to tell the truth when we promise one another, for example, to repay a loan – would be a world in which promises would thus lose their meaning. Specifically, in this case, the attempt to lie in order to acquire a loan I have no intention of repaying becomes self-contradictory: if everyone else allows himself or herself the same act – which would result from universalizing the maxim at work here – then no one would accept my promise at the outset. But if I cannot universalize lying in this way – i.e., make it a universal law acceptable for everyone – then for Kant it is wrong, even when it seems convenient or important. That is, it is always wrong, no matter the consequences.

In our case, a Kantian analysis would be to ask the question: what sort of social/moral order would result if everyone were to break a promise whenever doing so would result in at least more immediate, short-term pleasure? It seems likely that we would never be able to trust anyone's promise – which would make promise-making self-contradictory and meaningless. Hence, breaking a promise is always wrong – no matter the consequences.

Finally, deontology is apparent in the widely shared belief that there are ethical absolutes such as human rights. The discussion and literature on rights is largely modern: so Thomas Jefferson, inspired by John Locke, insisted in the Declaration of Independence, "We hold these truths to be self-evident: that all men are created equal; that they are endowed by their Creator with inherent and unalienable Rights; that among these are Life, Liberty and the pursuit of Happiness" ([1776] 1984: 19). The belief in human rights inspired the American and French revolutions – and, subsequently, much of the political transformations that define modern Western states.

But the belief that rights exist as absolutes that must be recognized and protected is not simply a Western phenomenon. In 1948, the United Nations issued its Universal Declaration of Human Rights – a document that goes well beyond what some scholars call the first-generation or primarily negative set of rights articulated by Locke and Jefferson to include second-generation or positive rights – e.g., the rights to education and health care. These rights have been realized, for example, as duties of the state in Western Europe and Scandinavia, while the right to health care remains hotly disputed in the United States. For that, a deontological notion of basic human rights has driven much of the political activism and transformation of modernity, both within and beyond the boundaries of "the West."

We will see that the claims that human rights exist as universal values will lead to important questions regarding the role of culture in shaping our ethics – questions that become especially pressing as digital media increasingly make it possible for individuals from diverse cultures around the globe to communicate quickly and easily with one another.

Difficulties . . .

As these examples suggest, deontology is open to criticism precisely because of its absolute nature.

On the one hand, we may agree, for example, that consequentialism becomes suspect when it leads us to violate what we may take to be absolute human rights. That is, using the utilitarian mantra of "the greatest good for the greatest number," we might argue that the sacrifice of the few for the good of the many is justifiable. We certainly make this argument in wartime, when soldiers, by definition, are those whose lives are potential sacrifices for the good of the many. But, these days, we may be less sympathetic to similar arguments that could be made, for example, regarding enslavement. That is, a utilitarian might argue that, just as it would be ethically justified to sacrifice a comparatively small portion of the population (soldiers) for the sake of the greater good, so we can justify the loss of certain freedoms and rights of a few (slaves) if we can show that these costs are overridden by the greater benefits such slaves would provide for the larger society. If we wish to argue against the utilitarian at this point, we may do so by reaching for some notion of (near) absolute human rights – e.g., rights to life, liberty, and the pursuit of property.[2] If, as modern deontologists would argue, these rights exist and are (near) absolute, then they may never be violated – e.g., by turning some portion of the population into slaves – even if to do so might lead to greater pleasure and enjoyment on the part of everyone else.

Likewise, we might admire the courage of protesters – e.g., during the civil rights movement of the 1960s or in more recent political protest movements around the world – who practice the nonviolent pacifism of a Gandhi or a King, sometimes with remarkable success. If we are deontologists, we would say that they are doing the right thing – even if it costs them great personal pain, and even if they are not always successful in gaining their intended political outcomes.

But many people are not always willing to accept a Kant-like absolute not to lie, for example. Sometimes, it seems quite clear that lying would be justified – e.g., if it were to save a life, much less many lives.

Indeed, to be fair to Kant, he developed a more nuanced position in his later works, so as to make greater ethical room for deception: while we might deceive others for less than ideal reasons, as deception allows us to hide our more negative characteristics

---

2   This was Locke's original formulation; Jefferson changed it for the Declaration of Independence.

while nonetheless developing a more virtuous character, it can help us become better persons. (See Myskja 2008 for discussion and application to the question of how we develop trust online.) As Kant's own transformation suggests, whether or not deontological approaches can consistently make room for what appear to be justified and important "exceptions to the rule" is a central question for defenders of this approach.

DISCUSSION/REFLECTION/WRITING:
A FIRST GO AT ETHICAL THEORY

Given this initial overview of consequentialist vs. deontological approaches, review the initial example of promise-keeping vs. enjoying pizza and beer with friends. In particular:

A) How did you initially analyze the dilemma – i.e., more as a consequentialist and/or more as a deontologist? (As the use of the "and/or" suggests, while there are sharp differences between the two positions, it is possible for us to use both in some combination or another.)

B) Now that you've had a chance to review and explore these two frameworks, try applying them to another ethical dilemma – ideally, one affiliated with the use of digital media. In doing so,

    (i) Describe the dilemma as fully and accurately as you can.

    (ii) Explain what your own initial response to this dilemma might be. That is, what would you decide to do, and how would you decide what to do?

    (iii) Then apply each of these frameworks to the dilemma as best you can – perhaps with the help of cohorts and/or your instructor. Make clear how each framework leads to a given outcome or decision regarding possible acts or choices.

C) Given the dilemma you choose to analyze, does the consequentialist approach lead to the same ethical conclusion as a deontological approach or to a different one? Especially if the outcomes are different, which outcome more closely fits with your own initial response to this dilemma (i.e., your response in B.ii)?

D) Especially if your initial response(s) mesh(es) well with either a consequentialist and/or a deontological response, do you see any additional reasons, insights, arguments, analytical approaches, etc., offered by consequentialism and/or deontology beyond those that you initially used in approaching this problem?

What are these, and do you think that they may prove useful in approaching other ethical dilemmas as well? (In Kantian terms: can you universalize these – or are they just useful in this particular case?)

E) Especially if the outcomes of these two different approaches are different, what does this difference mean? That is, are we forced, for example, to choose between one or the other approach, such that one is always right and the other always wrong?

If you say "yes," can you justify (provide good reasons, argument, evidence for) your response?

If you say "no" – again, can you justify (provide good reasons, argument, evidence for) your response?

3. Meta-ethical frameworks:
relativism, absolutism (monism), pluralism

Ethical relativism

These contrasts between utilitarian and deontological ethics suggest, on first glance, a meta-ethical view called ethical relativism. That is, in the face of (often radically) different ethical frameworks and claims, it is tempting to believe that these differences can only mean that there are no universally valid ethical norms, values, approaches, etc. Rather, it is argued, all such norms, values, and approaches are valid only relative to (i.e., within the domain of) a given culture or group of people. Such ethical relativism is even more tempting as we gain more knowledge and experience of how people live, think, and feel in cultures different from our own – a knowledge increasingly easy to acquire in a world more and more interconnected by digital media.

Ethical relativism offers us two chief advantages. First, it allows us to tolerate the views and practices of "Others" – i.e., those who are different from ourselves. Such toleration is itself an important ethical value; generally, it seems, the world could do with much more tolerance of important ethical (and cultural) differences, not less. Second, ethical relativism offers a certain kind of relief: if values and practices are always and only legitimate in relation to a specific culture, then we are under no obligation to look further for values, practices, frameworks, etc., that might claim genuinely universal validity. This latter task is indeed very hard work – a task that is perhaps too much to ask of all but professional philosophers and ethicists. Ethical relativism gives us the excuse and rationale we need to dismiss this task.

In my view, ethical relativism enjoys a third virtue: in at least some instances, it seems to be true. For example, in Switzerland and Germany, there is a strong obligation to show respect for one's cohorts at a party by shaking hands with each of them (i.e., not only the hosts, but also all the guests) before leaving. In the United States, there is no such compunction. On the other hand, it is very common for US persons to hug one another when greeting – including (at least in my Midwestern university) colleagues. Doing so in a Germanic culture, by contrast, is almost never appropriate. At least on first glance, it appears that there is no absolute right or wrong regarding such greeting rituals. Rather, what is right in Germanic cultures often seems strange in a US context, and what is right in the US can border on the offensive in Germanic cultures.

(That said, we will see in the discussion of ethical pluralism that these differences in greeting rituals may not be quite so absolutely relative as they first appear; but, for now, it seems that we can safely say that what is right in one cultural domain is wrong in another, and vice versa.)

But ethical relativism also faces two especially important difficulties. First, it is logically incoherent – and this in two ways. To begin with, the ethical relativist faces a simple, but fundamental contradiction: on the one hand, she or he wants to argue that there are no universally valid values, norms, practices, etc.; on the other hand, she or he concludes that we must thereby be tolerant of peoples and cultures whose ethical norms and practices may be different from our own. (Just to be clear: we can get to this tolerance in other ways, as we will see below in the section on ethical pluralism.) But tolerance thereby appears to emerge as itself a universally valid ethical norm or value – i.e., one that the ethical relativist wants to say we all should agree upon and follow.

Hence, the position of ethical relativism seems caught in a fundamental contradiction: if all ethical values, norms, and practices are indeed valid or legitimate only in relation to a given culture or time, then it would seem that tolerance must likewise count as only a relative value. And so, if there are those who are rigidly intolerant on some point – e.g., the eighteenth-century white racist's intolerance for people of color – it is not at all clear how the ethical relativist can coherently insist that such a person, as a product of a given culture and time, should rather have exercised tolerance.

The second logical problem for the ethical relativist is somewhat more difficult to show and understand – but let's try. The primary argument for ethical relativism can be put as follows:

- (*Premise 1*): If there are no universally valid values, practices, beliefs, etc., then we would expect to find diverse ethical values, practices, beliefs, etc., in diverse cultures and times.
- (*Premise 2*): We do find diverse ethical values, practices, beliefs, etc., in diverse cultures and times.
- (*Conclusion*): Therefore, there are no universally valid values, practices, beliefs, etc.

In logical terms, this argument commits the basic fallacy of affirming the consequent.

To see that this argument is a fallacy, consider another argument that uses the same form as this one:

- (*Premise 1*): If you like strawberry-flavored gum, then we can expect to find a red-colored packet of gum in your pocket.

- (*Premise 2*): We do find a red-colored packet of gum in your pocket.
- (*Conclusion*): Therefore, you must like strawberry-flavored gum.

While this seems sensible enough, it takes only a little reflection to see that both the first and second premises could be true, but the conclusion must not be true: perhaps you've switched to cinnamon-flavored gum today, which also comes in a red-colored packet.

To return to the original argument: the argument is a fallacy – meaning, the conclusion does not necessary follow – because it is possible that we find diverse values, beliefs, practices, etc., in diverse cultures for other reasons besides the one offered in the first premise (i.e., that there are no universally valid values, beliefs, practices, etc.). As we will explore more fully below, the meta-ethical position of ethical pluralism argues precisely that these diverse values, beliefs, practices, etc., are the result of diverse interpretations/applications/ understandings of shared ethical norms.

The debate between ethical relativists and ethical pluralists is an open, ongoing, and important one – one that we will reflect upon further in additional reflection and writing questions. But, at this juncture, the crucial point is this: if there are plausible alternative reasons for our observing diverse practices, beliefs, norms, etc., than just the one claimed by the ethical relativist (i.e., that there are no universally valid norms in the first place), then the argument for relativism is not a valid one.

The second set of objections against ethical relativism center on the arguments that seek to show that ethical relativism can actu-ally work against the sort of tolerance and mutual understanding that it seems to endorse and that makes it so attractive. Again, this involves two elements. To begin with, ethical relativism – by design – will not let us make any sort of ethical judgment about "the Other" – i.e., the person whose values, beliefs, practices, etc., are different from our own because, it is argued, they are the product of a different culture, time, etc. But this means, for example, that those raised in the United States and the United

Kingdom can neither praise a Mother Teresa in India as a moral hero, nor condemn a Hitler in Germany as a moral monster. In this way, ethical relativism leads to a paralysis of moral judgment – a paralysis that would require us to accept, say, genocide in Rwanda, rape-rooms and rape as terror in war, the use of babies and children as carriers of explosives in suicide bombings, etc., etc. (Indeed, ethical relativism could be used to paralyze moral judgment within one's own backyard: systematic violence against women, for example, could be excused as part of the "culture" of a given religious group, even if I personally am appalled by it.)

Moreover, Mary Midgley ([1981] 1996) has argued that ethical relativism further leads to what she calls moral isolationism. On this view, we presume that there is a water-tight boundary between specific cultures. This boundary not only prevents us from making ethical judgments about the values, beliefs, practices, etc., of "the Other," but thereby suggests that the members of one culture can never learn or gain anything of value (ethical or otherwise) from the members of another culture. But the history of how diverse cultures have emerged over time – i.e., precisely through processes of intermixing and hybridization with others – shows this to be false:

> If there were really an isolating barrier, of course, our own culture could never have been formed. It is no sealed box, but a fertile jungle of different influences – Greek, Jewish, Roman, Norse, Celtic and so forth, into which further influences are still pouring – American, Indian, Japanese, Jamaican, you name it. The moral isolationist's picture of separate, unmixable cultures is quite unreal. . . . Except for the very smallest and most remote, all cultures are formed out of many streams. All have the problem of digesting and assimilating things which, at the start, they do not understand. All have the choice of learning something from this challenge, or, alternatively, of refusing to learn, and fighting it mindlessly instead. (Midgley [1981] 1996: 119)[3]

Especially as digital media dramatically accelerate these processes of encountering other cultures, we can indeed see rapid cultural change in our own day – described in part in terms of cultural hybridization and the development of "third cultures." (Such third

---

3 For a more complete summary of Midgley's arguments, see www.drury.edu/ess/values/MMidgley.html.

cultures represent an amalgamation of elements from two or more diverse cultures that come into contact with one another. So we saw in chapter 2, for example, youth in Asian countries insisting on a more Western-like individual privacy, presumably under the influence of their exposure to Western cultures through diverse media, including the Internet and the Web. The resulting sense of privacy remains marked by indigenous roots in Confucian thought, Buddhism, Thai tradition, etc., so that the resulting sense of privacy remains somewhat limited in comparison with Western conceptions. But this gives us a third culture of privacy, one that blends elements of two distinctive cultures into a unique combination that begins to take on a life of its own.) To be sure, digital media confront us with a seemingly overwhelming range of cultural diversity – thus dramatically heightening the temptation towards ethical relativism. At the same time, however, in a world increasingly interwoven precisely by digital media and computer networks, the force of Midgley's insistence, quoted at the outset of this chapter – "Morally as well as physically, there is only one world, and we all have to live in it" – is only amplified. Not surprisingly, then, the realities of contemporary cultural hybridization reinforce Midgley's argument. Insofar as ethical relativism leads to moral isolationism and a perhaps fatal paralysis of moral judgment, these logical outcomes fly in the face of what we actually do in the contemporary world: we evaluate and make judgments about those elements of cultural practices, beliefs, norms, etc., different from our own that we will accept or reject.

Ethical absolutism (monism)

At the polar extreme of ethical relativism is a position often called ethical absolutism or ethical monism. Briefly, this view insists on the following:

> There are universally valid norms, beliefs, practices, etc. – i.e., such norms, beliefs, practices, etc., define what is right and good for all people at all times and in all places.

What is often tacit or unstated for the ethical absolutist is the additional claim:

> I/we know what those norms, beliefs, practices, etc., are – completely, clearly, unequivocally.

This may seem like an odd claim to spell out, but, as we will see, this is an especially crucial element of the ethical absolutist's position. Finally, the ethical absolutist will thereby have to argue:

> Those norms, beliefs, practices, etc., that are different from the ones we know to be universally valid must therefore be wrong (evil, invalid, etc.).

In this way, the ethical absolutist is in the position both to applaud those beliefs and behaviors that agree with his or her own view of what is universally valid and to condemn those beliefs and behaviors that differ from his or her own.

Given this meta-ethical framework, the ethical absolutist enjoys at least one advantage over the ethical relativist: the ethical absolutist can coherently and forthrightly applaud or condemn the values, beliefs, practices, etc., of others – e.g., she or he could applaud a Mother Teresa in India and condemn a Hitler in Germany. At the same time, however, this leads, obviously, to the intolerance of diversity that the ethical relativist finds so distasteful and destructive (and rightly, at least up to a point).

The contrasts between the ethical relativist and the ethical absolutist usually work around what we can call first-order ethical norms, values, practices, etc. – e.g., matters of abortion and euthanasia, war and peace, sexual identity/identities and relationships, freedom of expression, our treatment of animals and the environment at large, the role of the law vs. individual conscience, etc. For example, one could take an absolutist position either for or against abortion. An ethical absolutist might hold that all life is sacred – and that the baby/fetus in the mother's womb is a sacred life that must be protected at all costs, including, unfortunately, the cost of the life of the mother in certain circumstances. And, hence, abortion is never justified, even to save the life of the mother. Another ethical absolutist might agree that all life is sacred – including that of the mother; and so, if, say, a monstrously deformed baby/fetus thereby directly threatens the life of the mother, it is morally permissible – indeed, morally required – to remove and destroy the baby/fetus for the sake of saving the mother's life. While the two absolutists will thus profoundly disagree with each other, an ethical relativist will say, in effect, to each his or her own; neither position is ultimately "right," but we should learn to tolerate important ethical differences such as these and go on.

Suffice it to say that the ethical relativist's response here will satisfy neither of our ethical absolutists. But, for our purposes, the primary point at this juncture is to move to the second-order or meta-ethical level of discussion – i.e., to apply these meta-ethical positions to the ethical frameworks of utilitarianism and deontology. Hence we can ask: how would these two positions have us respond to the differences between utilitarian and deontological approaches? (As you might guess, we will ask the same question with regard to further differences as we explore additional ethical frameworks below.)

Roughly, it would appear that the ethical absolutist would require us to accept one of these approaches – and thereby reject the other. The ethical relativist, by contrast, would likely say: it doesn't matter – neither view can claim universal validity. Indeed, it's a waste of time to wrestle with this question, since there is no ultimate right or wrong in any event – it's all a matter of culture, individual preference, etc.

REFLECTION/DISCUSSION/WRITING:
RELATIVISM AND ABSOLUTISM

I. Given the accounts of ethical relativism and ethical absolutism, which of these positions better describes your own with regard to the following (first-order) ethical claims and issues?

A) The destruction of human life – and most especially innocent human life – is always wrong; hence, abortion is never justified.

B) Our right to determine what happens to our own bodies is the most fundamental of human rights. Hence, a woman has an absolute right to determine what happens to her body – and this includes the right to abortion, especially if her own life is imperiled by a pregnancy.

C) Killing is always wrong – even in self-defense.
D) Killing is sometimes justified – beginning with self-defense.
E) You should always keep a promise.
F) Sex before marriage is morally acceptable.
G) (Suggest additional "hot-button" moral issues for discussion and reflection.)

2. In response to these – and/or other – issues, it is probable that you will find that you are an ethical relativist with regard to some and an ethical absolutist with regard to others. Insofar as this is the case, can you begin to sort out and articulate what arguments, evidence, and/or other sorts of reasons you might have for supporting your position (i.e., as either an absolutist or a relativist) vis-à-vis a given issue?

Beyond relativism and absolutism: ethical pluralism
At this point, I hope it is beginning to be clear that, whatever the strengths and advantages of both ethical absolutism and ethical relativism, neither position is fully satisfactory. To begin with, if the previous reflection and writing exercise has been successful, it should have helped you discover that – like most people in my experience – there are ethical issues about which you may be profoundly absolutist and others that seem to be best left to a sort of relativist tolerance (if not indifference).

But this is not especially coherent: ethical absolutism and ethical relativism make mutually exclusive claims – there are/are not universally valid norms, values, practices, etc. How can we coherently hold both of these claims together?

As you've likely guessed, there is a third position – ethical pluralism – that seeks to resolve some of the problems faced by relativism and absolutism.

At its most basic, ethical pluralism argues that the ethical absolutist may be right – at least with regard to his or her opening premise: there are values, norms, practices, etc., that are valid for all human beings at all time and in all places. But the pluralist quickly parts company with the absolutist on a second point: rather than insisting that there is thus a single set of values, norms, practices, etc., that apply in exactly the same way at all times and in all places, the pluralist argues that it is possible (indeed, inevitable and desirable) to interpret/understand/apply these norms in diverse ways in diverse contexts. In this way, the ethical pluralist is able to agree at least partially with the empirical observation highlighted by the ethical relativist. Obviously, we do observe that there are different practices in diverse times and cultures. But, rather than interpreting these different practices as evidence for the absence of universally valid norms and values (as the relativist's argument does – and invalidly, as we have seen), the ethical pluralist argues that these diverse practices are the result of how different contexts will require us to interpret and apply the same norm in sometimes strikingly different ways.

To use a favorite example: it is easy to observe that people with kidney disease are treated differently in different cultures and places. In the United States – at least for those who can afford good health insurance – kidney dialysis, despite its enormous expense, will be made available more or less without regard for the patient's age. By contrast, the national health-care system of the United Kingdom has set an upper age limit of 65 on patients for whom it will subsidize such treatments (Annis 2006: 310). Lastly, at least early in the twentieth century, in the harsh environment of the Canadian arctic, an elderly member of the Kabloona community who was no longer able to contribute to the well-being of the community might voluntarily commit a form of suicide (Boss 2005: 9f.; see Ess 2007).

Again, the ethical relativist will argue that these three different practices clearly show that there are no values or norms shared universally across cultures. But, for the ethical pluralist, these three practices stand as three diverse interpretations, applications, and/or judgments as to how to apply a single norm – namely, the health and well-being of the community – in three very different environments and cultures. So, at least the relatively affluent in the US can afford the health insurance that will provide kidney dialysis without age limit; but, even in a relatively wealthy nation such as the UK, failure to set limits on subsidized treatments would quickly bankrupt the nationalized health system. Finally, in the unforgiving environments of the Kabloona, the well-being of the community would be jeopardized if scarce resources were diverted to caring for those who no longer could contribute to the community. Hence, such care is literally not affordable by the community, nor, apparently, is it expected by the individual. So, the practices of each of these communities clearly differ. But, for the ethical pluralist, these different practices rest upon a basic agreement on the well-being of the community as a shared norm or value. Each practice, simply, represents a distinctive interpretation of that norm; the diverse contexts of these communities require each of them to interpret and apply that norm differently.

In this way, the ethical pluralist can agree with the ethical relativist that (a) we do observe diverse practices as we move through different cultures and times, and that (b) we should tolerate these differences – rather than condemn them straight out, as the ethical absolutist is forced to do – at least insofar as we can understand them to be different interpretations of a shared norm or value. But the ethical pluralist, unlike the ethical relativist, does not thereby tolerate any and all practices. (Recall: such tolerance entails for the ethical relativist a serious logical contradiction.) On the contrary, if a practice – e.g., genocide – can be shown to violate a basic norm or value (in this case, the well-being of the community, at least as understood as an inclusive human community rather than an exclusive tribal community), then the ethical pluralist can condemn such a practice as immoral.

And so, the ethical pluralist can overcome some of the chief difficulties of ethical relativism, including its logical incoherence and its inability to distinguish between a Mother Teresa and a Hitler. At the same time, however, the ethical pluralist shies away from the sort of intolerance for difference that often follows from ethical absolutism. To recall: the ethical absolutist seems restricted to one and only one set of values and norms that must be interpreted, applied, and practiced the same way by all people in all places and at all times – and so any variation from this one set of norms and practices must be rejected as morally wrong. (In the example of kidney dialysis, a moral absolutist located, say, in the US might then well condemn the practices of the Kabloona as immoral.) By contrast, the ethical pluralist can tolerate – indeed, endorse – these differences in practice, insofar as they can be shown to reflect diverse interpretations and applications of a shared norm or value.

In these ways, ethical pluralism seeks to take up at least a limited version of the tolerance for difference enjoined by the ethical relativist, while avoiding a tolerance so complete as to paralyze ethical judgment entirely. An ethical pluralist does so while at the same time taking up at least a limited affirmation of universally valid values, norms, and practices as endorsed by an ethical absolutist, yet avoiding the ethical monism and intolerance of difference that such absolutism easily falls into.

Strengths and limits of ethical pluralism   Ethical pluralism thus provides us with an important way of understanding and responding to the sometimes radical differences that we encounter, especially at a global level.

To put it negatively: if we can choose only between ethical relativism and ethical monism, then any effort to undertake a digital media ethics that might "work" cross-culturally would seem doomed to two equally unattractive choices: either we follow the relativist and tolerate any and all practices (saving us, it must be admitted, the difficult work of having to think about any of this at all . . .), or we adopt an absolutism that would result in a kind of ethical colonialism – i.e., the imposition of a single set of practices upon all peoples, because any difference from the right set of values and practices must be wrong.

To put it positively: ethical pluralism allows us to see – in some important cases, at least – how people in diverse cultures may share important norms and values; but, at the same time, we are able to interpret and apply these norms and values in sometimes very different sorts of practices – ones that reflect our own cultural contexts and traditions. This means that ethical pluralism allows us to have a global digital media ethics – one that provides a shared set of guidelines for how we may ethically behave in relationship with one another. But these shared norms and values are interpreted through the lenses of different traditions and applied in different cultural contexts. These different interpretations or applications thereby allow us to preserve the practices and characteristics that make each culture distinctive and unique. In this way, ethical pluralism is a crucial element of the "ethical toolkit" we need if we are to develop a global ethics that respects and preserves diverse cultural traditions and identities.

Ethical pluralism enjoys two additional strengths. First, it is a way of approaching ethical matters that is found not only within Western traditions (beginning, at least, with Plato and Aristotle, but extending into contemporary ethical frameworks such as feminism [see Warren 1990]) but also in fact throughout diverse religious and philosophical traditions such as Islam (Eickelman 2003), Confucian thought (Chan 2003), and others. This is to say that ethical pluralism appears to be a widely shared and recognized way of approaching ethical differences – not simply a provincially Western way.

Second, ethical pluralism appears in fact to "work" in contemporary practices. Perhaps the most important example here is the issue of privacy. As we have seen in chapter 2, expectations of privacy and correlative data privacy protection laws vary from country to country – in part as they rest on dramatically different, if not contradictory, understandings of human beings. But it is arguable that there is increasing recognition of a shared notion of privacy that holds for both Western and non-Western countries and cultures. This shared notion is interpreted and applied in different ways, reflecting first of all the differences between cultures in terms of the importance they place on the individual vis-à-vis the community. The diverse practices of data privacy protection thereby reflect – and, more importantly, preserve – some of the fundamental values and traditions of each culture. In this way, ethical pluralism seems to "work" as an important component of a global information and computing ethics. And so we might expect that, in other issues of digital media ethics, pluralism will likewise emerge as an important strategy for preserving cultural differences while developing a shared, genuinely global ethics.

At the same time, however, ethical pluralism will not resolve all the differences we encounter as different cultures and traditions approach the ethical issues of digital media. To use the example of the Muhammad cartoons (Debatin 2007), for at least many (though by no means all) religious believers, cartoons that can only be seen as blasphemy must not be published. For the editors of the Danish newpaper *Jyllands-Posten*, however, essential ethical and political values were at stake in commissioning and publishing the cartoons – namely, freedom of expression and freedom of the press (Warburton 2009: 18–21, 52). Add to this the cultural observation that, for most Danes, anything – even the queen – is an appropriate occasion for humor (at least, up to a point). It is by no means clear how the conflict here can be resolved in a pluralist fashion. Such an analysis would have to show that these two views are in fact not as contradictory as they appear – that they are rather simply diverse interpretations of a shared ethical norm (which one[s]?). (Additional critiques are offered by Hiruta 2006 and Capurro 2008.)

Hence, in the face of diverse cultural norms, beliefs, and practices, we will not always be able to resolve these sometimes deep and irreducible differences by way of an ethical pluralism. More broadly, then, in the face of such differences, we are obliged to discern whether we most justifiably understand and respond to these differences as an ethical relativist, an ethical absolutist, and/ or an ethical pluralist.

REFLECTION/DISCUSSION/WRITING QUESTIONS:
META-ETHICS – A FIRST RUN

As many of the examples we've explored in this book should make clear, the culture(s) which surround us, whether during our upbringing and/or in our work and leisure as mature people, play a central role in shaping our ethical thinking. (At the same time, readers should keep in mind here the important caveats and difficulties of using cultural generalizations: see chapter 2, Interlude, pp. 47–51).

In particular, the comparative ethicist Bernd Carsten Stahl notes that, since the twentieth century, at least within the English-speaking world, utilitarian approaches have dominated over alternatives. By contrast, deontological approaches – especially as rooted in Kant and then the contemporary German philosopher Jürgen Habermas – have been favored in the Germanic countries, including much of Scandinavia. These in turn contrast with what Stahl characterizes as French moralism in Montaigne and Ricoeur. On Stahl's analysis, this approach to ethics is teleological – i.e., oriented towards the goal or *telos* of discerning and doing what is necessary for the sake of an ethical and social order that makes both individual and community life more fulfilling, productive, etc., through "the propagation of peace and avoidance of violence" (Stahl 2004: 17).

As we will see more fully below, these views in turn contrast with non-Western traditions. Briefly (and somewhat misleadingly), modern Western traditions emphasize the individual as the primary agent of ethical reflection and action, especially as reinforced by Western notions of individual rights. Certainly, these traditions further recognize that individuals' actions are made within and affect a larger community; and, as we will see, there are ethical traditions in the modern West that indeed emphasize greater attention to community, not simply individual, action and good. But, at least in comparison with modern Western traditions, non-Western traditions – including various forms of Buddhism, Confucian thought, and indigenous traditions in Africa, Australia, and the Americas – lay greater emphasis on the community and community well-being as the primary focus for ethical reflection and choice.

This ethical map becomes even more complicated, first of all, as we recognize that these generalizations will only go so far: again, each cultural generalization immediately implies counterexamples, additional layers and influences, etc. The complexity grows further as we add both (a) pre-modern and contemporary ethical traditions – as we are about to see, the virtue ethics expressed by Socrates and Aristotle and its contemporary expressions – and (b) contemporary ethical frameworks such as feminism, and especially the ethics of care, along with environmental ethics.

While overwhelming at first, exploring these diverse ethical approaches is both (a) unavoidable, especially as digital media allow more and more people around the globe to communicate and interact with one another, and (b) necessary – first of all in order to overcome our own ethnocentrism and its attendant dangers. Such exploration should further help us make better-informed choices regarding our own ethical frameworks and norms – and, ideally, assist us in moving towards a more inclusive, genuinely global digital media ethics that recognizes and fosters our ethical differences alongside our shared norms and values.

At this stage, however, it may be helpful to pause to take a first run at learning how to apply the meta-theoretical positions of ethical relativism, monism, and pluralism.

1. Presuming your own prevailing cultural context(s) and/or culture(s) of origin are primarily Western, review Stahl's characterization of various national cultures as principally utilitarian, deontological, and teleological.

   A) Which, if any, of these frameworks seems closest to what you observe in your culture to be a prevailing way of making ethical decisions? Illustrate your response with an example or two – ideally, one drawn from an ethical issue evoked by the use of digital media.
   B) Which, if any, of these frameworks seems furthest away from what you observe in your culture to be a prevailing way of making ethical decisions? You can illustrate and support your response here by applying this framework to the example(s) you describe in (1.A).
   C) What are the results? That is, do the two frameworks that you identify and apply in (1.A) and (1.B) issue in conflicting ethical conclusions (e.g., undertaking otherwise illegal music downloading because the benefits of doing so seem to outweigh the costs – i.e., a utilitarian analysis – vis-à-vis rejecting such an activity because it violates what may be argued to be a just law – i.e., a deontological analysis)?
      And/or: do these two frameworks end up endorsing the same, or least coherent and complementary, ethical conclusions or claims? (For example, we saw in chapter 2 how both deontological and utilitarian approaches to privacy in the

West endorse individual privacy rights as essential – though for characteristically different reasons.)

And/or: do these two frameworks issue in (at least, seemingly) contradictory results?

D) Especially if these two frameworks issue in different, perhaps contradictory, results, how do you respond? That is: do you interpret or understand these differences primarily as

    (i)   an ethical relativist?

    (ii) an ethical monist?

    (iii) an ethical pluralist?

However you respond to these differences, do your best to support and justify your answer with one or more arguments, elements of evidence, etc.

2. The same set of questions – but now encompassing a global range of ethical frameworks – may be asked. In particular: if your cultural context(s) and/or culture(s) of origin are non-Western, so that you already have a strong familiarity with especially non-Western ethical frameworks, now might be a good time to undertake the more global version of these questions. (And/or: you and/or your instructor may decide it's better to wait on these until further review of the discussion of these frameworks that is about to follow.)

Either way, this exercise should begin by asking you to take up two frameworks – one characteristically Western (e.g., utilitarianism) and one characteristically non-Western (e.g., Confucian, Buddhist, Hindu, African, etc.). With these two frameworks as your starting point, the questions in (1) can then be pursued.

4. Feminist ethics

As the discussion so far demonstrates, virtually all of the philosophers who have developed important ethical frameworks in Western (and, as we will see, Eastern) traditions are men. Especially for the second-wave feminists of the 1960s and 1970s, this observation naturally leads to an important question: is it possible that the conceptions, approaches, values, etc., that make up prevailing ethical (and other philosophical) frameworks reflect characteristically "male" or "masculinist" ways of knowing and thinking? Or, to state it negatively: is it possible that these prevailing ethical frameworks thus tend to ignore or exclude what are characteristically women's ways of knowing and reflecting on ethical issues?

In the domain of ethics – specifically, in the area of developmental psychology concerned with how people reflect on and seek to resolve ethical difficulties – these questions were given particular force through the work of Carol Gilligan. Gilligan's landmark book *In a Different Voice* (1982) documented both important parallels and distinctive differences between the ways in which men and women characteristically approached important ethical dilemmas. Briefly put, Gilligan's interviews with women facing difficult ethical choices (including the possibility of abortion) challenged the then prevailing schema of ethical development established through the work of Lawrence Kohlberg – work that, in fact, built on observations of and interviews with men exclusively. On the one hand, for both Gilligan and Kohlberg, the evidence of their interviews and observations suggested that individuals develop their abilities to recognize and come to grips with ethical issues over time and in ways that can be described by a three-stage schema (with each stage in turn involving two sub-stages). Pre-conventional morality, describing how pre-adolescents grapple with ethical matters, works on a simple reward–punishment schema: one is "good" because good acts are rewarded, and one (usually) avoids being "bad" because bad acts are punished. Conventional morality, characteristically the moral stage of young adolescents and adults, reflects the values, practices, and expectations prevailing in the larger society, with an emphasis on justice and correlative notions of recognizing and preserving basic individual rights – at least as these contribute to the maintenance of the status quo. Post-conventional morality, by contrast, represents a move into significant sorts of ethical autonomy (in Kant's term), as individuals take conscious responsibility for their ethical principles and reflections in new ways, so as perhaps to radically critique and re-evaluate prevailing social claims regarding rights and justice. As is often the case, such reflections can lead individuals to draw new ethical conclusions regarding right and wrong that run against the prevailing morality of their larger society. Historically, such post-conventional moralists have been important for what we think of as ethical and social progress: their post-conventional morality has led them to challenge prevailing social practices and values and, in the view of subsequent generations, helped lead society more broadly to a set of values and practices that are seen as ethically preferable over earlier ones. (To be sure, as the experience of these exemplary thinkers makes clear, moving to a post-conventional stage is difficult; indeed, Kohlberg claimed that most people never move beyond the conventional stage.)

While her findings support the outlines of this large framework, Gilligan found that, as they moved through these stages, women's moral experiences demonstrated important differences. For our purposes, the most important differences are as follows. For Kohlberg (and, to be fair, for most ethicists in the modern West), the key to moving beyond conventional morality is the critical use of reason – where reason is understood to focus especially on general principles, including rules of social justice and individual rights. So a Martin Luther King, Jr., for example, can argue that segregation laws are unjust because they violate the basic principle of justice in a democracy and the modern liberal state; only those laws that rest on the consent of the governed are just. But segregation laws were passed by a white population, in states where the people of color also affected by these laws had no vote – and hence no possibility of exercising consent. Hence such laws are unjust. On the basis of such arguments, King can then justify disobeying the law of the land – in developmental terms, going beyond conventional morality to a post-conventional morality based on clear principles of justice and rights (King [1963] 1964).

To be sure, Gilligan found that women certainly employ reason – minimally, the capacity for inference and the recognition of important general principles – in confronting their ethical quandaries. But, in addition to reflection on general principles, she found that women as a group tended to make three distinctive maneuvers. To begin with, as Piaget had already observed, little girls may be less concerned than their male counterparts with making sure, for example, that all the rules of a game are followed (justice), while they may be more concerned that everyone within a given group has the feeling of being treated fairly, of being included, etc., even if this sometimes means breaking the rules (Gilligan 1982: 32–8). But this means, second, that women as a group tend to focus on the emotive dimensions of an ethical problem. Third, a problem is seen to be ethical especially as it involves a web of inter-personal relationships, not simply individuals as "nodes" in those relationships marked only by defined sets of rights, etc.

So, for example, Kohlberg asked his (male) interviewees to respond to the "Heinz dilemma." In this scenario, a husband (Heinz) needs to obtain life-saving medicine for his wife; but he cannot afford to do so, and so his pharmacist refuses to provide him with the medicine. In Kohlberg's analysis, men as a group tended to analyze this dilemma in terms of the rights and prin-ciples involved – e.g., the right of the pharmacist to protect his property (and sources of profit and livelihood) vs. the wife's osten-sible right to life. But as young women were presented with this dilemma, as a group they tended to want more information – first of all, about the relationships between the three protagonists. For example: would Heinz's wife really want him to risk going to jail for her sake? Is it possible that they could talk with the pharmacist and work out a way to pay for the drug over time (Gilligan 1982: 25–32)?

In these ways, the women's questions often teased out specific details about the possibilities and relationships in play that might otherwise be ignored through an exclusive focus on general principles of justice and abstract rights. In doing so, the women's questions may suggest alternatives to the simple, "either/or" dilemma presented at the outset – i.e., either respect the law (and lose your wife) or disobey the law (but save your wife). So, as some of my own students have suggested: if the pharmacist is a friend who knows and trusts Heinz and his wife, why couldn't he arrange for Heinz to pay for the needed drug over time, rather than insisting on an all-or-nothing payment?

For Gilligan, women's ethical development could thus be char-acterized as an ethics of care and responsibility for both others and oneself (the latter, at least, in the post-conventional stage), in contrast with (but not in opposition to) the ethics of principles, rules, and justice that characterized the ethical focus of many (but by no means all) men. Finally, Gilligan emphasized that these two patterns of ethical development, while clearly different, are not mutually exclusive. Rather, both patterns are essential – and, ideally, conjoined in a synthesis that holds both together.

Of course, there are any number of controversial and highly contested assumptions and claims at work here, as the subsequent development and debates regarding feminist ethics bring to the forefront. To stick with just one: does Gilligan's schema run the risk of essentialism – of assuming or arguing that there is something (an "essence") about being biologically female that strongly directs (or simply determines) that all women must follow the lines of ethical development it articulates? Because such essentialism risks throwing us back to gender stereotypes that have been used throughout the history of patriarchy to justify women's subordination to men, it is argued to be a mistaken assumption from the outset. And Gilligan would deny that she is making such an essentialist assumption. But it remains a very great problem for feminist theorists both to avoid such essentialism and simultaneously to seek to argue and claim that women as a group tend to think, feel, etc., in ways that are distinct and legitimate alternatives to the ways more characteristic of their male counterparts.

Despite these and related difficulties, however, Gilligan's work inaugurated important new developments in ethical theory, beginning with greater respect for the positive role of emotions – specifically, care – as developed more extensively, to begin with, by Sara Ruddick (1989) explicitly in terms of an ethics of care. To be sure, one does not have to be a feminist to take up an ethics of care: early on in the modern West, David Hume famously argued that ethical reflection is fully reducible to emotions; but, for some of us, this goes too far, especially as it runs the risk of thereby reducing all ethical claims to purely relative ones.

Despite this risk, as we will see again in the context of virtue ethics (section 5, below), there is a growing recognition from a variety of sources – feminist ethics, virtue ethics, neurobiology, and comparative philosophy more broadly – of the central roles played by emotions in ethical decision-making. For example, some evidence suggests that a lack of emotion, as resulting from certain forms of brain damage, makes it impossible for people to make ethical decisions in their daily lives. Simply put, our internal sensibilities regarding the relative ethical importance of various possible acts (i.e., how far an act or choice may be good, really good, a little evil, really evil, etc.) appear to be felt as much as they may be rationally sorted out in a kind of calculus. So, if our capacities for emotion are damaged, we are no longer able to sort through the ethical choices confronting us: "Without an affective element the agent will be unable to rank the items to be judged in order of their significance to her directly, or to her indirectly by the affect they are likely to have on those about whom she is concerned" (Stuart 2007: 144). What is striking about these turns towards recognizing the integral role played by emotions in our decision-making process is that such insights thereby point us both towards pre-modern Western understandings of our ethical life as involving both thought and feeling (e.g., in the Socratic and Aristotelian conception of *phronesis*, a practical ethical judgment that is felt as much as thought) and towards non-Western understandings – e.g., the Confucian view of the human being as incorporating *xin*, what Ames and Rosemont translate as "heart-and-mind," to make the point that "there are no altogether disembodied thoughts for Confucius, nor any raw feelings altogether lacking (what in English would be called) 'cognitive content'" (1998: 56). The role of emotions in ethics is thus a shared understanding across a literally global scale; as feminist ethics brings this role to the foreground, it thereby points towards what may be a "bridge" concept, a shared understanding between both Western and Eastern views that will play an important role in any global digital media ethics.

Moreover, in emphasizing the importance of webs of interdependent relationships, in contrast with a prevailing emphasis on individual rights, feminist ethics thereby supported and developed alongside (then) new forms of environmental or ecological ethics. Briefly, such ethics extends the modern Western focus on the rational individual human being as the primary moral agent who deserves moral status, so as to argue that non-human entities, including not only living beings but the larger ecological systems they constitute in relationship with the natural order, also deserve and require moral status and respect in our ethical reflections.

In these ways, feminist ethics helps us move to a more inclusive and comprehensive account of how we may come to grips with the ethical challenges we face.

Applications to digital media ethics

Arguably, an ethics of care is at already at work in a number of choices and behaviors associated with digital media. For example, using one's mobile phone simply to check in on friends and loved ones – "just to say 'hi'" – seems like a clear expression of care and concern, one that nicely reinforces existing relationships.

As we've also seen, for those who enjoy using digital media to copy and distribute songs, videos, etc., that they enjoy, "sharing is caring." That is, it would appear that a primary motive in such sharing is our pleasure in giving to friends and loved ones the chance to enjoy the same music and videos that we have enjoyed.

These examples, however, also highlight one of the important limitations to an ethics of care. Insofar as such an ethics stresses the importance of our emotional bonds with one another, it thereby runs the risk of restricting our ethical focus too narrowly – i.e., upon a relatively small circle of family, friends, and loved ones. Taken to its extreme, an ethics of care could thus justify our ignoring whole populations around the globe because, simply, we do not experience a relationship of care with such populations. But in a world ever more interwoven via digital media – unless these media help us learn how to care for others beyond our immediate circles – the ethics of care runs the risk of an increasingly inappropriate provincialism.

REFLECTION/DISCUSSION/WRITING QUESTIONS:
FEMINIST ETHICS AND DIGITAL MEDIA

1. Choose an important ethical dilemma concerning the use of digital media – either one that has been explicitly articulated

and addressed in this book, or one of your own choosing. (So, for example, you may recall the scenario from the beginning of chapter 3 – one that raises the possibility of stealing a desired CD from a music store. The dilemma presented there appears to be a simple either/or: either steal the CD and enjoy the music (but risk possible legal problems, including fines and jail time) or don't steal the CD and fail to enjoy the music (but avoid possible legal problems, including fines and jail time).)

A) Identify the dilemma carefully, making sure that you identify as much of the ethically relevant values, principles, etc., that you see coming into play.

B) After reviewing the account given above regarding possible contrasts between an ethics of rights/principles and an ethics of care and responsibility, does your own analysis of the dilemma you have identified tend to follow one or the other (possibly both) of these ethical approaches?

C) In particular, in your analysis, do you tend to remain with an "either/or" conflict that seems to be generated by considerations of the principles, rights, etc., that come into play here; and/or are you further inclined to want to know more specific details regarding the context of a given ethical choice – including, for example, the sorts of relationships and feelings at work?

D) Insofar as these sorts of differences emerge – perhaps in a group and/or class discussion – do they seem to be correlated with gender in the ways Gilligan has claimed? If so, what might this correlation suggest for how we think about "doing ethics"? That is, are there important differences between masculine and feminine approaches to ethics – and, if so, what is our ethical responsibility for taking these differences into consideration?

2. In my view, one of the most important contributions of feminist ethics and an ethics of care is not only that they require us to acknowledge the significance of emotions, including feelings of care, but also that they help us learn to think beyond more

dualistic, "either/or" approaches that have been emphasized in modern Western reflection and teaching about ethics. By moving towards a "both/and" logic (or logic of complementarity), in particular, we are sometimes able to see a third alternative or possibility (or more) – overlooked by more dualistic ways of thinking – that thereby may help us resolve what otherwise seem to be intractable dilemmas of the sort faced by Heinz.

These (for the modern West, new) ways of thinking, moreover, are valuable not only as they help sustain a much needed environmental ethics but, further, as such relational thinking may closely resonate with (i) contemporary non-Western ethical frameworks (explored more fully below) and (ii) especially the networked or distributed character of ICTs and other digital media linked together through the Internet and the Web.

A) Given what you are able to understand about these two different logics – a logic of dualism as based on the exclusive "either/or" and a logic of complementarity of "both/and" (discussed in chapter 1, pp. 25–7) – as you observe the larger culture around you, which of these two logics appears to be at work more predominantly than the other? Be sure to provide an example or two to help illustrate your point.

B) Identify a central issue in digital media ethics that you have already analyzed and responded to with some care in the course of your working through this volume. Review your response: do you seem to rely on one of these logics more than the other in your analyses and resolution(s) of this issues? Be sure to explain carefully how the logic you identify is apparent in your analysis/resolution.

C) After reviewing your analyses and resolution(s), insofar as they seem to rest on using one logic more than another, would they be any different in any significant ways if you were to attempt to make them using the other logic instead? If so, how? Be sure to explain carefully how this is so.

5. Virtue ethics

Virtue ethics is both ancient in the West (associated with especially Socrates and Aristotle) and global, in the sense that we find versions of virtue ethics in diverse philosophical and religious traditions around the world (including, as we will see in the next section, in Confucian and Buddhist thought). In this way, virtue ethics is an important common ground for ethicists from diverse traditions, one that has clear potential to serve as a significant component of a shared global ethics. Indeed, virtue ethics has enjoyed something of a renaissance in recent decades among Western philosophers for a number of important reasons – including precisely its potential for providing a common ethical ground for global ethics. In particular, as we explore in chapter 4, virtue ethics emphasizes the central importance of our relationships with others, beginning with friendship: it is hence an especially appropriate framework in an age of social media, as (a) our sense of selfhood appears to emphasize relationality more and more, in part as (b) our relationships – beginning with our "friends" on social networking sites – are precisely what such venues are designed to facilitate and foster.

Virtue ethics begins with the sensibility that what we ought to do as human beings is, first of all, become excellent human beings. Becoming an excellent human being, more precisely, means to develop and fulfill our most important capacities as human beings. Clearly, as individuals we may have a distinctive set of potential abilities, such as athletic or musical abilities. But, for Socrates and Aristotle, our most important abilities as human beings as such, not simply as individuals, are our capacities to reason – and this in two ways. What Aristotle (and later Kant) identified as the "theoretical" function of reason centers on what we now think of as a scientific understanding of the laws and principles that guide the workings of the physical world. For the ancient and medieval thinkers in the West, this capacity to understand reality was important on a number of grounds. In particular, by understanding reality properly, we as human beings can then "attune" ourselves to that reality: that is, we can better know both what to expect of it and how to behave within and in relationship with it, in order to achieve what the Greeks called *eudaimonia* – often translated as "happiness" but better understood as a kind of fundamental sense of well-being and contentment.

But, if our goal as human beings is to achieve such contentment or *eudaimonia*, then it is equally important that we develop what Aristotle (and, subsequently, Kant) identified as practical reason. Such practical reason involves first of all our ability – given our best knowledge of reality and thus of our possible choices and actions – to make the sorts of analyses and ethical judgments required for us to do "the right thing," both for ourselves as individuals (the ethical for Aristotle) and for our larger communities (for Aristotle, the political). As we have seen, these sorts of ethical decision-making further require what Socrates and Aristotle term *phronesis* – a practical judgment that is able to discern the right choice (or, sometimes, choices) among the possibilities before us.

This capacity for judgment, we can notice, is one that is capable of learning from its mistakes. So Socrates (as related by Plato) uses the ship's pilot and the physician in the *Republic* as primary exemplars of people who exercise such judgment, and notes:

> a first-rate pilot [*cybernetes*] or physician for example, *feels* [*diaisthanetai*] the difference between the impossibilities and possibilities in his art and attempts the one and lets the others go; and then, too, if he does happen to trip, he is equal to correcting his error. (*Republic*, 360e–361a [Plato 1991]; emphasis added; cf. *Republic* I, 332c–e; VI, 489c; X, 618b–619a/301)

And learning from mistakes means, as Aristotle emphasized, that our developing these capacities of ethical judgment and analysis, and of reason more broadly, is an ongoing task: just as the athlete or physician must constantly practice if she or he is to maintain, much less improve, his or her abilities, so we as human beings must likewise cultivate in a conscious and ongoing way our rational abilities, including our use of *phronesis*.

To put it somewhat differently: being a human being is not something that is simply given or taken for granted. Rather, becoming a human being – meaning, a being capable of (among other things) making the ethical and political judgments required for living a good ("happy") life in a community thereby marked by harmony and well-being – is an ongoing task.

Finally, it is important to emphasize that, while developing our other capacities – e.g., as athletes, musicians, lovers, friends, parents, game-players, etc. – is important, for Socrates and Aristotle it is very clear that there is nothing more important than the task of cultivating and practicing excellence as a human being – meaning, as a human being engaged with making ethical and political judgments and choices. In particular, if we subordinate our cultivation of excellence as ethical and political beings to any other activity – e.g., the pursuit of wealth or power – we thereby put our capacity for reason and ethical judgment at risk. Indeed, Socrates and Aristotle argue that, if we allow our interests in wealth and power to persuade us to judge and act against our reason and better judgment, we thereby harm these capacities (just as we would harm a race-horse, to use Socrates' analogy, by using it as a plow-horse instead). But, if we harm and thereby diminish these capacities, we thereby undermine the capacities most central to our discerning what is genuinely good, pursuing it, and thereby achieving *eudaimonia* or well-being.

This is not to say, as some later moralists argued, that we can achieve *eudaimonia* only by abstaining from the pursuit of, say, wealth and power. Rather, Socrates and Aristotle are optimistic that both *eudaimonia*, as resulting from pursuing our excellence as ethical and political beings, and (at least a moderate amount of) wealth and power can be had together. (Indeed, for Aristotle, a moderate amount of wealth and power is a necessary condition of cultivating theoretical and practical reason, and thereby of achieving *eudaimonia*.) But the constant danger is to let our interests in wealth and power overshadow our pursuit of excellence as ethical and political beings – and thereby, to paraphrase Jesus four centuries later, to gain the whole world but lose our souls.

So Socrates (again as related by Plato) says, in *The Apology*:

> It is God's bidding, you must understand that; and I myself believe no greater blessing has ever come to you or to your city than this service of mine to God. I have gone about doing one thing and one thing only,

– exhorting all of you, young and old, not to care for your bodies or for money *above* or *beyond* your souls and their welfare, telling you that *virtue* does not come from wealth, but *wealth* from virtue, even as all other goods, public or private, that man can need. (*The Apology*, 29e–30b [Plato 1892]; emphasis added)

In this way, Socrates argues for the absolute priority of human excellence over all other interests if we are to achieve *eudaimonia* or well-being, but insists thereby that our pursuit of excellence will also lead to the other human goods that we desire and need.

While deontology and consequentialism dominated much of the ethical discussion among Western philosophers in the twentieth century, within the last four decades virtue ethics has enjoyed a considerable revival. Rosalind Hursthouse nicely summarizes why: for all of their strengths, neither deontology nor consequentialism seems to address a number of topics required for a complete moral philosophy, including "moral wisdom or discernment, friendship and family relationships, a deep concept of happiness, the role of the emotions in our moral life, and the questions of what sort of person I should be" (1999: 3).

All of these elements are important, in my view; but I would highlight here that an initial strength of virtue ethics is precisely the attention it gives to the emotions. As feminist philosophers made abundantly clear in their various critiques of received Western traditions, especially the modern emphasis on reason in ethical reflection rested on a terribly destructive dualism inherited from René Descartes ([1637] 1972; [1641] 1972), one that set mind radically apart from body – and thereby from emotions. This dualism both derived from and reinforced earlier gender stereotypes – roughly, men think, women feel – that not only worked to perpetuate the subordination of women in modern societies (and their exclusion from the academy, most especially philosophy departments) but also resulted in understandings of ethical reflection that systematically ignored and denigrated the emotional. Yet it seems that we often make good and justifiable ethical decisions in part as we pay attention to our feelings – "what my gut tells me," in idiomatic American. Indeed, it seems increasingly clear that we must pay attention to emotions and feelings. Briefly, emotions are part and parcel of what it means to help or harm a human being (i.e., such help usually results in some sort of pleasure, while harm usually involves some sort of pain). Moreover, emotions appear to play a critical role in motivating us to behave ethically in the first place (Gazzaniga 2005: 167). In addition, as we saw in the discussion of emotions in the previous section on feminist ethics, there is interesting evidence to suggest that a lack of emotion – e.g., as caused by specific forms of brain damage – incapacitates moral judgment. Emotions play a crucial role in our sense of what is important and what is not – i.e., we act on the basis of a felt set of values, not simply on an intellectual calculus of comparative weights (see Stuart 2007). Finally, as we saw, this attention to emotion helps to bridge Western ethics with non-Western views, such as Confucian thought. Again, in contrast with the Cartesian mind–body split, Ames and Rosemont (1998: 56) translate *xin* as "heart-and-mind," in order to emphasize that thought and feeling always accompany each other. As in the case of feminist ethics, when virtue ethics brings to the foreground the importance of emotions in our ethical lives, it thereby points to a post-Cartesian view – one that brings Western ethics closer to at least some of its non-Western counterparts. Doing so may be an essential step in the development of a more global digital media ethics – i.e., one that "works" in both Western and non-Western cultures and traditions.

Moreover, virtue ethics, as including a focus on the development of moral judgment, thereby highlights a critical element of learning how to be human – both alone and with others: most importantly, as it is only through developing and exercising such judgment that we can claim to be autonomous and (self-)responsible human beings. Without such judgment, simply, we are likely only to follow the dictates of others.

Finally, we have seen that some modern Western ethical frameworks contrast starkly with their non-Western counterparts. Aristotle's virtue ethics, however, resonates with similar emphases on becoming an excellent or exemplary human being as a focus of one's life that are found in a number of philosophical and religious traditions around the world, including Buddhism and

Confucian thought. We will explore this more fully below, but here it is worth pointing out this resonance precisely in terms of the notions of judgment and self-correction: so Theptawee Chokvasin, for example, highlights in Buddhist thought the importance of Attasammapanidhi, "the characteristic of a person who can set herself in the right course, right direction in self-guidance, perfect self-adjustment" (2007: 78). For Chokvasin, this notion of self-guidance closely parallels modern Western notions of moral autonomy, specifically as articulated by Kant and Habermas. In addition to this important resonance with modern Western ethics, as Soraj Hongladarom and I have discussed, the Buddhist concept of Attasammapanidhi further resonates closely with the emphasis in Western virtue ethics, beginning with Socrates, on the central importance of moral judgment, especially as it allows us to take up the responsibility of choosing and guiding our actions as we navigate among the various ethical choices we face. (Socrates, in fact, expresses this point using the *cybernetes* – the pilot or steersman – as his model: cf. Hongladarom and Ess 2007: xix, xxiii, xxixf.)

Virtue ethics: sample applications to digital media

An initial way of applying a virtue ethics to digital media, as noted in the previous chapter, is to ask the question: what sort of person do I want/need to become to be content – not simply in the immediate present, but across the course of my entire (I hope, long) life? Along these lines: what sorts of habits should I cultivate in my behaviors that will lead to fostering my reason (both theoretical and practical) and thereby lead to greater harmony in myself and with others, including the larger natural (and, for religious folk, supernatural) orders?

As part of its resurgence in the contemporary West, virtue ethics has found wide application, including to such increasingly urgent topics as designing ethics for robots (e.g., Coleman 2001; cf. Beavers 2012; Hughes 2012). Perhaps most broadly, Julie Cohen (2012) draws on the work of virtue ethicist Martha Nussbaum and communitarian political philosopher Amartya Sen vis-à-vis a range of issues facing contemporary users of digital media, including copyright (chapter 3) and privacy (chapters 5, 6). We can recognize in Cohen's account of a decentered or situated self what we have explored in this volume in terms of the relational self: while not invoking virtue ethics per se, Cohen orients her analyses and recommendations towards the classic goal of virtue ethics, namely human flourishing (reflecting in part Nussbaum's role here).

In this volume, I have applied virtue ethics especially to the topic of friendship online (chapter 4) and to pornography* and sex and violence in computer games in chapter 5 (see pp. 127–33, 178, 187–8, 190–3).

REFLECTION/DISCUSSION/WRITING QUESTIONS:
THE VIRTUES OF GAMES

1. A virtue ethicist critical of violence in video games (and other forms of play) might argue that we as human beings should cultivate those feelings and behaviors that lead to greater under-standing and harmony between human beings – especially those from different cultures, who believe and act in ways sometimes strikingly different from our own. Such cultivation is not always fun: while rewarding in the long run, it is almost always hard work and time-consuming.

By contrast, the pleasure and enjoyment generated by some (but by no means all) computer games – whether in the form of first-person shooter (FPS) games played in solitude on one's own PC or game console or in the form of massively multiplayer online games such as "World of Warcraft" – derive from our focusing on the practices and skills of annihilating others (at least virtually). A critical virtue ethicist might acknowledge that playing games of this sort is ethically justifiable up to a point. But he or she is likely to make at least two arguments against an excessive use of such games. First, as with all our other choices, choosing to spend our time, energy, talents, and abilities in this particular way represents what we might think of as an "opportunity cost": that is, spending two or three hours a day on games of this sort represents the cost of two or three hours possibly spent on other activities – including those activities that might more directly foster the habits and excel-lences necessary to my becoming a more complete and content human being in community with others. Second, as playing such games reinforces both a basic fear of "the Other" – whether in the form of an alien or an enemy soldier – and my primary response to this Other as one of violence and killing, then it appears that such game-playing thereby reinforces beliefs and attitudes that do not simply supplant, but arguably work against, the cultivation of other habits and excellences that may well be more important for human development and contentment.

Taking the perspective of a virtue ethicist, can you provide additional argument, evidence, reasons, etc., that either support or contradict these claims as made by a critical virtue ethicist?

To do so might require, for example, that you consider additional habits of excellence needed for a life of contentment (*eudaimonia*) or happiness.

Then your question would be: How far does the consumption and use of video games that feature violence in the ways described above foster and/or hinder the pursuit and practice of those habits of excellence?

2. Develop (if you haven't already) a utilitarian approach to the questions of violence in games.

3. Given this more developed perspective, how do you respond to the following claims:

A) Video games are a harmless pastime, and it is only because "the media" like to focus in on them in trying to explain the acts of a few disturbed people that anyone would believe that violence in video games is some sort of threat.

B) Violence in video games demonstrably leads – in at least enough cases to be of legitimate concern to the larger society – to genuine violence and thus harm to others; hence they must be very carefully regulated in order to protect the larger society.

6. Confucian ethics

Confucian thought begins with a very different understanding of the human being than that held in modern Western theories.

Modern Western thought tends strongly to assume that human beings are "atomic" individuals – i.e., that the human being as an individual is the most basic element or component of society, one that begins and can remain in complete solitude from others. (This atomism is traceable to the English philosopher Thomas Hobbes and the French philosopher René Descartes, but that story is too long to develop here.) Henry Rosemont (2006) has characterized this as the "peach-pit" view of human beings. That is, a peach presents us with a surface – one that grows, changes, and finally dies over time. But underneath these surface changes is the peach-pit – a stony, hard core that remains (relatively) unchanged over time. The peach-pit is thus closely analogous to traditional Christian and Islamic conceptions of the soul and modern conceptions of the atomistic self. That is, underlying a surface body that grows, changes, and ultimately dies with time there is thought to be the "real" self, the identity that remains the same through time, "underneath" the outward and surface appearances of the mortal body. To be sure, this conception of the self resolves some important philosophical and ethical problems concerning identity – e.g., if there is no substantive, real self underneath the constant changes of a body, then who or what is responsible for that body's actions? That is, if the body associated with "you" committed a terrible crime five years ago, is it reasonable to say something like "that wasn't really me – I [meaning, my body] have changed and can no longer be held responsible for what I [my body] did five years ago"? Generally, in the modern West we do think that individuals remain responsible for their acts through time; thinking this way makes sense on the assumption of a "peach-pit" or atomistic self/identity that remains more or less the same over the life-course.

Such a conception of the self, however, can be understood as the result of a long development in Western societies, primarily in the last five hundred years, beginning with the Protestant Reformation. The Protestant emphasis on the individual soul and salvation is then philosophically refined and secularized in figures such as Descartes. Making real such a conception of the self further appears to depend on the wealth generated through industrialization. (As we have seen in the discussion of privacy, such a conception of the self, while initially alien to such Eastern societies as China, Japan, and Thailand, is becoming increasingly apparent – in part, as these societies develop the wealth that make individual privacy realizable, e.g., through the luxury of private rooms for children, etc.)

By contrast, in classical Confucian thought (and elsewhere, as we will see), human beings are understood first of all as relational beings: we are who we always and only as we are taken up in specific relationships with others. For me, this means that I am always and only someone's son, brother, spouse, father, uncle, friend, employee, boss, beneficiary, etc.; and how I am – i.e., my choices, attitudes, behaviors, etc. – is always shaped in specific ways by each specific relationship. And so, how I am in relationship with my parents is different from how I am in relationship with my spouse, my siblings, my own children, my students, etc. To continue with Henry Rosemont's (2006) organic metaphors, in classical Chinese thought, human beings are like onions, not peaches: each of our distinctive relationships with others – including the larger social and political communities and, finally, the natural order at large (*Tian*) – constitutes one of the multiple layers that in turn make up who we are as human beings. In contrast with the peach-pit model, however, if we remove the layers of relationship from the onion, there's nothing left.

In ways closely analogous to the virtue ethics in the West, this understanding of the human being as a relational being means that ethics is primarily about becoming a (more) complete human being – first of all, by cultivating the behaviors and attitudes required for establishing harmony both among members of the human community (beginning with the family) and with the larger order (*Tian*) as such. In classical Confucian thought, this begins with learning and practicing filial piety, respect and care for one's parents, and ritual propriety. But the ultimate aim is to become an exemplary person (*junzi*) – someone who has cultivated and practiced appropriate attention to and care for others to such a degree that this exemplary behavior is who that person is. So Confucius describes the exemplary person as follows:

> The Master said, "Having a sense of appropriate conduct (*yi*) as one's basic disposition (*zhi*), developing it in observing ritual propriety (*li*), expressing it with modesty, and consummating it in making good on one's word (*xin*): this then is an exemplary person (*junzi*)." (15.18; Ames and Rosemont 1998: 188)

The exemplary person, in short, is one who has shaped his or her basic character or disposition through the practice of appropriate conduct and ritual propriety. The primary markers of such a character are modesty and integrity.

Much as Socrates and Aristotle emphasized achieving human excellence through cultivating and practicing the right habits throughout one's lifetime, Confucian ethics emphasizes that the project of becoming an exemplary person (always in relationship with others) is a life-long project. As one of the most famous of the Analects has it,

> At fifteen my heart-and-mind was set on learning.
> At thirty my character had been formed.
> At forty I had no more perplexities.
> At fifty I realized the propensities of *tian* (*T'ian-ming*).
> At sixty I was at ease with whatever I heard.
> At seventy I could give my heart-and-mind free rein without overstepping the boundaries.
>
> (2:4; Ames and Rosemont 1998: 76f.)

This is to say, for Confucius, cultivating the virtues or excellences, beginning with filial piety, leads to a sense of harmony or resonant relationship both with other human beings and with the larger order or things – a sort of freedom and contentment that can be achieved in no other way.

And because, finally, it is believed that such ultimate freedom and contentment can be achieved only through the cultivation of excellence as a human being, we are always mistaken when we believe we will achieve happiness through other means instead, such as wealth and honor. So, just as Socrates and Aristotle later emphasized the importance of putting such human excellence first, in the same way Confucius insists that such excellence or virtue – for Confucius, following the proper *dao* or path – must always come first:

The Master said, "Wealth and honor are what people want, but if they are the consequence of deviating from the way (*dao*), I would have no part of them. Poverty and disgrace are what people deplore, but if they are the consequence of staying on the way, I would not avoid them." (4.5; Ames and Rosemont 1998: 90; see also 4.11)

Confucian ethics and digital media: example applications
We have seen that Confucian ethics is at the center of a major conflict between Western and Eastern attitudes and practices regarding copyright (chapter 3). As a reminder, within a Confucian framework, an exemplary person, as benevolent towards others, would want to share the important insights that have allowed him or her to become such a person with others who likewise seek such excellence. Hence, the text he or she produces to record such insights is seen not primarily as a matter of personal property, but rather as a gift to be given to others – one that, indeed, may work as a kind of essential toolkit for the larger life-project of becoming an exemplary person. The appropriate response of those benefiting from this gift might include copying it and giving it to others – first of all, as a mark of respect and gratitude for the work of the exemplary person. In this light, copying and distributing a text is not principally a matter of violating one's personal property as articulated in terms of copyright limitations; it is rather a matter of showing respect and gratitude for the gift of a benevolent master.

More recently, Pak Wong (forthcoming) has sought to apply Confucian thought to a range of ethical issues affiliated with Web 2.0 technologies and venues, including social networking sites. So his "Confucian Social Media: An Oxymoron?" addresses conflicts between Confucian values and those ostensibly embedded in the design of the contemporary Internet and Web. Endorsing a Confucian virtue ethics approach, Wong provides three recommendations for practices (or virtues), beginning with "A skilful engagement with social media" that includes careful use of privacy settings and techniques such as "social steganography" (so boyd 2010) for sustaining a strong sense of who one's audience is. His further recommendations – a "reinvigoration of rites in the online world" and "prioritisation of the offline world" – likewise seek to sustain Confucian virtues in our use of social media. Wong further adds two (re)design recommendations, namely "Designing contextual awareness into social media" and "(re)introduction of role responsibility into social media."

7. Additional perspectives – African

Colleagues engaged in the global dialogues on information and computing ethics represent a number of important linguistic/cultural domains – certainly Western perspectives (the US, the UK, Australia, Northern and Southern Europe, including Scandinavia) as well as Asian perspectives (including China, Japan, Thailand, India). To my knowledge, there has been comparatively less representation and participation (at least in the English-language literature) from Latin American countries (e.g., Capurro 2012). For their part, however, African thinkers have recently become more engaged in these global dialogues – sparked in part by the first African Information Ethics conference, held in Pretoria, South Africa, in February 2007.

In his opening address to the conference, Rafael Capurro (2007: 6) emphasized the importance of *ubuntu* as an indigenous philosophical tradition and framework for developing an information ethics appropriate to the African context. As we saw in an introductory way in the discussion of Open Source and FLOSS (chapter 3), *ubuntu* (as inspiring the popular Ubuntu distribution of Linux) emphasizes that we are human beings in and through our relationships with other human beings: "to be human is to affirm one's humanity by recognizing the humanity of others and, on that basis, establish humane respectful relations with them" (Ramose 2002: 644; cited in Capurro 2007: 6; cf. Capurro 2012: 120f.). While not all peoples and traditions in Africa recognize the term *ubuntu*, this notion of being human as involving an intrinsic interrelationship with and interdependence upon others is widely characteristic of African thought. So Barbara Paterson has observed that, "In African philosophy, a person is defined through his or her *relationships* with other persons, not through an isolated quality such as rationality [Menkiti 1979; Shutte 1993]" (Paterson

2007: 157; emphasis added). And just as Confucian thought, in beginning with the person as a relational being, thereby stresses interaction with the larger community (both human and natural), so, Paterson continues, in African thought, in community, "Through being affirmed by others and through the desire to help and support others, the individual grows, personhood is developed, and personal freedom comes into being" (ibid.: 158). This means that personhood is not a given, but rather an ongoing project: "African thought sees a person as *a being under construction* whose character changes as *the relations to other persons* change. *To grow older* means *to become more of a person* and more worthy of respect" (ibid.; emphasis added). Again, given this concept of the individual, engagement with the community is paramount: "The individual belongs to the group and is linked to members of the group through interaction; conversation and dialogue are both purpose and activity of the community" (ibid.).

What kind of person we are to become is articulated by no less a moral authority than Archbishop Desmond Tutu:

> A person with ubuntu is open and available to others, affirming of others, does not feel threatened that others are able and good, for he or she has a proper self-assurance that comes from knowing that he or she belongs in a greater whole and is diminished when others are humiliated or diminished, when others are tortured or oppressed. (https://help.ubuntu.com/10.04/about-ubuntu/C/about-ubuntu-name.html)

In other terms, *ubuntu* involves the project of acquiring and practicing certain virtues, including a strong sense of interconnectedness with one's larger community and the states and fates of others in that community – in part as this contributes to the virtue of "proper self-assurance."

It would appear, then, that African traditions closely parallel both Confucian thought and Aristotelian virtue ethics, beginning with their shared emphasis on the individual human being as first of all engaged with the larger human (and natural) communities for the sake of both individual and community harmony and flourishing. Hence, Confucian and Aristotelian approaches may provide helpful analogues for African thinkers as they explore and develop their own forms of information and computing ethics. But this exploration and development are just now emerging, and it will be very interesting to see where they take African philosophers and users of digital media – both for their own sake, and for the sake of the larger global dialogue regarding ICE and digital ethics more generally.

REFLECTION/DISCUSSION/WRITING QUESTIONS:
ETHICS AND META-ETHICS

Now that you have reviewed a global range of ethical frameworks, review one or two of the specific issues/cases of digital media ethics that you have analyzed and perhaps resolved with some care in the course of working through this volume.

1. Which of the ethical frameworks that we have now explored, i.e.,

- utilitarianism
- deontology
- feminist ethics/ethics of care
- virtue ethics
- Confucian ethics
- African ethics

seem(s) to have been most in play in your reflections and decision-making? Explain your response here with some care, making clear for yourself (and your reader, if applicable) how your analyses and resolutions fit the patterns and approaches of a given ethical framework.

2. Choose a framework that seems very far away from your own ethical starting points (identified in (1)). Take up this same ethical issue and, as best you can, provide an analysis and resolution of the issue using this alternative framework. How far are the results similar to and/or different from the results using your original ethical theory/theories?

3. How do you respond to these differences? That is, given what we've now learned about

- ethical relativism
- ethical monism/absolutism
- ethical pluralism

which of these three meta-ethical frameworks are you most likely/able to apply to any differences that may emerge between the analyses and resolutions you have developed in (1) and (2)?

FOR FURTHER READING, RESEARCH

ETHICAL THEORIES

There is an enormous number of excellent textbooks that provide a more extensive introduction to and analysis of the ethical frameworks discussed here. If you are interested in learning more about these sorts of theories, the following will be useful:

Boss, Judith A. (2005) *Analyzing Moral Issues* (3rd edn). Boston: McGraw-Hill.

Boss's text is exemplary for its introduction of various issues and approaches in ethics, with an especially strong emphasis on their application to current, real-world issues.

Hinman, Lawrence M. (2008) *Ethics: A Pluralistic Approach to Moral Theory* (4th edn). Belmont, CA: Wadsworth.

In addition to providing excellent overviews of basic theoretical frameworks such as utilitarianism (Hinman's chapter 5), deontology (chapter 6), and virtue ethics (chapter 9), Hinman's text is useful for pursuing the meta-theoretical issues raised in this chapter regarding relativism, absolutism, and pluralism (his chapters 2 and 9; in the latter, he helpfully connects pluralism with Aristotle's virtue ethics and notion of *phronesis* – see esp. 285–8). Moreover, Hinman's "Ethics Updates" – http://ethics.sandiego. edu/ – is one of the most comprehensive and genuinely useful online resources for both theoretical and applied ethics.

Hursthouse, Rosalind (1999) *On Virtue Ethics*. Oxford: Oxford University Press.

——(2012) Virtue Ethics, *Stanford Encyclopedia of Philosophy* (summer 2012 edn), ed. Edward N. Zalta, http://plato. stanford.edu/archives/sum2012/entries/ethics-virtue/ (accessed December 16, 2012).
Hursthouse provides a useful overview of the re-emergence of virtue ethics in recent decades, along with discussion of current approaches and issues.
Thomson, Anne (1999) *Critical Reasoning in Ethics: A Practical Introduction.* London: Routledge.
This is one of the most accessible and genuinely practical approaches to logic and critical thinking in ethics for the non-specialist (meaning, first of all, students and faculty outside the field of philosophy) that I have seen.
Yu, Jiyuan (2007) *The Ethics of Confucius and Aristotle: Mirrors of Virtue.* New York: Routledge.
Provides one of the most complete comparisons and contrasts between these two major forms and traditions of virtue ethics.

INFORMATION AND COMPUTER ETHICS *(ICE)*

Because computers and then computer networks were among the earliest digital technologies, much of the extant reflection and literature on ethics and digital media is constituted by information and computing ethics. The literature, accordingly, is huge. Here are simply a few recommendations for further reading:
Himma, Kenneth Einar, and Herman T. Tavani (eds) (2008) *The Handbook of Information and Computer Ethics.* Hoboken, NJ: Wiley.
An authoritative survey of foundational issues, methodological frameworks, and their applications in key foci (e.g., privacy, intellectual property, security), along with major sections on professional ethics, responsibility issues and risk assessment, regulatory issues, and access and equity issues.
Weber-Wulff, Debora, Christina Class, Wolfgang Coy, Constanze Kurz, and David Zellhöfer (eds) (2009) Gewissensbisse: Ethische Probleme der Informatik [Pricks of Conscience: Ethical Problems of Informatics]. Bielefeld: transcript.

This explores central problems evoked by biometric technologies, data protection issues, and matters of intellectual property. It is accompanied by a frequently updated website – http://gewissens bits.gi.de/ – that offers current case studies and analyses.

Tavani, Herman T. (2013) *Ethics and Technology: Ethical Issues in an Age of Information and Communication Technology* (4th edn). Hoboken, NJ: Wiley.

One of the single most comprehensive and clear books in this domain, especially useful for teaching, as it includes an extensive array of real-world case-studies.

van den Hoven, Jeroen, and John Weckert (eds) (2008) *Information Technology and Moral Philosophy*. Cambridge: Cambridge University Press.

An essential collection of philosophically sophisticated analyses of a wide range of issues and topics in ICE by some of its most significant and well-known figures. It nicely complements the Himma and Tavani *Handbook* by providing more specialized articles.

INTERCULTURAL INFORMATION ETHICS

Capurro, Rafael (2008) Intercultural Information Ethics, pp. 639–65 in Kenneth Einar Himma and Herman T. Tavani (eds), *The Handbook of Information and Computer Ethics*. Hoboken, NJ: Wiley.

Capurro coined the term "intercultural information ethics" (IIE) and here provides a masterful overview of the growing field of literature, topics, traditions, and approaches. See also Capurro (2012), especially pp. 119–20, for an overview of Information Ethics in Latin America.

Nakada, Makoto (2012) Robots and Privacy in Japanese, Thai and Chinese Cultures: Discussions on Robots and Privacy as Topics of Intercultural Information Ethics in "Far East," pp. 478–92 in Michele Strano, Herbert Hrachovec, Fay Sudweeks, and Charles Ess (eds), *Cultural Attitudes Towards Technology and Communi-cation 2012*. Murdoch, Western Australia: Murdoch University, www.catacconference.org/ (accessed December 19, 2012).

Nakada, Makoto, and Rafael Capurro (2009) The Public/Private Debate: A Contribution to Intercultural Information Ethics, pp. 335–53 in Rocci Luppicini and Rebecca Adell (eds), *Handbook of Research on Technoethics*. Hershey, PA: IGI Global.

Stahl, Bernd Carsten (2006) Emancipation in Cross-Cultural IS [Information Systems] Research: The Fine Line between Relativism and Dictatorship of the Intellectual, *Ethics and Information Technology*, 8(3): 97–108.

Stahl (2004) has developed his own framework for information ethics in cross-cultural contexts, one resting especially on the procedural approaches highlighted in the work of Jürgen Habermas. Here, Stahl explores ways of avoiding cultural imperialism while nonetheless advocating emancipation as a central ethical goal and norm. His article is usefully read in conjunction with that by Wheeler below.

ETHICAL RELATIVISM AND PLURALISM

Brey, Philip (2007) Is Information Ethics Culture-Relative?, *Journal of Technology and Human Interaction*, 3(3): 12–24.

Brey – also known for his development of an approach to information ethics he denotes as "disclosive ethics" – works through in considerable detail how (and, if so, how far) we may move beyond ethical and cultural relativism.

Ess, Charles (2007) Cybernetic Pluralism in an Emerging Global Information and Computing Ethics, *International Review of Information Ethics*, 7 (September), www.-i--r--i--e.net/inhalt/007/11-ess.pdf (accessed September 23, 2008).

An extensive review of ethical pluralism in information and computing ethics, including more detailed attention to both Confucian and African contexts.

Floridi, Luciano (2007) Global Information Ethics: The Importance of Being Environmentally Earnest, *Journal of Technology and Human Interaction*, 3(3): 1–11.

Floridi – the author of a widely influential framework for information and computing ethics – takes up here the specific challenges of cultural diversity to a global ICE. He argues specifically for an ethical pluralism in the form of what he calls a "lite" information ontology.

Hiruta, Kei (2006) What Pluralism, Why Pluralism, and How? A Response to Charles Ess, *Ethics and Information Technology*, 8(4): 227–36.

Hiruta responds to my earlier effort to sketch out a particular version of ethical pluralism – namely, a *pros hen* or focal pluralism as based on Aristotle (Ess 2006). While generally sympathetic to the project, Hiruta helpfully notes some important weaknesses and potential alternatives.

Wheeler, Deborah (2006) Gender sensitivity and the drive for IT: Lessons from the NetCorps Jordan Project, *Ethics and Information Technology*, 8(3): 131–42.

Wheeler is one of the most prolific ethnographers of women and IT in the Middle East. Here she highlights an approach to an ICT4D (ICT for Development) project in Jordan and its differential impacts on women and men. Arguably, the introduction of IT in this project has led to a form of emancipation for women in Jordan, but one that is understood pluralistically – i.e., one that retains and preserves some of the essential differences defining local culture(s) in particular and Arab-Islamic cultures more broadly.

See also discussion of Mackenzie (2008) in the last "Advanced topics" section below: Mackenzie's account of relational autonomy includes a "value pluralism".

FEMINIST APPROACHES TO DIGITAL MEDIA ETHICS

Adam, Alison (2005) *Gender, Ethics and Information Technology*. New York: Palgrave MacMillan.

Includes introductory chapters on ethics, computer ethics, and issues of gender, and then applies these to problems of "Internet Dating, Cyberstalking and Internet Pornography" (chapter 6), "Hacking into Hacking: Gender and the Hacker Phenomenon" (chapter 7), and "Someone to Watch Over me – Gender, Technologies, Privacy and Surveillance" (chapter 8).

Adam, Alison (2008) The Gender Agenda in Computer Ethics, pp. 589–619 in Kenneth E. Himma and Herman T. Tavani (eds),

The Handbook of Information and Computer Ethics. Hoboken, NJ: Wiley .

Provides a critical review of current accounts of women's and men's decision-making, underlining the need for better theorizing concerning gender. Adam highlights cyberstalking and hacker ethics as important areas for feminist analysis and points towards a cyberfeminism that conjoins political goals, subversion, and playfulness as dimensions of feminist ethics and the ethics of care that would help further develop a feminist computer ethics.

van der Velden, Maya (2009) Design for a Common World: On Ethical Agency and Cognitive Justice, *Ethics and Information Technology*, 11(1): 37–47. doi: 10.1007/s10676-008-9178-2.

Uses a feminist critique of positivist understandings of technology and science as ethically neutral, in order to develop an alternative notion of moral agency as distributed among interconnected designers, the technologies they design, and the users of these technologies.

Such feminist approaches, finally, often overlap with the final advanced topic, below.

ADVANCED TOPICS IN APPLIED ETHICS:
DEVELOPING A DIGITAL MEDIA ETHICS ON THE BASIS OF
AFRICAN THOUGHT

The first African Information Ethics conference in 2007, mentioned above, resulted in a significant collection of essays and reflections – both from within more prevailing Western frameworks and from within distinctively African perspectives. Review the papers contributed to the *International Review of Information Ethics* for Volume 7 (www.i-r-i-e.net/issue7.htm). It is strongly recommended that you begin with Rafael Capurro's opening address (2007), but in the listing for the first fifteen papers you will no doubt see others that will also provide distinctive introductions to African frameworks and issues in ICE.

ADVANCED TOPICS IN APPLIED ETHICS:
EMERGING NOTIONS OF RELATIONAL SELFHOOD AND
DISTRIBUTED MORALITY

As we have seen, the (high modern) ethical frameworks of utilitarianism and deontology begin with assumptions of the moral agent as primarily an individual – in Kantian terms, a rational autonomy – such that responsibility for our choices and actions lies squarely with us as individual beings. This emphasis on a primarily individual moral self, however, contrasts with earlier emphases globally on the more relational aspects of selfhood and identity. Specifically, the (more) relational self underlies the ethical traditions we've explored here of Buddhist, Confucian, and African societies. At the same time, Western moral thought has turned more and more towards relational conceptions of selfhood, perhaps most explicitly in feminist and virtue ethics, as well as in Habermasian notions of communicative reason and identity as "from the start interwoven with relations of mutual recognition" and a correlative requirement "to preserve both the integrity of individual persons and the web of interpersonal relations in which their identities are formed and maintained" (McCarthy [1978] 1981: 47). Finally, as we explored especially in chapter 2 in conjunction with changing notions of privacy, it is arguable that these changing notions of privacy in "Western" societies – i.e., away from more individual and exclusive privacy towards more relational and inclusive notions, e.g., of group privacy – in part index precisely a shift towards more relational understandings of selfhood.

Review one or more of the resources listed below, with a view towards

A) articulating and defining more carefully your own sense of selfhood and identity – i.e., as more relational or more individual and/or as more emotive or more rational – and thereby

B) how far you (and your larger communities) may need to shift from a more individual sense of ethical responsibility towards a more distributed sense of responsibility (as has been characteristic previously of "Eastern" societies and traditions) *or* from a more distributed sense of responsibility (if you are, say, from a society historically shaped by Buddhist, Confucian, or African traditions, for example) towards a more individual sense of responsibility. And thereby

C) what these shifts might mean for how ethical agency and responsibility should be understood and evaluated in our usages of digital media – perhaps beginning with the examples suggested by Floridi (2012) as starting points for reflection.

Christman, John (2011) Autonomy in Moral and Political Philosophy, *Stanford Encyclopedia of Philosophy* (spring 2011 edn), ed. Edward N. Zalta, http://plato.stanford.edu/archives/spr2011/entries/autonomy-moral/.

Provides a useful overview of diverse notions of autonomy, especially as critical to (high modern) ethical and liberal political theory. A brief section (3.3) on relational autonomy provides a useful introduction.

Mackenzie, Catriona (2008) Relational Autonomy, Normative Authority and Perfectionism, *Journal of Social Philosophy*, 39(4): 512–33.

Mackenzie is a leading expositor of a feminist understanding of relational autonomy. Here she refines her earlier accounts to offer a "weak substantive, relational approach to autonomy that grounds an agent's normative authority over decisions of import to her life in her practical identity and in relations of intersubjective recognition" (p. 512) – in part as such autonomy is central to a life of flourishing, i.e., the overriding focus of a virtue ethics (p. 529).

For parallel considerations, compare with Julie Cohen's account of the "decentered" or situated self (2012) – in our terms, a relational self – and her correlative re-evaluations of central issues including privacy (chapter 6).

Ess, Charles (2012) At the Intersections Between Internet Studies and Philosophy: "Who Am I Online?," *Philosophy and Technology*, doi: 10.1007/s13347-012-0085-4.

This introduces a recent special journal issue conjoining both philosophical and Internet Studies approaches to our senses of selfhood and identity in both online and offline contexts. The intro-duction summarizes the articles making up the special issue and then connects them to larger contexts and philosophical problems.

Hongladarom, Soraj (2011) Pervasive Computing, Privacy and Distribution of the Self, *Information*, 2(2): 360–71.

Hongladarom is one of the foremost theorists and expositors of Buddhist approaches to ethical matters involving new tech-nologies. This article continues some of his earlier explorations of Buddhist conceptions of selfhood, as perhaps changing in "Western" directions, vis-à-vis specific expectations and practices of privacy.

Floridi, Luciano (2012) Distributed Morality in an Information Society, *Science and Engineering Ethics*, doi: 10.1007/s11948-012-9413-4.

Floridi describes what distributed morality "looks like," as ethical responsibility is increasingly diffused across our networks of communication – both among diverse human agents (includ-ing infrastructure and program designers) and among artificial agents (AAs) and multi-agent systems (MASs). He offers several positive examples of distributed agency and responsibility, such as "the Shopping Samaritan" (whose purchases of RED prod-ucts benefits AIDs victims in Africa) and forms of "Socially Oriented Capitalism," namely, "Peer-to-Peer Lending". He then addresses some of the major difficulties facing these (relatively) new conceptions.

Simon, Judith (2013) Distributed Epistemic Responsibility in a Hyperconnected Era, pp. 135–51 in Stefana Broadbent et al.

Simon conjoins important recent work in distributed notions of knowing, including that of Lucy Suchman and Karen Barad, in order to clarify what we mean by notions of (epistemic) agency, accountability and responsibility.

Wong, Pak (2012) Dao, Harmony and Personhood: Towards a Confucian Ethics of Technology, *Philosophy and Technology*, 25(1) 67–86, doi: 10.1007/s13347-011-0021-z.

Wong's article here nicely supplements the one referred to above, applying specifically to social media, as it provides a more general introduction and discussion of basic Confucian concepts and how they may contribute to a specifically Confucian ethics of technology.

See also Cohen (2012) and Papacharissi (2012) for attention to "the networked self."

Glossary

Affirming the consequent: a common logical fallacy (invalid argument). Formulaically, the argument looks like this: A → B (If A is true, then B is true). B (B is true). Therefore A (A is true).

CMC: computer-mediated communication – e.g., email and list-servs, chat, videoconferencing, etc., all of which depend upon both computers and computer networks to function.

Copyleft: a range of schemes for protecting authors' rights to their work, but in ways that are less restrictive with regard to how others may take up such work, as compared with prevailing copyright frameworks. Primary examples of such copyleft schemes are the GNU Free Documentation License and the Creative Commons Licenses.

Cyberbullying: using various communicative venues (e.g., message boards on a MySpace or Facebook profile, email, etc.) to attack and intimidate another person.

Cyberstalking: using the Internet and/or other digital media (e.g., "buddy-locators" on cellphones) to stalk or harass a person.

Exclusive or: "Either one or the other – but not both." More formulaically: either A may be true or B may be true, but both A and B may not be true at the same time.

While the exclusive or describes many relationships properly (e.g., a standard light may be on or off, but not both), when applied to contexts and examples that in fact admit of a third possibility (or more), it then becomes a false dichotomy. It is noted in this volume because of its prevalence in media reporting fostering "moral panics."

Flaming: sending especially aggressive, insulting, hostile messages, sometimes anonymously or under a pseudonym. Flaming sometimes results in "flame-wars" – intensively hostile exchanges between a few members of a listserv or other online group. Such flame-wars, in turn, can destroy online communities, as they make further participation in the listserv too unpleasant and insufficiently rewarding to be justified.

FLOSS: Free/Libre/Open Source Software (see chapter 3, pp. 94–7).

F2F: "face-to-face": direct (face-to-face) conversation/ communication, in contrast to communication mediated through such information and communication technologies as cellphones, text-messaging, email, etc.

ICTs: information and communication technologies.

Inclusive or: "Either one or the other – possibly both." More formulaically: either A may be true or B may be true, or both A and B may be true at the same time.

Internet: the Internet (perhaps more accurately, a global collection of internets) is made up of computer networks based upon a standardized collection of machine communication protocols – clustered around the TCP (Transmission Control Protocol)/IP (Internet Protocol) suite.

The World Wide Web – familiar to most users in the form of webpages accessed through browsers such as Windows Explorer, Mozilla Firefox, and others – may be considered a subset of the Internet, one built upon HTML (Hypertext Mark-up Language) coding that facilitates moving quickly from any one page to another (wherever such pages may be located on a given computer/server) in the form of links.

Questionable analogy: an analogy argument compares two (or more) examples/cases/contexts in order to conclude that what is accepted as true in a first example/case/context should be true of the second, because of the relevant *similarities* between the two. But if, upon analysis, one or more relevant *differences* between the two cases can be pointed out, then the analogy is *questionable* and the conclusion is not warranted. It is more idiomatically thought of as "comparing apples and oranges."

Trolling: a troll joins a listserv or other online community with the intention of attracting attention to himself or herself, his or her ideas, favorite theories, etc., and thereby taking over the communicative bandwidth of the group. Trolls may not always intend to be destructive, but they are infamously so, especially for groups that are comparatively vulnerable and/or populated by relatively new users of CMC. See Herring et al. (2002).

World Wide Web: see "Internet."

References

Abramson, Jeffrey, Christopher Arterton, and Gary Orren (1988) *The Electronic Commonwealth: The Impact of New Media Technologies on Democratic Politics*. New York: Basic Books.

ACM (Association for Computing Machinery) (1999) *Software Engineering Code of Ethics and Professional Practice*, www.acm.org/about/se-code (accessed December 16, 2012).

Adams, Carol J. (1996) "This Is Not Our Fathers' Pornography": Sex, Lies, and Computers, pp. 147–70 in Charles Ess (ed.), *Philosophical Perspectives on Computer-Mediated Communication*. Albany: State University of New York Press.

Albrechtslund, A. (2008) Online Social Networking as Participatory Surveillance, *First Monday*, 13(3), http://firstmonday.org/article/view/2142/1949 (accessed November 14, 2012).

Alexander, Leigh (2009) And You Thought Grand Theft Auto Was Bad: Should the United States Ban a Japanese "Rape Simulator' Game? *Slate*, March 9, www.slate.com/articles/technology/gaming/2009/03/and_you_thought_grand_theft_auto_was_bad.html?GT1=38001 (accessed December 1, 2012).

Ames, Roger, and Henry Rosemont, Jr. (1998) *The Analects of Confucius: A Philosophical Translation*. New York: Ballantine Books.

Annis, Joseph (2006) *Reports of Council on Medical Service* (American Medical Association), www.ama-assn.org/resources/doc/hod/a-06cms.pdf (accessed February 10, 2013).

AoIR (Association of Internet Researchers) Ethics Working Group (2002) *Ethical Decision-Making and Internet Research: Recommendations from the AoIR Ethics Working Committee*, www.aoir.org/reports/ethics.pdf (accessed February 10, 2012).

Article 29 Data Protection Working Party (2012a) *Opinion 04/2012 on Cookie Consent Exemption* (00879/12/EN WP 194), http://ec.europa.eu/justice/data-protection/article-29/documentation/opinion-recommendation/files/2012/wp194_en.pdf (accessed December 19, 2012).

—(2012b) *Opinion 08/2012 providing Further Input on the Data Protection Reform Discussions* (01574/12/EN WP199), http://ec.europa.eu/justice/data-protection/article-29/documentation/opinion-recommendation/files/2012/wp199_en.pdf (accessed December 18, 2012).

Bäcke, Maria (2011) Make-Believe and Make-Belief in Second Life Role-Playing Communities, *Convergence: The International Journal of Research into New Media Technologies*, 18(1): 85–92, doi: 10.1177/1354856511419917

Barber, Trudy (2004) A Pleasure Prophecy: Predictions for the Sex Tourist of the Future, pp. 322–36 in Dennis D. Waskul (ed.), *net.seXXX: Readings on Sex, Pornography, and the Internet*. New York: Peter Lang.

Baron, Naomi (2008) *Always On: Language in an Online and Mobile World*. Oxford: Oxford University Press.

Baumol, William J. and Alan S. Blinder (2011) *Economics: Principles and Policy* (12th edn). Mason, OH: South-Western Cengage Learning.

Baym, Nancy (2011) Social Networks 2.0, pp. 384–405 in Mia Consalvo and Charles Ess (eds), *The Handbook of Internet Studies*. Oxford: Wiley-Blackwell.

BBC News (2012a) Automatic Bar on Net Porn Considered, June 28, www.bbc.co.uk/news/uk-politics-18616909 (accessed November 28, 2012).

—(2012b) Phone Hacking: Accused Protest their Innocence, July 24, www.bbc.co.uk/news/uk-18972742 (accessed November 17, 2012).

Beavers, Anthony (2012) Moral Machines and the Threat of Ethical Nihilism, pp. 333–44 in Patrick Lin, Keith Abney, and George A. Bekey (eds), *Robot Ethics: The Ethical and Social Implications of Robotics*. Cambridge, MA: MIT Press.

Bechmann, Anja, Charles Ess, and Anne Marit Waade (under review) Studying Locative Mobile Media: Analytical Framework, Communicative Functions and Ethics.

Becker, Barbara (2001) The Disappearance of Materiality?, pp. 58–77 in V. Lemecha and R. Stone (eds), *The Multiple and the Mutable Subject*. Winnipeg: St. Norbert Arts Centre.

Benhabib, Seyla (1986) *Critique, Norm, and Utopia: A Study of the Foundations of Critical Theory*. New York: Columbia University Press.

Bizer, Johann (2003) Grundrechte im Netz: Von der freien Meinungsäußerung bis zum Recht auf Eigentum, pp. 21–9 in Christiane Schulzki-Haddouti (ed.), *Bürgerrechte im Netz*. Bonn: Bundeszentrale für politische Bildung, www.bpb.de/files/FPQOF9.pdf (accessed September 23, 2008).

Bleaney, Rob (2012) Amanda Todd: Suicide girl's Mum Reveals More Harrowing Details of Cyber Bullying Campaign that Drove her Daughter to her Death. *Daily Mirror*, October 15, www.mirror. co.uk/news/world-news/amanda-todd-suicide-girls-mum-1379909 (accessed December 18, 2012).

Boss, Judith (2005) *Analyzing Moral Issues* (3rd edn). Boston: McGraw-Hill.

Bowell, Tracy, and Gary Kemp (2005) *Critical Thinking: A Concise Guide* (2nd edn). London: Routledge.

boyd, danah (2010) Social Steganography: Learning to Hide in Plain Sight, Digital Media and Learning blog, 23 August, http://dmlcentral. net/blog/danah-boyd/social-steganography-learning-hide-plain-sight (accessed December 16, 2012).

boyd, danah, and Alice Marwick (2011) Social Privacy in Networked Publics: Teens' Attitudes, Practices, and Strategies, pp. 1–29 in Proceedings of the "A Decade in Internet Time: OII Symposium on the Dynamics of the Internet and Society, " 21–4 September 2011, University of Oxford, http://papers.ssrn.com/sol3/papers. cfm?abstract_id=1925128 (accessed 9 April 2013).

Briggs, Asa, and Peter Burke (2005) *A Social History of the Media* (2nd edn). Cambridge, and Malden, MA: Polity.

Broadbent, Stefana, Nicole Dewandre, Charles Ess, Luciano Floridi, Jean-Gabriel Ganascia, Mireille Hildebrandt, Yiannis Laouris, Claire Lobet-Maris, Sarah Oates, Ugo Pagallo, Judith Simon, May Thorseth, and Peter-Paul Verbeek (2013) The Onlife Initiative. Brussels: European Commission, https://ec.europa.eu/digital-agenda/sites/ digital-agenda/files/Onlife_Initiative.pdf (accessed March 15, 2013).

Bromseth, Janne, and Jenny Sundén (2011) Queering Internet Studies: Intersections of Gender and Sexuality, pp. 270–99 in Mia Consalvo and Charles Ess (eds), *The Handbook of Internet Studies*. Oxford: Wiley-Blackwell.

Buchanan, Elizabeth, and Kathrine Andrews Henderson (2008) *Case Studies in Library and Information Science Ethics*. Jefferson, NC: McFarland.

Burk, Dan (2007) Privacy and Property in the Global Datasphere, pp. 94–107 in Soraj Hongladarom and Charles Ess (eds), *Information Technology Ethics: Cultural Perspectives*. Hershey, PA: Idea Group Reference.

Bynum, Terrell Ward (2000) A Very Short History of Computer Ethics, *Newsletter on Philosophy and Computers* (American Philosophical Association), http://southernct.edu/organizations/rccs/a-very-short-history-of-computer-ethics (accessed November 21, 2012).

Capurro, Rafael (2005) Privacy: An Intercultural Perspective, *Ethics and Information Technology*, 7(1): 37–47.

—(2007) Information Ethics for and from Africa, *IRIE International Review of Information Ethics*, 7(09), www.i-r-i-e.net/inhalt/007/01-capurro.pdf (accessed February 10, 2013).

—(2008) Intercultural Information Ethics, pp. 639–65 in Kenneth Einar Himma and Herman T. Tavani (eds), *The Handbook of Information and Computer Ethics*. Hoboken, NJ: Wiley.

—(2012) Intercultural Aspects of Digitally Mediated Whoness, Privacy and Freedom, pp. 113–22 in Johannes Buchmann (ed.), *Internet Privacy: Eine multidisziplinäre Bestandsaufnahme/A Multidisciplinary Analysis*. Berlin: Deutsche Akademie der Technikwissenschaften, www.acatech.de/de/publikationen/publikationssuche/detail/artikel/internet-privacy.html (accessed December 18, 2012).

Carbo, Toni, and Martha M. Smith (2008) Global Information Ethics: Intercultural Perspectives on Past and Future Research, *Journal of the American Society for Information Science and Technology*, 59(7): 1111–23, http://onlinelibrary.wiley.com/doi/10.1002/asi.20851/full (accessed December 16, 2012).

Carey, James (1989) *Communication as Culture: Essays on Media and Society*. Boston: Unwin Hyman.

Chan, Joseph (2003) Confucian Attitudes towards Ethical Pluralism, pp. 129–53 in Richard Madsen and Tracy B. Strong (eds), *The Many and the One: Religious and Secular Perspectives on Ethical Pluralism in the Modern World*. Princeton, NJ: Princeton University Press.

Cheong, Pauline Hope, Judith N. Martin, and Leah P. Macfadyen (2012) *New Media and Intercultural Communication: Identity, Community and Politics*. Oxford: Peter Lang.

Chokvasin, Theptawee (2007) Mobile Phone and Autonomy, pp. 68–80 in Soraj Hongladarom and Charles Ess (eds), *Information Technology Ethics: Cultural Perspectives*. Hershey, PA: Idea Group Reference.

Clifford, Stephanie (2009) Teaching Teenagers about Harassment, *New York Times*, January 26, www.nytimes.com/2009/01/27/business/media/27adco.html?ref=meganmeier&_r=0 (accessed December 5, 2012).

CNN (2012) Massacre at Batman Premier, CNN transcripts, July 20, http://transcripts.cnn.com/TRANSCRIPTS/1207/20/cnr.01.html (accessed December 2, 2012).

Cohen, Julie E. (2012) *Configuring the Networked Self: Law, Code, and the Play of Everyday Practice*. New Haven, CT: Yale University Press, www.juliecohen.com/page5.php (accessed December 16, 2012).

Coleman, Kari Gwen (2001) Android Arête: Toward a Virtue Ethic for Computational Agents, *Ethics and Information Technology*, 3(4): 247–65.

Coomes, Phil (2012) Comment on "The Media Mix-Up that Ruined my Life," November 14, www.bbc.co.uk/news/correspondents/philcoomes/ (accessed December 13, 2012).

Couldry, Nick (2012) *Media, Society, World: Social Theory and Digital Media Practice*. Cambridge: Polity.

Council of Europe (1950) *The European Convention on Human Rights and its Five Protocols*, www.hri.org/docs/ECHR50.html (accessed December 10, 2007).

Daily Mail Reporter (2012) Are We Creating a Generation of Murderers? Shoot 'em ups Such as Call of Duty "Train" Gamers to Shoot Real Guns – and Hit Victims in the Head, May 1, www.dailymail.co.uk/sciencetech/article-2137757/Are-creating-generation-murderers-Shoot-em-ups-train-gamers-shoot-real-guns-accurately-hit-victims-head.html#ixzz2DsrpAbjh (accessed December 2, 2012).

David, Gabriela (2009) Clarifying the Mysteries of an Exposed Intimacy: Another Intimate Representation Mise-en-scène, pp. 77–86 in Kristóf Nyíri (ed.), *Engagement and Exposure: Mobile Communication and the Ethics of Social Networking*. Vienna: Passagen.

Debatin, Bernhard (ed.) (2007) *The Cartoon Debate and the Freedom of the Press: Conflicting Norms and Values in the Global Media Culture/Der Karikaturenstreit und die Pressefreiheit: Wert- und Normenkonflikte in der globalen Medienkultur*. Berlin: LIT.

Debatin, Bernhard (2011) Ethics, Privacy, and Self-Restraint in Social Networking, pp. 47–60 in S. Trepte and L. Reinecke (eds), *Privacy Online*. Berlin: Springer.

DeCew, Judith W. (1997) *The Pursuit of Privacy: Law, Ethics, and the Rise of Technology*. Ithaca, NY: Cornell University Press.

Descartes, René ([1637] 1972) *Discourse on Method*, pp. 81–130 in *The Philosophical Works of Descartes*, trans E. S. Haldane and G. R. T. Ross, Vol. 1. Cambridge: Cambridge University Press.

—([1641] 1972) *Meditations on First Philosophy*, pp. 135–99 in *The Philosophical Works of Descartes*, trans. E. S. Haldane and G. R. T. Ross, Vol. 1. Cambridge: Cambridge University Press.

Dibbell, Julian ([1993] 2012) A Rape in Cyberspace, pp. 30–44 in C. Thorn and J. Dibbell (eds), *Violation: Rape in Gaming*. CreateSpace Independent Publishing Platform; www.juliandibbell.com/articles/a-rape-in-cyberspace/ (accessed March 9, 2013).

Duhigg, Charles (2012) How Companies Learn Your Secrets, *New York Times*, February 16, www.nytimes.com/2012/02/19/magazine/shopping-habits.html?emc=eta1 (accessed November 14, 2012).

Eickelman, Dale F. (2003) Islam and Ethical Pluralism, pp. 161–80 in Richard Madsen and Tracy B. Strong (eds), *The Many and the One: Religious and Secular Perspectives on Ethical Pluralism in the Modern World*. Princeton, NJ: Princeton University Press.

Elshtain, Jean Beth (1982) Interactive TV: Democracy and the QUBE Tube, *The Nation*, August 7–14: 108.

Ess, Charles (1996) The Political Computer: Democracy, CMC, and Habermas, pp. 197–230 in C. Ess (ed.), *Philosophical Perspectives on Computer-Mediated Communication*. Albany: State University of New York Press.

—(1998) The Letter from the Birmingham Jail: Critical Thinking Notes http://www.drury.edu/ess/alpha/mlking.html (accessed March 15, 2013).

—(2005) "Lost in Translation"? Intercultural Dialogues on Privacy and Information Ethics, *Ethics and Information Technology*, 7(1): 1–6 [introduction to special issue on privacy and data privacy protection in Asia].

—(2006) Ethical Pluralism and Global Information Ethics, *Ethics and Information Technology*, 8(4): 215–26.

—(2007) Cybernetic Pluralism in an Emerging Global Information and Computing Ethics, *International Review of Information Ethics*, 7 (September), www.-i--r--i--e.net/inhalt/007/11-ess.pdf (accessed February 10, 2013).

—(2010) The Embodied Self in a Digital Age: Possibilities, Risks, and Prospects for a Pluralistic (Democratic/Liberal) Future?, *Nordicom Information*, 32(2): 105–118, www.nordicom.gu.se/?portal=publ&main= info_publ2.php&ex=320 (accessed November 17, 2012).

—(2011) Self, Community, and Ethics in Digital Mediatized Worlds, pp. 3–30 in C. Ess and M. Thorseth (eds), *Trust and Virtual Worlds: Contemporary Perspectives*. New York: Peter Lang.

—(2012) At the Intersections between Internet Studies and Philosophy: "Who Am I Online?," *Philosophy and Technology*, doi: 10.1007/ s13347-012-0085-4.

Ess, Charles, and Mia Consalvo (2011) What is "Internet Studies"?, pp. 1–7 in Mia Consalvo and Charles Ess (eds), *The Handbook of Internet Studies*. Oxford: Wiley-Blackwell.

European Union (1995) Directive 95/46/EC of the European Parliament and of the Council of 24 October 1995, http://eur-lex.europa.eu/ LexUriServ/LexUriServ.do?uri=CELEX:31995L0046:EN:HTML (accessed February 10, 2013).

Finnemann, Niels Ole (2005) *Internettet i mediehistorisk perspektiv* [The Internet in Media-Historical Perspective]. Frederiksberg, Denmark: Samfundslitteratur.

Floridi, Luciano (2005) The Ontological Interpretation of Informational Privacy, *Ethics and Information Technology*, 7(4): 185–200.

—(2006) Four Challenges for a Theory of Informational Privacy, *Ethics and Information Technology*, 8(3): 109–19.

—(2008) Foundations of Information Ethics, pp. 3–23 in Kenneth Einar Himma and Herman T. Tavani (eds.), *The Handbook of Computer and Information Ethics*. Hoboken, NJ: Wiley.

—(2012) Distributed Morality in an Information Society, *Science and Engineering Ethics*, doi: 10.1007/s11948-012-9413-4.

Fornaciari, Federica (2012) Privacy is Dead, Long Live Privacy! Framing the Economy of Information in the Digital Age, paper given at the Association of Internet Researchers conference, Manchester, UK, October 19–21.

Foucault, M (1987) The Ethic of Care for the Self as a Practice of Freedom, in J. Bernhauer and D. Rasmussen (eds), *The Final Foucault*. Cambridge, MA: MIT Press.

—(1988) Technologies of the Self, pp. 16–49 in L. H. Martin, H. Gutman, and P. Hutton (eds), *Technologies of the Self: A Seminar with Michel Foucault*. Amherst: University of Massachusetts Press.

Fuchs, Christian, and Nick Dyer-Witheford (2012) Karl Marx @ Internet Studies, *New Media & Society*, doi: 10.1177/1461444812462854.

Gapper, John (2012) Google Protests at EU Privacy Rules Draft, *Financial Times*, January 27, www.ft.com/intl/cms/s/0/492190ce-490a-11e1-954a-00144feabdco.html#axzz2CBqC9oOE (accessed November 14, 2012).

Gazzaniga, Michael S. (2005) *The Ethical Brain*. Washington, DC: Dana Press.

Ghosh, S. (2006) The Troubled Existence of Sex and Sexuality: Feminists Engage with Censorship, pp. 255–85 in B. Bose (ed.), *Gender and Censorship*. New Delhi: Women Unlimited.

Gibson, William (1984). *Neuromancer*. New York: Ace Books.

Giddens, Anthony (1991) *Modernity and Self-Identity: Self and Society in the Late Modern Age*. Stanford, CA: Stanford University Press.

Gilbert, Françoise (2012) European Data Protection 2.0: New Compliance Requirements in Sight – What the Proposed EU Data Protection Regulation Means for U.S. Companies, *Santa Clara Computer & High Technology Law Journal*, 28: 815–63, http://digitalcommons.law.scu.edu/chtlj/vol28/iss4/3 (accessed December 19, 2012).

Gilligan, Carol (1982) *In a Different Voice: Psychological Theory and Women's Development*. Cambridge, MA: Harvard University Press.

Goffman, Erving (1959) *The Presentation of Self in Everyday Life*. Garden City, NY: Doubleday.

—(1966) *Behavior in Public Spaces: Notes on the Social Organization of Gatherings*. New York: Simon & Schuster.

Greenleaf, Graham (2011) *Asia-Pacific Data Privacy: 2011, Year of Revolution?* UNSW Law Research Paper No. 2011-29, http://papers. ssrn.com/sol3/papers.cfm?abstract_id=1914212 (accessed November 18, 2012).

Grodzinsky, Frances S., Keith Miller, and Marty J. Wolf (2008) The Ethics of Designing Artificial Agents, *Ethics and Information Technology*, 10(2–3): 115–21, doi: 10.1007/s10676-008-9163-9.

GVU (Graphic, Visualization, and Usability Center, Georgia Technological University) (1998) GVU's 10th WWW User Survey, www.cc.gatech.edu/gvu/user_surveys/survey-1998-10/graphs/ general/q50.htm (accessed January 19, 2008).

Haddon, Leslie, and Gitte Stald (2009) Cultures of Research and Policy in Europe, pp. 55–70 in S. Livingston and L. Haddon (eds), *Kids Online: Opportunities and Risks for Children*. Bristol: Policy Press.

Haid, G. M., N. M. Malamuth, and C. Yuen (2010) Pornography and Attitudes Supporting Violence against Women: Revisiting the Relationship in Non-Experimental Studies, *Aggressive Behaviour*, 36: 14–20.

Hansen, Mette Halskov, and Rune Svarverud (eds) (2010) *The Rise of the Individual in Modern Chinese Society*. Copenhagen: Nordic Institute of Asian Studies.

Henaff, Marcel, and Tracy Strong (2001) *Public Space and Democracy*. Minneapolis: University of Minnesota Press.

Herman, Susan N. (2011) *Taking Liberties: The War on Terror and the Erosion of American Democracy*. Oxford: Oxford University Press.

Herring, Susan, Kirk Job-Sluder, and Sasha Barab (2002) Searching for Safety Online: "Trolling" in a Feminist Forum. *Information Society*, 18(5): 371–83.

Hiruta, Kei (2006) What Pluralism, Why Pluralism, and How? A Response to Charles Ess, *Ethics and Information Technology*, 8(4): 227–36.

Hongladarom, Soraj (2007) Analysis and Justification of Privacy from a Buddhist Perspective, pp. 108–22 in Soraj Hongladarom and Charles Ess (eds), *Information Technology Ethics: Cultural Perspectives*. Hershey, PA: Idea Group Reference.

Hongladarom, Soraj, and Charles Ess (2007) Preface, pp. xi–xxxv in Soraj Hongladarom and Charles Ess (eds), *Information Technology Ethics: Cultural Perspectives*. Hershey, PA: Idea Group Reference.

Hornung, Peter Michael (2010) ARoS tager Eros på tapetet [ARoS – the
    Aarhus Art Museum – puts Eros on the agenda], *Politiken*, March 28
    [The online version of this story, including the uncensored image of
    the Jeff Koons painting, is no longer available. The curious can easily
    find the image online, though you will have to turn off any filtering
    software, including Google's for images. US readers should be advised
    that the image would be X-rated, though of a more softcore sort].
Howard, Phillip N., Aiden Duffy, Deen Freelon, Muzammil Hussain,
    Will Mari, and Marwa Mazaid (2011) *Opening Closed Regimes:
    What Was the Role of Social Media During the Arab Spring?* Project
    on Information Technology and Political Islam. Research Memo
    2011.1. Seattle: University of Washington, http://www.scribd.com/
    doc/66443833/Opening-Closed-Regimes-What-Was-the-Role-of-
    Social-Media-During-the-Arab-Spring (accessed February 10, 2013).
Hsu, Shang Hwa, Ming-Hui Wen, and Muh-Cherng Wu (2009)
    Exploring User Experiences as Predictors of MMORPG Addiction,
    Computers & Education, 53: 990–9.
Hughes, James (2012) Compassionate AI and Selfless Robots: A Buddhist
    Approach, pp. 69–83 in Patrick Lin, Keith Abney, and George
    A. Bekey (eds), *Robot Ethics: The Ethical and Social Implications of
    Robotics*. Cambridge, MA: MIT Press.
Huizinga, Johan ([1938] 1955) *Homo Ludens: A Study of the Play-Element in
    Culture*. Boston: Beacon Press.
Hursthouse, Rosalind (1999) *On Virtue Ethics*. Oxford: Oxford University
    Press.
Jefferson, Thomas ([1776] 1984) A Declaration by the Representatives of
    the United States of America, in General Congress Assembled, pp.
    19–24 in Merrill D. Peterson (ed.), *Thomas Jefferson: Writings*. New
    York: Library of America.
Jenkins, Henry (2006) *Convergence Culture: Where Old and New Media
    Collide*. New York: New York University Press.
Jensen, Jakob Linaa (2007) The Internet Omnopticon, pp. 351–80 in
    H. Bang and A. Esmark (eds), *New Publics with/out Democracy*.
    Frederiksberg, Denmark: Samfundslitteratur/NORDICOM.
Johnson, Deborah (2001) *Computer Ethics* (3rd edn). Upper Saddle River,
    NJ: Prentice-Hall.
Kant, Immanuel ([1788] 1956) *Critique of Practical Reason*, trans. Lewis
    White Beck. Indianapolis: Bobbs-Merrill.
—([1785] 1959) *Foundations of the Metaphysics of Morals*, trans. Lewis
    White Beck. Indianapolis: Bobbs-Merrill.
Khatib, Firas, Frank DiMaio, Foldit Contenders Group, Foldit Void
    Crushers Group, Seth Cooper, et al. (2011) Crystal Structure of a

Monomeric Retroviral Protease Solved by Protein Folding Game Players *Nature Structural & Molecular Biology*, 18: 1175–7, doi: 10.1038/nsmb.2119.<http://www.nature.com/nsmb/journal/v18/n10/full/nsmb.2119.html>, accessed December 1, 2012.

King, Martin Luther King, Jr. ([1963] 1964) Letter from the Birmingham Jail, pp. 77–100 in Martin Luther King, Jr. (ed.), *Why We Can't Wait*. New York: Mentor.

Kiss, Jemima (2012) Facebook Hits 1 Billion Users a Month, *The Guardian*, October 4, www.guardian.co.uk/technology/2012/oct/04/facebook-hits-billion-users-a-month (accessed December 5, 2012).

Kitiyadisai, Krisana (2005) Privacy Rights and Protection: Foreign Values in Modern Thai Context, *Ethics and Information Technology*, 7(1): 17–26.

Kondor, Zsuzsanna (2009) Communication and the Metaphysics of Practice: Sellarsian Ethics Revisited, pp. 179–87 in Kristóf Nyíri (ed.), *Engagement and Exposure: Mobile Communication and the Ethics of Social Networking*. Vienna: Passagen.

Lange, Patricia G. (2007) Publicly Private and Privately Public: Social Networking on YouTube, *Journal of Computer-Mediated Communication*, 13(1), article 18, http://jcmc.indiana.edu/vol13/issue1/lange.html (accessed November 17, 2012).

Lenhart, Amanda, and Mary Madden (2007) *Teens, Privacy and Online Social Networks: How Teens Manage their Online Identities and Personal Information in the Age of MySpace*. Washington, DC: Pew Internet and American Life Project, www.pewinternet.org/PPF/r/211/report_display.asp (accessed January 20, 2008).

Levinas, Emmanuel (1987) *Time and the Other and Additional Essays*, trans. Richard A. Cohen. Pittsburgh: Duquesne University Press.

Lievrouw, Leah A., and Sonia Livingstone (eds) (2006) *The Handbook of New Media: Social Shaping and Social Consequences of ICTs* (updated student edn). Thousand Oaks, CA: Sage.

Lim, Merlyna (2006) Democracy, Conspiracy, Pornography: The Internet and Political Activism in Indonesia. Lecture at IR 7.0: Internet Convergences Conference, Brisbane, September 28.

Lin, Pei-Chun, and Caroline Henkes (2004) Privacy Research: Privacy Sense in China, Hong Kong and Taiwan, unpublished MS, Universität Trier.

Liptak, Adam (2011) Justices Reject Ban on Violent Video Games for Children, *New York Times*, June 27, www.nytimes.com/2011/06/28/us/28scotus.html?pagewanted=all (accessed December 2, 2012).

Livingstone, Sonia (2011) Internet, Children, and Youth, pp. 348–68 in Mia Consalvo and Charles Ess (eds), *The Handbook of Internet Studies*. Oxford: Wiley-Blackwell.

Livingstone, Sonia, Leslie Haddon, Anke Görzig, and Kjartan Ólafsson (2011) *EU Kids Online: Final Report 2011*, http://eprints.lse.ac.uk/45490/ (accessed November 30, 2012).

Lomborg, Stine (2012) Negotiating Privacy through Phatic Communication: A Case Study of the Blogging Self, *Philosophy and Technology*, 25: 415–34, doi: 10.1007/s13347-011-0018-7.

Lomborg, Stine, and Charles Ess (2012) "Keeping the Line Open and Warm": An Activist Danish Church and its Presence on Facebook, pp. 169–90 in Pauline Cheong, Judith N. Martin, and Leah P. Macfadyen (eds), *New Media and Intercultural Communication: Identity, Community and Politics*. Oxford: Peter Lang.

Lü, Yao-Hui (2005) Privacy and Data Privacy Issues in Contemporary China, *Ethics and Information Technology*, 7(1): 7–15.

Lüders, Marika (2011) Why and How Online Sociability Became Part and Parcel of Teenage Life, pp. 456–73 in Mia Consalvo and Charles Ess (eds), *The Handbook of Internet Studies*. Oxford: Wiley-Blackwell.

Lukesch, Helmut (2012a) Computerspiele und "Spielsucht" [Computer Games and Pathological Gambling], pp. 147–68 in Martin K. W Schweer (ed.), *Medien in unserer Gesellschaft: Chancen und Risiken* [Media in Our Society: Opportunities and Risks]. Frankfurt am Main: Lang.

—(2012b) Jugendmedienschutz als gesellschaftliche Herausforderung [Youth Media Protection as a Social Challenge], paper presented at "Wissen im Netz – auf der Suche nach einer Ethik des Internetzeitalters" [Knowledge on the Net – in Search of an Ethics in the Internet Age], 2nd Tübingen International Conference on Ethics and Society. Tübingen, Germany, October 11–12.

Maag, Christopher (2007) A Hoax Turned Fatal Draws Anger but No Charges, *New York Times*, November 27, www.nytimes.com/2007/11/28/us/28hoax.html?ref=meganmeier (accessed December 5, 2012).

Mahr, Krista (2009) Top 10 Heroes, 2: Neda Agha-Soltan, *Time Lists*, December 8, www.time.com/time/specials/packages/article/0,28804,1945379_1944701_1944705,00.html (accessed December 13, 2012).

Markham, Annette, and Elizabeth Buchanan (2012) *Ethical Decision-Making and Internet Research, Version 2.0: Recommendations from the AoIR Ethics Working Committee*, www.aoir.org/reports/ethics2.pdf (accessed February 10, 2013).

Martin, Daniel (2012) School Groping Surge Blamed on Internet Porn: Third of Sixth-Form Girls Have Been Abused by Classmates, *Daily Mail*, November 13, www.dailymail.co.uk/news/article-2232582/

School-groping-surge-blamed-net-porn-Third-sixth-form-girls-abused-classmates.html (accessed November 28, 2012).

Martin, John. P (2011) Another Webcam Claim Settled in Lower Marion, *Philadelphia Inquirer*, August 23, www.philly.com/philly/hp/news_update/20110823_Lower_Merion_board_settles_4th_webcam_claim.html (accessed November 17, 2012).

Massumi, Brian (2002) *Parables for the Virtual: Movement, Affect, Sensation*. Durham, NC, and London: Duke University Press.

Mauger, Jeremy John (2012) Internet Filtering in Denmark: The Case of Pirate Bay, paper given at the Association of Internet Researchers conference, Manchester, UK, October 19–21.

McCarthy, Thomas ([1978] 1981) *The Critical Theory of Jürgen Habermas*. Cambridge, MA: MIT Press.

McElroy, Wendy (1995) *XXX: A Woman's Right to Pornography*. New York: St. Martin's Press. Available from http://www.wendymcelroy.com/xxx/

McFarland, Michael C. (2004) Intellectual Property, Information, and the Common Good, pp. 294–304 in Richard A. Spinello and Herman T. Tavani (eds), *Readings in Cyberethics* (2nd edn). Sudbury, MA: Jones & Bartlett.

McKenna, Michael (2009) Compatibilism, *Stanford Encyclopedia of Philosophy* (winter 2009 edn), ed. Edward N. Zalta, http://plato.stanford.edu/archives/win2009/entries/compatibilism/ (accessed November 29, 2012).

Menkiti, Ifeanyi A. (1979) Person and Community in African Traditional Thought, pp. 157–68 in Richard A. Wright (ed.), *African Philosophy*. New York: New York University Press.

Meyrowitz, Joshua (1985) *No Sense of Place: The Impact of Electronic Media on Social Behavior*. Oxford: Oxford University Press.

Midgley, Mary ([1981] 1996) Trying Out One's New Sword, pp. 116–19 in John Arthur (ed.), *Morality and Moral Controversies* (4th edn). Upper Saddle River, NJ: Simon & Schuster.

Moor, James (2000) Toward a Theory of Privacy in the Information Age, pp. 200–12 in R. M. Baird, R. Ramsower, and S. E. Rosenbaum (eds), *Cyberethics: Social & Moral Issues in the Computer Age*. Amherst, NY: Prometheus Books.

Moore, Adam D. (2003) Privacy: Its Meaning and Value, *American Philosophical Quarterly*, 40(3): 215–27.

Mora, Maria (2012) More than Mommy Porn: "Why I Read Smut," *SheKnows Parenting*, July 31, www.sheknows.com/parenting/articles/966571/moms-who-read-erotica (accessed November 30, 2012).

Mullins, Phil (1996) Sacred Text in the Sea of Texts: The Bible in North American Electronic Culture, pp. 271–302 in Charles Ess (ed.), *Philosophical Perspectives on Computer-Mediated Communication.* Albany: State University of New York Press.

Myskja, Bjørn (2008) The Categorical Imperative and the Ethics of Trust, *Ethics and Information Technology,* 10(4): 213–20.

Nakada, Makoto, and Takanori Tamura (2005) Japanese Conceptions of Privacy: An Intercultural Perspective, *Ethics and Information Technology,* 7(1): 27–36.

NESH ([Norwegian] National Committee for Research Ethics in the Social Sciences and the Humanities) (2006) *Forskningsetiske retningslinjer for samfunnsvitenskap, humaniora, juss og teologi [Research ethics guidelines for social sciences, the humanities, law and theology],* www.etikkom. no/Documents/Publikasjoner-som-PDF/Forskningsetiske%20 retningslinjer%20for%20samfunnsvitenskap,%20humaniora,%20 juss%20og%20teologi%20%282006%29.pdf (accessed April 9, 2013).

Nissenbaum, Helen (2010) *Privacy in Context: Technology, Policy, and the Integrity of Social Life.* Palo Alto, CA: Stanford University Press.

Nordstrøm, Jon (2012) *Dansk porno/Danish Porn.* Copenhagen: Nordstrøms Forlag.

Ong, Walter (1988) *Orality and Literacy: The Technologizing of the Word.* London: Routledge.

Paasonen, Susanna (2010) Labors of Love: Netporn, Web 2.0 and the Meanings of Amateurism, *New Media & Society,* 12(8): 1297–312.

—(2011) Online Pornography: Ubiquitous and Effaced, pp. 424–39 in Mia Consalvo and Charles Ess (eds), *The Handbook of Internet Studies.* Oxford: Wiley-Blackwell.

Paasonen, Susanna, Kaarina Nikunen, and Laura Saarenmaa Paasonen (eds) (2007) *Pornification: Sex and Sexuality in Media Culture.* Oxford, New York: Berg.

Papacharissi, Zisi (2010) *A Private Sphere: Democracy in a Digital Age.* Cambridge, and Malden, MA: Polity.

—(ed.) (2012) *A Networked Self: Identity, Community, and Culture on Social Network Sites.* New York and London: Routledge.

Paterson, Barbara (2007) We Cannot Eat Data: The Need for Computer Ethics to Address the Cultural and Ecological Impacts of Computing, pp. 153–68 in Soraj Hongladarom and Charles Ess (eds), *Information Technology Ethics: Cultural Perspectives.* Hershey, PA: Idea Group Reference.

Pedersen, Jens Ehlers-Kristian (2011) 5 cm afgjorde forårsdyst [5 cm Ruled the Spring Contest], *Jyllands-Posten,* April 30, http://jyllands-posten. dk/aarhus/article2415426.ece (accessed December 4, 2012).

Perlroth, Nicholas (2012) Trying to Keep Your E-Mails Secret When the C.I.A. Chief Couldn't, *New York Times*, November 17, p. B1, www.nytimes.com/2012/11/17/technology/trying-to-keep-your-e-mails-secret-when-the-cia-chief-couldnt.html?pagewanted=all&_r=0 (accessed November 18, 2012).

Pew Forum on Religion and Public Life (2008) *U.S. Religious Landscape Survey*, http://religions.pewforum.org/reports (accessed November 29, 2012).

Plato (1892) *The Apology*, pp. 109–35 in *The Dialogues of Plato* (3rd edn), vol. 2, trans. B. Jowett. Oxford: Oxford University Press.

—(1991) *The Republic*, trans. Allan Bloom, with notes, an interpretive essay and a new introduction. New York: Basic Books.

Politiken (2012) Redegørelse: Tegnet børneporno er uskadeligt [Study: Cartoon Child Pornography is Harmless], *Politiken*, July 23, http://politiken.dk/indland/ECE1696551/redegoerelse-tegnet-boerneporno-er-uskadeligt/ (accessed December 11, 2012).

Possin, Kevin (2005) *Critical Thinking: A Computer-Assisted Introduction to Logic and Critical Thinking*. Winona, MN: Critical Thinking Lab [CD].

Raasch, Chuck, and Kevin Johnson (2012). NRA is Mum amid Calls for Change after Newtown Shooting, *USA Today*, December 18, www.freep.com/usatoday/article/1776557?odyssey=mod|newswell|text|FRONTPAGE|s (accessed December 18, 2012).

Ramasoota, Pirongrong (2001) Privacy: A Philosophical Sketch and a Search for a Thai Perception, *Manusya: Journal of Humanities*, 4(2): 89–107.

Ramose, Mogobe B. (2002) Globalization and Ubuntu, pp. 626–50 in Pieter Coetzee and Abraham Roux (eds), *Philosophy from Africa: A Text with Readings* (2nd edn). Oxford: Oxford University Press.

Reading, Anna (2009) The Playful Panopticon? Ethics and the Coded Self in Social Networking Sites, pp. 93–101 in Kristóf Nyíri (ed.), *Engagement and Exposure: Mobile Communication and the Ethics of Social Networking*. Vienna: Passagen.

Reidenberg, Joel (2000) Testimony of Joel R. Reidenberg . . . before the Subcommittee on Courts and Intellectual Property Committee on the Judiciary, United States House of Representatives: Oversight Hearing on Privacy and Electronic Commerce, May 18, 2000, http://reidenberg.home.sprynet.com/Reidenberg_Testimony.html (accessed December 10, 2007).

Rheingold, Howard (1993) *The Virtual Community: Homesteading on the Electronic Frontier*. New York: HarperCollins.

Richmond, Riva (2010) Facebook 'Dislike' Button Is a Scam, *New York Times*, Gadgetwise, August 17, http://gadgetwise.blogs.nytimes.

com/2010/08/17/facebook-dislike-button-is-a-scam (accessed December 16, 2012).

Rosemont, Henry, Jr. (2006) Individual Rights vs. Social Justice: A Confucian Meditation, lecture given at Drury University, Springfield, MO, April 6.

Röttgers, Kurt (2009) The Pornographic Turn – or: The Loss of Decency, pp. 87–91 in Kristóf Nyíri (ed.), *Engagement and Exposure: Mobile Communication and the Ethics of Social Networking*. Vienna: Passagen.

Ruddick, Sara (1975) Better Sex, pp. 83–104 in R. Baker and F. Elliston (eds), *Philosophy and Sex*. Amherst, NY: Prometheus Books.

—(1989) *Maternal Thinking: Towards a Politics of Peace*. Boston: Beacon Press.

Samuels, Julie (2010) Steve Jobs Is Watching You: Apple Seeking to Patent Spyware, Electronic Frontier Foundation, August 23, https://www.eff.org/deeplinks/2010/08/steve-jobs-watching-you-apple-seeking-patent-0 (accessed November 17, 2012).

Schulz, Stefan (2012) Polemik vom Podium [Polemics from the Podium], *Frankfurter Allgemeine Zeitung*, November 26.

Shelley, Mary Wollstonecraft ([1818] 1933) *Frankenstein: or, a Modern Prometheus*. New York: Dutton.

Shutte, Augustine (1993) *Philosophy for Africa*. Cape Town: University of Cape Town Press.

Sicart, Miguel (2009) *The Ethics of Computer Games*. Cambridge, MA: MIT Press.

Sigot, Nathalie (2002) Jevons's Debt to Bentham: Mathematical Economy, Morals and Psychology, *The Manchester School*, 70 (2): 262–78.

Sinnott-Armstrong, Walter (2012) Consequentialism, *Stanford Encyclopedia of Philosophy* (winter 2012 edn), ed. Edward N. Zalta, http://plato.stanford.edu/archives/win2012/entries/consequentialism/ (accessed April 6, 2013).

Smith, Clarissa, Feona Attwood, and Martin Barker (2012) Porn Research: Preliminary Findings, www.pornresearch.org/results.html (accessed November 29, 2012).

Stahl, Bernd Carsten (2004) *Responsible Management of Information Systems*. Hershey, PA: Idea Group.

Stelter, Brian (2008) Guilty Verdict in Cyberbullying Case Provokes Many Questions over Online Identity, *New York Times*, November 27, www.nytimes.com/2008/11/28/us/28internet.html?ref=meganmeier (accessed April 9, 2013).

Storsul, Tanja, and Dagny Stuedahl (eds) (2007) *Ambivalence towards Convergence: Digitalization and Media Change*. Gothenburg: NORDICOM.

Strikwerda, L. (2011) Virtual Child Pornography: Why Images Do Harm from a Moral Perspective, pp. 139–61 in Charles Ess and May Thorseth (eds), *Trust and Virtual Worlds: Contemporary Perspectives*. Oxford: Peter Lang.

Stromer-Galley, J., and Wichowski, A. (2011) Political Discussion Online, pp. 168–87 in Mia Consalvo and Charles Ess (eds), *The Handbook of Internet Studies*. Oxford: Wiley-Blackwell.

Stuart, Susan (2007) Conscious Machines: Memory, Melody and Muscular Imagination, pp. 141–6 in *AI and Consciousness: Theoretical Foundations and Current Approaches: Papers from the 2007 AAAI Fall Symposium*. Menlo Park, CA: Association for the Advancement of Artificial Intelligence Press.

—(2008) From Agency to Apperception: Through Kinaesthesia to Cognition and Creation, *Ethics and Information Technology*, 10(4): 255–64.

Subrahmanyam, Kaveri, and David Šmahel (2011) *Digital Youth: The Role of Media in Development*. New York: Springer.

Sui, S. (2011) The Law and Regulation on Privacy in China, paper presented at the Rising Pan European and International Awareness of Biometrics and Security Ethics (RISE) conference, Beijing, October 20–21.

Sunstein, Cass (2001) *republic.com*. Princeton, NJ: Princeton University Press.

Talmadge, Wright (2008) Violence and Media: From Media Effects to Moral Panics, pp. 549–57 in R. Andersen and J. Gray (eds), *Battleground: The Media*, Vol. 2. Westport, CT: Greenwood Press.

Tang, R. (2002) Approaches to Privacy – The Hong Kong Experience, www.pco.org.hk/english/infocentre/speech_20020222.html (accessed April 8, 2013).

Tavani, Herman T. (2008) Floridi's Ontological Theory of Informational Privacy: Some Implications and Challenges, *Ethics and Information Technology*, 10(2–3): 155–66.

—(2013) *Ethics and Technology: Ethical Issues in an Age of Information and Communication Technology* (4th edn). Hoboken, NJ: Wiley.

Thorn, Clarisse, and Julian Dibbell (eds) (2012) *Violation: Rape in Gaming*. CreateSpace Independent Publishing Platform.

Thorseth, May (2006) Worldwide Deliberation and Public Use of Reason Online, *Ethics and Information Technology*, 8(4): 243–52.

—(2011) Virtuality and Trust in Broadened Thinking Online, pp. 162–73 in C. Ess and M. Thorseth (eds), *Trust and Virtual Worlds: Contemporary Perspectives*. New York: Peter Lang.

Time (1969) Denmark: Pornography: What is Permitted is Boring, *Time*, June 6, www.time.com/time/magazine/article/0,9171,941672,00. html (accessed February 10, 2013).

Turkle, Sherry (1985) *The Second Self: Computers and the Human Spirit*. New York: Simon & Schuster.

—(1995) *Life on the Screen: Identity in the Age of the Internet*. New York: Simon & Schuster.

—(2011) *Alone Together: Why We Expect More from Technology and Less from Each Other*. New York: Basic Books.

Vallor, Shannon (2009) Social Networking Technology and the Virtues, *Ethics and Information Technology*, 12(2): 157–70.

—(2011) Flourishing on Facebook: Virtue Friendship & New Social Media, *Ethics and Information Technology*, 14(3): 185–99.

—(2012) Social Networking and Ethics, *Stanford Encyclopedia of Philosophy* (winter 2012 edn), ed. Edward N. Zalta (accessed February 28, 2013).

van der Velden, Maya (2009) Design for a Common World: On Ethical Agency and Cognitive Justice, *Ethics and Information Technology*, 11(1): 37–47, doi: 10.1007/s10676-008-9178-2.

Verrier, Antonin (2007) *Porte de Choisy*, www.festivalpocketfilms.fr/spip. php?article648 (accessed November 17, 2012).

Warburton, Nigel (2009) *Free Speech: A Very Short Introduction*. Oxford: OUP.

Ward, Stephen J. A. (2011) *Ethics and the Media: An Introduction*. Cambridge: Cambridge University Press.

Warren, Karen J. (1990) The Power and the Promise of Ecological Feminism, *Environmental Ethics*, 12(2): 123–46.

Warren, Lydia, and Meghan Keneally (2012) The Internet Vigilantes: Anonymous Hackers' Group Outs Man, 32, "Who Drove Girl, 15, to Suicide by Spreading Topless Photos of Her," *Daily Mail*, October 16, www.dailymail.co.uk/news/article-2218532/Amanda-Todd-Anonymous-names-man-drove-teen-kill-spreading-nude-pictures. html#ixzz2CC1ihYXx (accessed November 14, 2012).

Wellman, Barry, and Caroline Haythornthwaite (2002) *The Internet in Everyday Life*. Oxford and Malden, MA: Blackwell.

West, Caroline (2012) Pornography and Censorship, *Stanford Encyclopedia of Philosophy* (winter 2012 edn), ed. Edward N. Zalta, http://plato. stanford.edu/archives/win2012/entries/pornography-censorship/ (accessed November 30, 2012).

Weston, Anthony (2000) *A Rulebook for Arguments* (3rd edn). Indianapolis: Hackett.

White, Aoife (2008) IP Addresses Are Personal Data, E.U. Regulator

Says, *Washington Post*, January 22, p. D1, www.washingtonpost.
com/wp-dyn/content/article/2008/01/21/AR2008012101340.html
(accessed February 7, 2013).

Wiegand, Ralf (2012) Offen für alles [Open for All], *Suddeutsche Zeitung*,
November 26, p. 3.

Wiener, Norbert ([1950] 1954) *The Human Use of Human Beings:
Cybernetics and Society* (2nd edn). New York: Doubleday Anchor.

Wittkower, Dylan E. (ed.) (2010) *Facebook and Philosophy: What's on your
Mind?* Chicago: Open Court Press.

Wolf, Naomi (2003) The Porn Myth, *New York Magazine*, October
20, http://nymag.com/nymetro/news/trends/n_9437/ (accessed
December 20, 2012).

Wong, Pak (forthcoming) Confucian Social Media: An Oxymoron?, *Dao:
A Journal of Comparative Philosophy*

Woolf, Virginia (1929) *A Room of One's Own*. New York and London:
Hogarth Press.

Yan, Yunxiang (2010) The Chinese Path to Individualization, *British
Journal of Sociology*, 61 (3): 489–512.

Young, Iris Marion (2000) *Inclusion and Democracy*. Oxford: Oxford
University Press.

Index